Dimensions of *Musical* Learning and Teaching

A Different Kind of Classroom

Dimensions of *Musical* Learning and Teaching

A Different Kind of Classroom

Edited by
Eunice Boardman

The National Association for Music Education

ISBN 1-56545-146-5

Table of Contents

Foreword

The opening sentence of the foreword to *Dimensions of Musical Thinking* (MENC, 1989) read as follows: "Who would not agree that helping students learn to think, to use information in intelligent ways, has always been an important goal of schooling?" (p. v). Certainly, the research into issues related to thinking and learning as applied to classroom experience that have occurred since 1989 has only served to reinforce that observation. Simultaneously, the call for improved instruction for guiding young people to emerge from their school days prepared to function effectively in the new millennium continues to be sounded. There has been one important difference in the concerns and suggestions for reform that should be noted. Increasingly, the media, which both mold and reflect the beliefs of the public, have focused attention on the value of music and the other arts as an essential part of a curriculum designed to help students "learn how to learn."

Herbert Kupferberg, senior editor of *Parade Magazine,* summarized the public view, stating, "I'm increasingly impressed by the evidence that music in the schools has a ripple effect and actually improves many students' performance in other subject areas" ("The New Sounds of Success in School," *Parade Magazine,* Feb. 26, 1999, p. 18).

Likewise, the education profession has increasingly turned its attention to addressing the value of the arts to education. Two articles in the November 1998 special issue of *Educational Leadership* on "How the Brain Works" (published by the Association for Supervision and Curriculum Development) recognize the arts as an integral part of the school curriculum. As noted at the beginning of an article by Robert Sylwester, "From fine-tuning muscular systems to integrating emotion and logic, the arts have important biological value. For their unique contributions to brain development, the arts must take center stage in schools" ("Art for the Brain's Sake," *Educational Leadership 56,*

(3): 26). In "The Music in Our Minds," another article in the same issue of *Educational Leadership,* Norman Weinberger supports this statement, drawing on a wide variety of research to support his conclusion that music study (both performance and listening) enhances skills in other subjects such as reading and math. (It is important to note that a number of music educators and researchers have questioned the validity of the research on which these claims are based.[1])

I have taken time to mention this trend because I believe that the public, who, along with professional educators, ultimately determines what is or should be taught in the schools, is sending the music education profession a message. I am deeply concerned that (a) we are not hearing the call and/or (b) we are not prepared to answer. A goal of this new book, *Dimensions of Musical Learning and Teaching: A Different Kind of Classroom,* is to provide some information and guidelines for music educators so that they may be better prepared to answer the call by translating recent research into practice structuring classroom environments that truly engage students in thinking musically.

—Eunice Boardman

Note

1. For a detailed discussion of the research that has been focused on the relationship of music to various aspects of intelligence/academic achievement, see the Fall/Winter issue of *The Journal of Aesthetic Education, 34,* (3–4), which includes the following articles: E. Winner & L. Hetland, "The Arts in Education: Evaluating the Evidence," pp. 3–10; L. Hetland. "Listening to Music Enhances Spatial-Temporal Reasoning," pp. 104–48; K. Vaughn, "Music and Mathematics: Modest Support of the Oft-Claimed Relationship," pp. 149–66; R. Butzlaff, "Can Music Be Used to Teach Reading?," pp. 167–78; and L. Hetland, "Learning to Make Music Enhances Spatial Reasoning," pp. 178–238. Of importance are the authors' conclusions that most studies fail to reveal causal results; that is, while there is definite information that suggests a relationship between academic achievement and involvement in music, there is no proof that this relationship is causal (a result of participation in music study). Another valuable article on the relationship of music to extramusical values is B. Reimer, "Facing the Risks of the 'Mozart Effect,'" *Music Educators Journal, 86,* (1):37–43.

1

THE RELATIONSHIP OF MUSICAL THINKING AND LEARNING TO CLASSROOM INSTRUCTION

EUNICE BOARDMAN

Dimensions of Musical Thinking (Boardman, 1989) focused on relating the development of thinking processes to the acquisition of a particular body of content (music) from four perspectives: content areas as models and metaphors, as changing bodies of knowledge, and as special approaches to investigation, and content learning as schema dependent. While the information provided in that volume is still sound and its approaches to teaching and learning are still valid, recent research proposes a more holistic view of the learner and thereby the learning-teaching process.

Holistic views of learning and teaching come from a variety of research centers, but many center on recognition that, as summarized by Caine and Caine (1997): "The brain is not divided into individual segments marked 'feelings' or 'cognitive development' or 'physical activity.' Rather, active learners are totally immersed in their world and learn from their entire experience" (p. 18–19).

According to these researchers, more learning will take place when learners are situated in complex experiences where they are free to process, analyze, and examine experience for meaning and understanding and where they can relate what they have learned to their own purpose. The student who sees the relevance of a particular skill to his or her own purpose will readily engage in the type of practice, rehearsal, and refinement needed to polish that skill (Caine & Caine, 1997). Bruner (1997) has also spoken frequently of the holistic nature of learning, observing that "actions (anticipated, in progress, and recalled) infuse our representations of the world. Conceiving of a possible world includes conceiving of procedures for operating upon it" (p. 117). He further avers that, while we can abstract emotion, action, or cognition from the unified whole, if we do so too rigidly we lose sight of the fact that one of the functions of a culture is to keep them related in those images, stories, and the like by which our experience is given coherence and cultural relevance.

Educators have sought to translate the assumptions that form the basis for the holistic nature of learning into approaches to curriculum building and instructional practice that seek to reject the reductionist theories that have dictated educational practice for most of this century. They offer in their place approaches that may be variously characterized by terms such as integration, connectionism, multi- or cross-disciplinary study, collaboration, and so on.

While each of these approaches may emerge from somewhat different perspectives and may translate these terms into contrasting designs for instruction, I propose that most educators would agree that some common principles are basic to the organization of effective instruction:

- Seeing learning as a *constructive,* not a *receptive* process
- Recognizing the importance of context by emphasizing the *contextual,* socially interactive nature of knowledge, strategies, and expertise and their role in cognitive development
- Recognizing the importance of multiple *modes of representation* of knowledge
- Continuing to acknowledge the centrality of mental processes involved in critical and creative thinking and the crucial role of metacognition.

Seeing Learning as a Constructive Process

Constructivism as a theory of learning, as applied to a theory of teaching, has been growing in influence since Piaget (1998) proposed that children actively "construct" their knowledge of the world through a constantly evolving process of assimilation, accommodation, and adaptation. While numerous constructivist schools of thought have emerged, each with a somewhat different viewpoint, all seem to agree that knowing is not passive, but active, generating meanings in accordance with what an individual chooses to pay attention to. Thus, knowledge is developed in ways that are coherent and purposeful for the individual who is creating the meaning, while at the same time reflecting the social contexts within which the person functions. As stated by Benson and Hunter (1992), humans do not passively encounter knowledge in the world; rather, they actively generate meanings in accordance with what they choose to pay attention to. Knowledge is thus generated by individuals in ways that are coherent, meaningful, and purposeful for the person who is creating the meaning and in the social contexts in which the person functions.

The recognition that learning is a constructive process is not a new one. While one could possibly go back to Socrates, of more relevance may be Kant's view, which concluded that logical analysis by itself is not enough; neither is the view that experience generates new knowledge (Brooks & Brooks, 1999). One cannot infer relationships (analysis) among objects, events, or actions (experience) unless one has prior understanding through which these perceptions can be organized, as Bruner (Anglin, 1996) described them, into "mental constructions projected onto an objective world" (p. 316). Piaget's research led him to a similar conclusion—that the growth of knowledge is the result of individual constructions made by the learner. Furthermore, theories relevant for educators seem to support the proposition that learning is a process whereby learners actively select, retain, and transform information in order to "assimilate, accommodate and/or adapt" to their environment—thereby constructing meaning. "We construct meaning of the world in which we live by synthesizing new experiences into what we have previously come to understand" (Brooks & Brooks, 1999, p. 4). That, in a sense, is the essence of constructivism: humans do not find or discover knowledge, but rather construct or make it.

The implications for instructional change are challenging because the theory requires a truly different approach to teaching and learning. No longer is a simple, linear approach to education acceptable. In a truly constructivist classroom, according to Brooks and Brooks (1999), "The teacher searches for students' understandings of concepts, and then structures opportunities for students to refine or revise these understandings by posing contradictions, presenting new information, asking questions, encouraging research and/or engaging students in inquiries designed to challenge current concepts" (p. xii). This constructivist instructional approach is based on five principles that grow out of a primarily social-constructivist theory of learning:

- Teachers seek and value their students' points of view.
- Classroom activities challenge students' suppositions.
- Teachers pose problems of emerging relevance.
- Teachers build lessons around primary concepts and "big" ideas.
- Teachers assess student learning in the context of daily teaching (Brooks & Brooks, 1999, p. ix).

Recognizing the Importance of Context

Acknowledgment that learning is idiosyncratic is not meant to suggest that learning occurs in a cocoon. As observed by Bruner (1997), "For however much the individual may seem to operate on his or her own in carrying out the quest for meanings, nobody can do it unaided by the culture's symbolic systems. Culture … though itself man-made, both forms and makes possible the workings of a distinctively human mind. In this view learning and thinking are always situated in a cultural setting and always dependent upon the utilization of cultural resources" (pp. 3–4).

Bruner's assertion as to the impact of culture on how the mind works reinforces our understanding that the mental frameworks or cognitive structures that we use to guide us as we perceive, conceptualize, and symbolize the world around us are formed as a result of our interaction with the sociocultural field in which we live. As argued most convincingly by Vygotsky, cognitive development has its origin in interactions among people within the cultural setting. The very mental processes we use to solve problems, make connections, and draw conclusions are dependent upon (molded by) these initial social processes. Of importance to us as educators is Vygotsky's delineation of two types of concepts. He designates the first type as "spontaneous" concepts that the child develops naturally in the process of construction that emerge naturally from the child's own reflection on everyday experience; the second type is described as "scientific" concepts that arise during the structured activity of instruction and provide the child with more formalized concepts that are culturally agreed upon (Fosnot, 1996). His famous "zone of proximal development" occurs when the child's spontaneous concepts have reached a level that enables him or her to absorb a related scientific concept. "For example, historical concepts can begin to develop only when the child's everyday concept of the past is sufficiently differentiated—when he or she can make the distinction between "in the past and now" (Fosnot, 1996, p. 19; paraphrased from Vygotsky, 1962/68). Likewise, geographic and sociological concepts must grow out of the simple schema "here and elsewhere." One might speculate that such spontaneous and scientific concepts exist also in music when children grasp stylistic concepts as they connect with concepts of "past and now" or "here and elsewhere." Likewise, understanding the structure of music is dependent upon possessing a concept of "same and different." The point at which this ability to make the connection between spontaneous and scientific concepts occurs will vary from child to child (and, of course, be determined by the nature of the interaction with expert and novice within the classroom setting or other context).

Support for the influence of context on learning potential, as well as eventual achievement, arises from a variety of sources, including recent research into how the brain learns. While much of this research is still highly experimental, some emergent results hold promise when one considers the organization of instructional contexts. One aspect of such research addresses the nature/nurture controversy that has raged as long as people have been concerned with teaching and learning. Jensen (1998) points out that anywhere from 40 to 70 per cent of one's potential to learn and achieve is a result of environmental impact, dependent upon the richness of the experience in which the learner is immersed. Frequent new learning experiences and challenges are essential to brain growth. Experience, according to Dewey (1934), is the process of a person purposively interacting with environment and realizing the consequences of the interaction, rooted in insightful behavior. The contextual nature of experience was also stressed by Dewey (1934) in his observation, "An experience is always what it is because of a transaction taking place between an individual and what at the time constitutes his environment" (p. 44). Marian Diamond's recent research into brain development supports Dewey's statement, revealing that an enriched environment literally changes the structure of brain cells (Anglin, as quoted in Jensen, 1998). Jensen (1998) defines characteristics of enriching environments: first, the learning must be challenging (mere novelty is not enough), providing new information or experiences; and second, there must be some way to learn from the experience through interactive feedback.

I've loosely equated the terms "environment" and "context" in the previous discussion, although they are not synonymous terms. However, dictionary definitions of both terms imply that a particular event or situation occurs within a context or environment distinguished by particular qualities that influence the quality of that event or situation. In many educational writings, the term "context" is frequently seen as a more complex term that acknowledges that any learning event takes place, not within a single environment, but within a multiplicity of contexts, as illustrated in Figure 1, The contexts in which learning may take place. What does not come through clearly in this figure is the constant interaction and the potentially synergetic nature of these multiple contexts. Depending upon the nature of the specific learning event (a particular lesson), learners bring to this event a diverse body of knowledge, much of which they may not be aware, that they have collected as they move among these various contexts—music, its role in their lives, how it is organized, how it serves as an expressive force, and its perceived value. As teachers, it is our responsibility, first, to acknowledge and respect the body of knowledge that the learners bring with them and, second, to build on that knowledge to help them expand their understanding of (in Vygotsky's words) the scientific concepts of music.

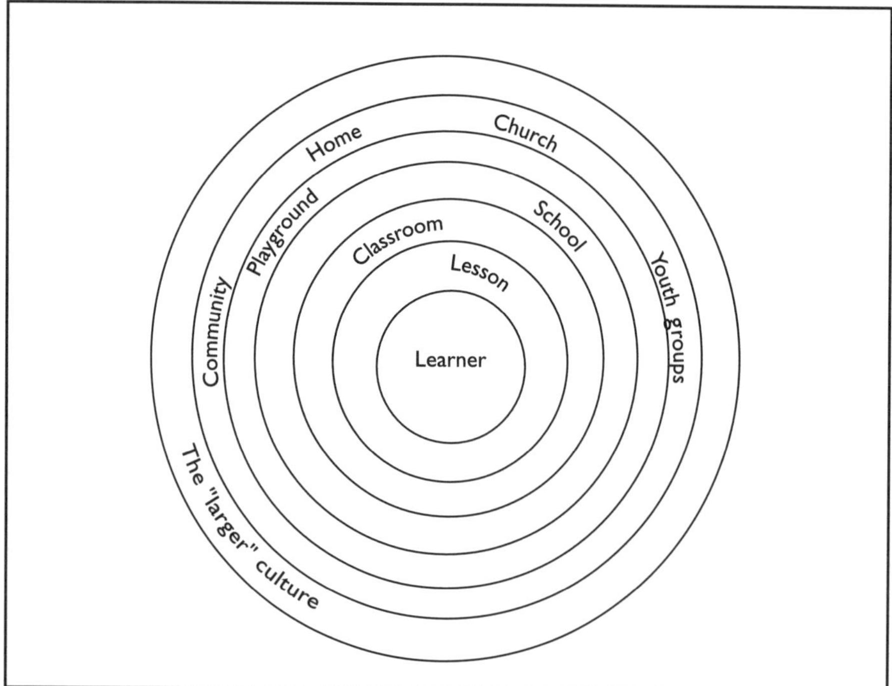

Figure 1. The contexts in which learning may take place

Another area of research that bears on the significance of context for learning is known as "situated learning." Theorists supportive of this concept state that all learning must be defined in relation to actional contexts, not to self-contained structures (Lave & Wenger, 1991). Thus, learning is recognized as increasing participation in communities of practice. Learning as legitimate peripheral participation means that learning is not simply a condition of membership in the community but is itself an evolving form of membership. One begins as a newcomer and, as learning is acquired, gradually moves to the position of "old-timer." Such a theory recognizes the importance of continuity in learning as the acquisition of culturally approved knowledge and practice. It is not, however, a static theory. As learners learn how to participate in the community (for example, the community of musicians), change, as a result of interactions among community members, is a fundamental property of such groups (Lave & Wenger, 1991, p. 117). This theory is important for music teachers because it stresses the belief that the learner should always be functioning as a musician, albeit as a novice. In situated learning contexts, the student does not learn "about" music or musicians; he or she learns music by functioning as a musician. As musical skills and understandings required by the community are gained, the learner moves into fuller membership within the community of musicians and, eventually, may contribute to the ever-changing body of knowledge that makes up the world of music.

Acknowledgment of the significance of context for learning and of the principles embedded in related theories such as situated learning is not a new idea for music educators. Most are familiar with Suzuki's description of the insight that caused him to develop his approach to learning and teaching violin when he realized that children learned the language of the culture to which they were born. What children learn is determined by their environment. If they live in Japan, they learn to speak Japanese; if they live in a home where violin music is played each day, they become violinists (Suzuki, 1969). And such, in simple form, is a basic premise of contextual teaching and learning: not only what children learn but how they learn is a function of the environment in which learning takes place.

Recognition of this basic premise is fundamental to the approach known as "contextual teaching and learning" (Contextual Teaching and Learning, 2000) from which the following definition has emerged:

> Contextual teaching and learning is a conception of teaching and learning that helps teachers relate subject matter content to real world situations and motivates students to make connections between knowledge and its applications to their lives as family members, citizens, and workers and engage in the hard work that learning requires.

The closely allied nature of the theories known as "constructivism" and "contextualism" as applied to teaching and learning is evident in the following list of phrases used by effective teachers that was compiled by the

Contextual Teaching and Learning Association. The similarities are quickly evident when comparing this list with that found at the end of the preceding section:

- Emphasize problem-solving.
- Recognize the need for teaching and learning to occur in a variety of contexts such as home, community, and work sites.
- Teach students to monitor and direct their own learning so they become self-regulated learners.
- Anchor teaching in students' diverse life-contexts.
- Encourage students to learn from each other and together.
- Employ authentic assessment (Contextual Teaching and Learning, 2000, p. 1).

Representation of Knowledge

Another theme that seems indelibly interwoven into current theories of learning is that of knowledge representation. A representation is something that stands for something else—it is a structure in the mind that preserves information about objects or events in the world (Sternberg, 1999). Just how these structures are shaped and the form they may take has been the subject of much research over the past forty-plus years. Most theorists seem to agree that such internalization is a result of perceptual interactions (involving any or all of the senses) between the individual and an object or event that are gradually formed into schema (cognitive maps, images, and so forth; I shall use these terms interchangeably, although each theorist may have a slightly different definition). Such a development is not a single sensory act but a cyclical activity that never ends. This is because what the individual perceives at any single moment is selective; it is dependent upon the nature of one's current schema, which is a result of the context in which the perceptual act takes place (see Neisser (1976), one of the early proponents of a cognitive approach to psychology, for an extensive but readable discussion of the relationship between perception and cognition). That is, a particular configuration is dependent upon the kinds of interactions that have previously shaped one's schema (i.e., "This is a big dog that will bite" v. "Nice doggie!") The importance of modes of representation lies in the fact that, according to Neisser (1996) and others, they serve as guides to action; they allow us to organize information and to anticipate subsequent events.

Various writers speak about the attributes of such mental constructions. For some writers, mental constructions seem to be basically symbolic in the more traditional sense of the word. For others, modes of representation are a reflection of the source of the sensory information, i.e., visual, aural, kinetic, and so forth. No matter the form, as noted by Fosnot (1996), "The very act of representing objects, interactions, or meaning embedded in experience within a medium such as language, paint, and canvas or mathematical model appears to create a dialectical tension beneficial to thought. Each medium has its own attributes and limits and thus elicits new connections, new variations on the contextually embedded meaning" (p. 22).

While Fosnot does not specifically identify music as a particular mode of representation, Eisner, as well as others, does: "Forms of representation are the devices that humans use to make public conceptions that are privately held. They are the vehicles through which concepts that are visual, auditory, kinesthetic, olfactory, gustatory, and tactile are given public status. This public status might take the form of words, pictures, music, mathematics, dance, and the like." (Eisner, 1994, p. 39). Gardner (1983) also recognizes the catholic nature of modes of representation, although he uses the term "symbol," defining it as any entity that can refer to any other entity, including words, diagrams, pictures, and the like, so long as it is used to represent some kind of information (including expressive information). He further notes that symbols may denote or connote by conveying moods, feelings, and tones, as well as other kinds of information, and he recognizes the importance of artistic symbols including music, visual art, dance, and so on (p. 301). (Gardner builds part of his theory of multiple intelligences on the existence of domain-specific symbol systems.)

While particular forms of representation may be domain-specific, including specific art forms as mentioned above, theories of representation, such as that proposed by Bruner, recognize that some modes may cross domains. Bruner defines representation as "a set of rules in terms of which one conserves one's encounters with events" (Bruner, 1997, p. 156). We may represent some events by the actions they require (enactive), by some form of picture (iconic), or with words or other symbolic modes or systems, such as mathematics. While Bruner originally proposed these three modes as being progressive, reflecting various stages in an individual's conceptual development, he later came to reject this aspect of the theory. He now suggests that it is useful to make the distinction among the modes on grounds other than developmental. The enactive, or procedural mode, guides activity, particularly skilled activity directed toward a particular action. Iconic representations serve as prototypes for classes of events, providing benchmarks against which to compare candidacy for membership in those classes. The power of the symbolic mode is in its key to membership in the culture—it allows individuals to share in the meanings that form their culture (Bruner, 1997).

Within many of the writings referenced, the implicit, if not explicit, message to educators is that the curriculum should provide students the opportunity to embrace multiple modes of representation. As observed by Eisner (1994), "Since meaning in the context of representation is always mediated through some form of representation, each form of representation has a special contribution to make to human experience. ... (in addition) education, I believe, ought to enable the young to learn how to access the meanings that have been created through what I have referred to as forms of representation. ... Education ought to help the young learn how to create their own meanings through these forms" (p. 19).

Both views of representation, as domain-specific and as domain-crossing, have significance for classroom planning. The expanding recognition by researchers other than those directly related to music education that music is a particular domain with a unique mode of representation, and thereby should be included within the curriculum, provides us with a special opportunity as well as a challenge. What is rarely explicitly stated, however, is the fact that a traditional, deconstructionist orientation toward music study will not necessarily result in students who can truly use music as a unique mode of representation. It's not just a case of patting ourselves on the back and continuing in the same instructional paths we've followed in the past. For music to take its rightful place in the curriculum, students in the music classroom must be involved in a search for meaning. Their focus must be on music's expressive intent—on ways in which it can present alternative views of the meaning of an event or feeling or represent feelings otherwise inexpressible. Within a classroom where music as a mode of representation is emphasized, attention will always be given first to this dimension. The teacher's role is to help students build schemata that encompass essential musical concepts and thus gain insight as to how musical elements contribute to musical meaning. This is not to suggest that what we might describe as basic knowledge and skills (such as fingering, reading notation, tone production, and the like) are neglected. These are addressed as the need for them arises out of the music itself—not as discrete tasks to be mastered.

Such a classroom will acknowledge the cross-domain aspect of representation as it impinges upon the development of meaning. As noted in the brief discussion at the beginning of this section, meaning may be represented in a variety of forms, but the development of concepts and schemata seems to require the same type of environment. The teacher focusing on meaning-making will simultaneously:

- make sure that the physical world contains the essential information
- ensure that the learner selects those aspects of the world most important to the problem solution
- recognize that the learner already possesses concepts and schema that also influence the selective process of the cycle.

If representations begin with sensory data, then it is readily apparent that the environment we prepare for our students must be rich with information that students can draw on as they explore musical meaning. Such an enriched environment will go far beyond the provision of a methods book or a preselected set of octavos. It will include many methods books, a wide variety of octavos, ample CDs representing a broad spectrum of music genres, a diverse selection of books about music, and visual materials designed to help students build understandings about style, form, and expression. And it will offer ample music-making objects that are far beyond the traditional ones. Such should be true whether the classroom is primarily a band or choral rehearsal room, a media lab, or a general music classroom.

These materials should not be offered to the students without guidance, however; it is the teacher's responsibility to help students determine how to locate needed information in response to questions, such as, "If the problem is one of fingering (or tone production or phrasing), what might be the best way to get an answer?" One answer might be "From the teacher." And that's all right. Sometimes it's the most efficient—provided that the teacher does not become the source for all answers. Other questions might be: "What might be the best way to decide how this composition by Vivaldi should be performed?" "On what basis should I choose a CD of Stravinsky's *Firebird Suite*?" "How can we best organize the information gained to help others in their search?" Students accustomed to traditional instructional approaches may need extensive guidance at first, until they realize that learning, and thus creating meaning, is their responsibility, not the teacher's. The teacher is there as a guide, as a problem poser, as a resource, but not as an all-knowing authority.

Finally, as noted in the discussion of constructivism, teachers must recognize that the student arrives in their classroom not as a tabla rasa, but with many concepts already formed. If we are to help students move forward as musicians, we must first seek to understand what concepts they currently possess, how these concepts influence their attitudes toward music involvement, and the level of actual music making they may currently possess, even if it is not in what we see as a traditional or accepted mode of performance.

Because the process of making meaning begins with development of concepts internalized as representations that may take any of several forms, the following principles of concept formation may provide guidance when a music teacher is planning classroom instruction, regardless of the age of the students or specific area of focus within the broad domain of music, band, choir, and so forth (Boardman, 1997).

Concept formation moves from whole to part. This chapter began with recognition of the holistic nature of learning. One of the ways that this holistic process reveals itself is through the ways that concepts are formed. Musical response begins with a sense of the expressive whole. With guidance, students will gradually become aware and form concepts of particular elements that contribute to the expressive whole. For example, melodic understanding may begin with an awareness of its contour, the "upness and downness." Only after many guided activities may the learner begin to focus on specific aspects, such as the distance between pitches (size of interval) or the fact that, in most music of the Western world, all pitches within a melody belong to the same scale or "pitch set."

Concept formation depends on the ability to perceive. The capacity of an individual to perceive the defining characteristics of an object or event is basic to concept formation. The relative ease with which a concept is attained depends directly on the clarity with which the individual may perceive the features to be conceptualized. When these features are perceived at multiple sensory levels (tactile, kinesthetic, visual, and aural), conceptualization occurs more readily. Translated into music methodology, this principle suggests the desirability of varied sensory experiences with music that involve not only the ears but also the eyes and the body. Active exploration, where the learner actually manipulates and experiments with the materials of sound, is superior to methods that are essentially passive or call for only verbal responses. Regardless of the type of classroom (band, choir, orchestra, or general music), activities should regularly include all kinds of musical participation: listening, singing, playing, moving, and creating (i.e., improvising and composing), as well as seeing visual representations of music (not just notation). The teacher's role is to plan experiences that will facilitate the student's perception of the musical features to be conceptualized and then help the learner formulate the appropriate concepts through experimentation as well as discussion. By providing for a variety of sensory levels, students for whom one form of perception is limited (such as for the visually or hearing impaired) will still be able to engage in meaningful musical experiences.

Concept formation proceeds from the concrete to the abstract. Concepts embedded in or represented by concrete objects and readily accessible events are most easily acquired by the novice learner. Many musical concepts are so abstract that the importance of providing concrete experiences with music cannot be overemphasized. The introduction of such melodic concepts as those represented by the terms "up-down" or "step-skip" must be planned around the use of materials and activities that represent these concepts as concretely as possible. Such concepts can best be grasped if they are related to spatial concepts that the learner already understands. Bodily movements that reflect the up-down character of the contour, performance on spatial instruments such as step bells, and the observation of visual diagrams that reflect the contour should be used to help novices make the association between what they hear, what they see, and the verbal symbol commonly used to describe the musical sound.

As children grow musically, concrete experiences are not as essential to concept formation. However, when new ideas are introduced, they should be couched in as concrete, thereby meaningful, terms as possible, no matter what the age of the student. For example, the concept of scale organization can be grasped readily by nine- and ten-year-olds if the introduction is presented in a setting that allows for physical manipulation of the items that produce the sounds. Experimentation that involves selecting the necessary bells from a set of chromatic resonator bells and placing them in the correct order will help the neophyte expand a generalized concept of "scale" as a set of pitches that consistently move upward or downward to an awareness of the necessity for this arrangement to include specific "whole" and "half" steps (terms that actually have little aural meaning) at particular points in the series. Such experiences will be more meaningful than any amount of time spent singing tonal syllables, memorizing key signatures, or practicing fingerings.

Concept formation depends on the complexity of the example. The amount of effort required to form a concept is directly related to the complexity of the context from which the concept must be derived. The selection of music examples in which the structure of the element to be stressed is clearly evident is one of the most difficult, yet essential, tasks of the teacher. The concept of "phrase," for instance, will be more readily grasped when the composition used as an introductory example has clearly defined phrases that are all of the same length, with tones of long duration and descending melodic lines marking the end of each. As the learner becomes sensitive to this clearly defined organization, examples where phrases are of varying length or where other characteristics are less clearly defined should be introduced, thus enabling the learner to gradually expand the concept to include a wider variety of possibilities.

Concept formation is a gradual process, dependent upon prior experience. The formation of any particular concept is a long, slow process that moves only gradually from vague to clear and from inexact to precise. Changes occur in the implications, relationships, and transfer possibilities that an individual senses as many sensory experiences gradually become synthesized and integrated into a single meaningful definition. A single musical experience cannot suffice for the development of musical understanding. Formulating the concepts of accent groups (meter) or rhythm pattern requires not only numerous concrete experiences, but also experiences that recur over a long period of time. Such repetition allows the individual to test a vaguely formed definition in new situations. Each new experience should allow the learner to become more convinced of the validity of the concept being evolved or to alter his or her present concept to accommodate the new information just acquired. Only by such recurrence will a concept be internalized to the point that it can become a useful tool in solving new musical problems.

While the above principles address the formation of concepts, the development of schemata is dependent upon a similar process. For some researchers, schema are dependent upon the organization of multiple concepts into a guide for action. Recognition that concepts are useful as guides for action only when they coalesce into a broad schema reminds us that concepts cannot be taught in isolation The teacher should not say, all in one lesson, "Today, we'll focus on rhythm. Here is a good song to introduce harmony. Let's drill on intervals." Every musical endeavor must involve consideration of the multiple ways in which elements combine to create the musical whole as it unfolds over time.

Continuing to Acknowledge the Centrality of Critical and Creative Thinking and the Crucial Role of Metacognition

The original book, *Dimensions of Thinking* (Marzano et al, 1988), ushered in an era for educators that had been simmering for many years—an era based on recognition that helping children learn is dependent upon helping children learn to think. *Dimensions of Musical Thinking* (Boardman, 1989) was based on the propositions presented in that text. Today, results of new research, some of which are summarized in this chapter, have provided additional insight into the teaching-learning process. What has not changed, however, is recognition that the individual's ability to learn is dependent upon that person's ability to make use of appropriate thinking processes. All of the suggestions for helping students learn offered by various educational practitioners in this new edition are based on an implicit, when not explicit, recognition that students must be guided in gaining the skills required for critical and creative thinking while engaging in problem solving and decision making.

For teachers concerned with helping children learn to make use of appropriate thinking strategies, a major problem is how to decide which type of thinking is most appropriate for a particular music learning context. Swartz and Perkins (1990) provide a helpful distinction among the four processes mentioned above (see Figure 2, The four thinking skills) that can readily be used to guide students toward effective thinking.

Critical thinking skills within a music classroom are essential in a variety of situations, such as when selecting the most valid recorded performance of a particular composition from a specific style period or comparing contrasting views as to whether the performance of a particular passage is stylistically or expressively acceptable. The role of creative thinking skills within the music classroom, while most apparent in a compositional/or improvisational situation, also is important in other roles, such as translating a musical idea

Type of skill	Goals	Component skills
Critical Thinking	To evaluate contrasting identify position or idea, analyze competing positions or the clarity of ideas	Identify position or idea, analyze competing views, weight evidence, gather new information
Creative Thinking	To generate new ideas, develop new products	Establish need for idea, restructure existing views of problem, generate possibilities
Decision Making	To reach an informed decision	Consider available information, evaluate information, identify options, weigh options, make decision
Problem Solving	To reach one or more adequate solutions to a problem	Identify, represent, select a strategy, implement the strategy, evaluate progress

Figure 2. The four thinking skills

into another mode of representation (e.g., dance or painting). Certainly, both decision making and problem solving are constantly needed as students consider alternative ways of performing a new piece of music, composing a composition in a particular form, or finding imaginative ways to describe music heard.

No matter what the type of skill students need to use to achieve a goal, a wide spectrum of basic cognitive tools must be accessible to the learner, any of which may be used by the student when engaging in critical or creative thinking, decision making, or problem solving. It is possible to locate a variety of lists of such tools; the following offers one such list that may guide the teacher when seeking to engage students in meaningful learning events (Boardman, 1998).

Focus (all components are familiar). This is a time to engage in a satisfying musical experience, where all components are known. It frequently is used as an introductory activity prior to moving on to other, more demanding, less familiar activities. It is also a valuable step to use to close a lesson, to help students consolidate what they have learned, and to reassure them that they have indeed made progress toward becoming independent musicians. Focusing involves such cognitive tools as attending, defining, and recalling.

Observe/Encode (all components remain the same as in the preceding lesson segment). In an observational lesson segment, the purpose of this type of cognitive processing is twofold: it involves focusing through identifying and/or clarifying possible problems, followed by engaging in activities that ensure that encoding has taken place by refining and reinforcing.

Apply (musical context changes from one segment to the next). In this option, the context—the music with which the learner has been interacting—changes while other components remains the same. The goal now is to apply what has been learned to a new musical event by identifying similarities and inferring or predicting how known information can be used in new situation. For example, the class may have learned how to interpret meter signatures while learning song A. Students are now asked to apply that solution while learning song B.

Refocus: Organize/Reorganize. As a lesson proceeds, in order for the total experience to be truly holistic, emphasis may need to shift from one aspect of the musical structure to another; this requires the learner to be flexible and able to shift attention. For example, children may have been focusing primarily on the rhythmic aspects of "On Top of Old Smoky"; then they are asked to focus on melodic aspects in order to learn to perform the song successfully. Organizing skills involve such specific processes as comparing, classifying, ordering, and translating.

Translate. In a translative activity, the context (the music), the content (the concept being stressed), and the mode of representation remain consistent—the same as in the preceding activity. The action category also remains the same, but the type of action changes. For example, if learners have been performing through singing, they would now be asked to "translate" their understanding into a different format by now performing through playing.

Transfer. In a transferring activity, the context, content, and mode continue as in the preceding activity, but the action changes. For example, if the learner has been describing a musical event, he or she now demonstrates the ability to transfer that knowledge or skill to a different action by performing or creating. Processes and skills such as identifying, recognizing, distinguishing, and detecting may be involved.

Generate/Integrate. The learner is now guided to move to a different mode of representation that has not been used to show an understanding of the concept (at this particular level of complexity) currently being stressed. For example, the learner who has been functioning enactively when showing the melodic contour is now helped to observe how a shape drawn in the air can be reproduced visually with an iconic representation. Or the student who is at the symbolic level when reading simple 2:1 rhythms may be guided to return to the iconic mode to help him or her grasp 3:1 relationships. In such situations, the learner changes his or her existing knowledge structure or "schema" to incorporate new information. Processes may include some of those used in other situations, including inferring, predicting, elaborating, diverging, restructuring, and, of course, transferring.

Analyze. One example of an analysis task might be when a more complex example of the same concept category is introduced. In this situation, some other components might also change, though not necessarily. For example, students have been learning to sight-sing songs that move primarily by steps or skips outlining the tonic chord; they are now challenged to deal with a piece that includes skips outlining the V^7 chord. In this situation, all components remain the same except for the particular aspect of the musical context: students have learned the first part of a song that includes only familiar relationships. They now examine part two and are confronted with unfamiliar relationships. They are guided to compare attributes and recognize relationships to determine the characteristics of the new pattern.

Synthesize/Evaluate/Verify. In many situations, any combination of components may change as the lesson unfolds. The learner is challenged by the situation to engage in higher-level thinking strategies. In order to engage in such strategies, the student needs to be able to draw on prior learnings and determine those that will be helpful in solving a new, holistic problem. In this option, the learner is expected to make decisions as to process; the teacher becomes an expediter. Creative activities frequently fall in this category. Any of a variety of specific cognitive skills may be involved as the process continues.

The extent to which the students are made aware of a particular tool they are using will determine the extent to which metacognitive processes may emerge. Brown (1980), who says that metacognition can be defined as the knowledge people have about their own thought processes, proposes that metacognition has two dimensions. The first is knowledge of cognition that includes three types of knowledge: declarative knowledge (about ourselves as learners); procedural knowledge (about strategies that may be undertaken, such as taking notes), and conditional knowledge (about knowing when and why to use a particular strategy). In order for students to become metacognitive learners, the teacher needs to constantly emphasize the types of skills and tools that are or should be used, as, for example, "To solve this problem, we probably need to compare the two performances. How many different ideas can you generate for the theme of your composition?" or "What would be the best way to decide which expressive qualities to emphasize in this passage?"

In other words, share with your students the thinking processes to be undertaken so that they realize that one needs to "think about thinking."

Conclusion

This chapter opened with the acknowledgment that recent research supports recognition that learning is a holistic enterprise: any learning that occurs is an amalgamation of action, emotion, and cognition. Likewise, it is hoped that the complementary nature of the various topics examined in this chapter—context, constructivism, modes of representation, and cognitive processes—combine to form a holistic view of learning and teaching. It would seem impossible to focus on only one of the theories presented herein and ignore all others. A truly successful approach to music instruction will be a synthesis of all of the issues addressed here, as well as other research not fully discussed, such as the research into the brain and implications for learning (see Jensen, 1998 for a highly readable discussion of the brain and how we learn). The development of such an approach is not an easy task, but the rewards in the form of student involvement and teacher excitement will be immeasurable.

References

Anglin, J. M. (Ed.) (1973). *Beyond the information given.* New York: W. W. Norton.

Benson, G. D., & Hunter, W. J. (1992). "Chaos theory: No strange attractor in teacher education." *Action in Teacher Education* 14, no. 4: 61–67.

Boardman, E. (Ed.). (1989). *Dimensions of musical thinking.* Reston, VA: MENC.

Boardman, E. (1998). *Thinking about thinking.* Unpublished manuscript.

Boardman, E. (1997). *Toward a theory of music instruction.* Unpublished manuscript.

Brooks, J. G., & Brooks, M. G. (1999). *In search of understanding: The case for constructivist classrooms.* Alexandria, VA: Association for Supervision and Curriculum Development.

Brown, A. L. (1980). Metacognition, executive control, self regulation, and other more mysterious mechanisms. In F. Weinert & R. Kluwe (Eds.) *Metacognition, motivation, and understanding.* (pp. 88–107). Hillsdale, NJ: Lawrence Erlbaum.

Bruner, J. (1986). *Actual minds, possible worlds.* Cambridge, MA: Harvard University Press.

Bruner, J. (1997). *The culture of education.* Cambridge, MA: Harvard University Press).

Caine, R. N., & Caine, G. (1997). *Education on the edge of possibility.* Alexandria, VA: Association for Supervision and Curriculum Development.

"Contextual Teaching and Learning." (2000). Contextual Teaching and Learning. contextual@services.netlogix.net

Dewey, J. *Art as experience.* New York: Minton Balch.

Eisner, E. (1994). *Cognition and curriculum reconsidered.* New York: Teachers College Press.

Fosnot, C. (1996). *Constructivism: Theory, perspectives, and practice.* New York: Teachers College Press.

Gardner, H. (1983). *Frames of mind: The theory of multiple intelligences.* New York: Basic Books.

Jensen, Eric. (1998). *Teaching with the brain in mind.* Alexandria, VA: Association for Supervision and Curriculum Development.

Marzano, R. J., Hughes, C. S., Jones, B. F., Presseisen, B. Z., Rankin, S. C., & Sughor, C. (1988). *Dimensions of thinking: A framework for curriculum and instruction.* Alexandria, VA: Association for Supervision and Curriculum Development.

Lave, J., & Wenger, E. (1991). *Situated learning: Legitimate peripheral participation.* Cambridge, England: Cambridge University Press.

Neisser, U. (1976). *Cognition and reality.* New York: W. H. Freeman

Piaget, J. (1998). *Selected works.* New York: Routledge.

Sternberg, R. J. (Ed.) (1999). *The nature of cognition.* Cambridge, MA: MIT Press.

Suzuki, S. (1969). *Nurtured by love.* Jericho, NY: Exposition Press.

Swartz, R. J., & Perkins, D. N. (1990). *Teaching thinking: Issues and approaches.* Pacific Grove, CA: Critical Thinking Press.

Eunice Boardman is professor emerita of music and education at the University of Illinois in Urbana–Champaign.

2

THE ROLE OF CONTEXT IN TEACHING AND LEARNING MUSIC

LENORE POGONOWSKI

Imagine the excitement of fifth graders reenacting the Battle of Bunker Hill by creating music for troops to march into action. Imagine the feelings they could develop and express in consideration of the fear men must have as they anticipate battle, potential wounds, and inevitable death. Imagine the barrenness of the landscape as it existed in 1775. How could we depict all of this through music? Pride, fear, insecurity, desperation, loneliness—all of these imagined feelings are feelings that we could expect in other settings or contexts as we reflect upon our own life experiences.

Context, for the purpose of this chapter, is a determined place and time, either real or simulated. Context is used to engage students in music making that describes real-life situations as closely as possible. It requires the use of higher-order thinking skills such as analysis, synthesis, and evaluation or what we often call critical-thinking skills.

How Does Learning Occur?

In a traditional music classroom, the teacher's role is generally characterized as that of a conveyor of musical knowledge. Information is transmitted from the teacher to the students. In a constructivist music classroom, knowledge is transmitted in several directions: from teacher to student, from student to student, and from student to teacher (Brooks & Brooks, 1993). Contextual teaching adds yet another dimension to this person-to-person transfer. According to Crawford and Witte (1999), "Transferring is a teaching strategy that we define as using knowledge in a new context or situation" (p. 38). Transferring is especially effective when students use newly acquired knowledge in unfamiliar situations as, for example, using issues relating to the Battle of Bunker Hill as a springboard for creating music.

Caine and Caine (in Crawford & Witte, 1999) point out that "emotions and cognition cannot be separated and the conjunction of the two is at the heart of learning" (p. 38). When we evoke curiosity and emotion as motivators in transferring social study ideas about the American Revolution to the music room, we acknowledge the distinctive nature of both subjects. We also permit the barriers between subjects to break down as students' curiosity impels them to draw upon information from all areas of human knowledge. Books, films, recordings, and other such tools serve this end. At the same time, we acknowledge the importance of transferring the meaning of ideas from one subject to another. Viewed from the perspective of music, the Battle of Bunker Hill takes on new meaning as students engage in creating and performing music based on aspects of the battle while interacting with each other.

Throughout the twentieth century, educators have grappled with educational issues in search of ways to make what children learn in school more accessible and useful in other contexts. In 1929, Whitehead complained that schools produce too much inert knowledge, molding students who know definitions of concepts but are unable to use them when it is appropriate to apply them (Borko & Putnam, 1988, p. 35). In her presidential address to the American Educational Research Association (AERA), Lauren Resnick (1987a) argued that "as long as school focuses mainly on individual forms of competence and on decontextualized skills, educating people to be good learners in school settings alone may not be sufficient to help them become strong out-of-school learners" (p. 18).

Educators have addressed these concerns about the irrelevance and inappropriateness of school learning in numerous ways. E. L. Thorndike (1922), for example, viewed the educational problem in relationship to the learning of content. He approached learning as the systematic accumulation of stimulus-response bonds acquired through practice. Much of the skill, drill, and practice in classrooms, textbooks, and computer software is a direct outcome of the work done by Thorndike and his followers. As Caine and Caine (1997b) point out, "Learning came to mean absorbing fragmented and categorized pieces of information. Students were evaluated on how much of this information they absorbed, and they were considered educated if they could prove that they had the basic concepts and skills needed to work in more or less predictable jobs they would have for a lifetime" (p. 3).

Unlike Thorndike, John Dewey (1916) developed compelling arguments for schools to be realistic in terms of resembling out-of-school life. He maintained that the child is not born with a ready-made faculty called thinking that can be drilled like multiplication tables. Students need to learn by engaging in meaningful and purposeful activities that feel like life itself, rather than rehearse abstract content transmitted by teachers and textbooks. In his view, schools are social places where experiences and ideas are exchanged and subjected to intellectual and common-sense scrutiny. They are places where misconceptions are realized, and new lines of thought and inquiry are set up, as opposed to places where students show off to the teacher and the other children the amount of information they have committed to memory.

According to John Dewey, the development of the mind begins with the child's self-perceptions or personal here-and-now world. For example, a song can be a child's song just as his or her neighbor has a song; it is an accompaniment as he or she sculpts in the sandbox, grocery shops with dad, and plays with peers in and out of school. A child may recognize that although his or her neighbor's song is different, they are both songs. Hearing a rap song on MTV, the child may decide that his or her song is sweeter than the aggressive beat of rap music. Or, upon hearing the demonic element of Mozart in the cemetery scene in the last finale of *Don Giovanni,* the child may decide that it's a song—someone else's song. A child's knowledge of song is organized around his or her own experiences and his or her perceptions of similarities and differences between those experiences in which song is involved.

As the ability to think matures, the child is able to organize facts logically, that is, in terms of their relationship to each other. The formulated, logically organized knowledge of "song" is that all songs have melodies and rhythms; that his or her song belongs to a personal genre akin to folk music; that rap music has less melody and a heavy emphasis on rhythm; and that an aria from an opera can be very solemn in communicating the emotional content of the words. As Dewey saw it, education must engage the whole child mentally, socially, physically, and emotionally. The purpose of the teacher in nurturing thinking is to encourage in the learner a habit of establishing connections between the everyday life of human beings and the materials of formal instruction in a way that has meaning and application.

The observations of Jerome Bruner (1996) and others resonate with Dewey's argument. Bruner contends that learning is an interactive process in which people learn from each other, and not just by showing and telling. He proposes that the classroom be reconceived as a subcommunity within which are modeled ways of doing or knowing, opportunities for emulation, dialogue, and reflective practices. Contrary to some criticism of his ideas regarding the teachers's role in his ideal classroom, Bruner believes that "such subcommunities do not reduce the teacher's role nor his or her authority. Instead, the teacher orchestrates the proceedings, rescues cognitive activity from implicitness, making it more public, negotiable, and solidary" (p. 24).

As I reflect on my own lifelong quest for learning, some of my most significant memories are associated with contexts in which others were involved in the learning process. Interactions with other people are a source of "disequilibration" (Piaget, 1985), whereby students progress in three phases. First, students are satisfied with their mode of thought and therefore are in a state of equilibrium. Then, through their interactions with others, they become aware of the shortcomings in their existing thinking and are dissatisfied (i.e., are in a state of disequilibration or, said another way, they experience cognitive dissonance). Finally, they adopt a more sophisticated mode of thought that eliminates the shortcomings of the old one (i.e., reach a more stable equilibrium). Piaget approached his work from the perspective of individuals, while sociocultural theorists conceptualize learning as participating more fully in the discourse and practices of a particular community as they simultaneously contribute to the growth and change of that community (e.g., Cobb, 1994). From this view, learning is as much a matter of enculturation in a community's ways of thinking and dispositions as it is a result of explicit instruction in specific concepts, skills, and procedures (Driver et al., 1994; Resnick, 1987a; Schoenfeld, 1992). Learning, then, involves the use of critical thinking skills that help us objectify realities within our personal and subjective modes for interpreting experience.

Students learn by participating in the activities of the classroom community along with more knowledgeable members, garnering for themselves new understandings and ways of thinking. At the same time, these students influence the understandings and practices of others in the classroom community. The role of teacher as presenter of information or stimulator of individual thinking is replaced by images of the teacher as coach, mentor, or master craftsperson working alongside apprentices. These images underscore the fact that, in the world outside of school, thinking, knowing, and learning are often collaborative or, to put it another way, distributed and shared across people and their environments (Borko & Putnam, 1998).

Writing about classroom as community and the manifest excitement that comes from the importance of our own and others' contributions to the educational process in higher education, Hooks (1994) contends that our capacity to generate excitement is deeply affected by our interest in one another, in hearing one another's voices, and in recognizing one another's presence. Our collective listening to one another affirms the value and uniqueness of each voice. It helps create a communal awareness of the diversity of our experiences and provides a limited sense of the experiences that may inform how we think and what we say.

What Is the Teacher's Role?

Regarding the role of the teacher in the classroom community, Hooks (1994) says that the teacher must genuinely value everyone's presence. There must be an ongoing recognition that everyone influences the classroom dynamic and that everyone contributes. These contributions are resources. Used constructively, they enhance the capacity of any class to create an open learning community. Often, before this process can begin, there has to be some deconstruction of the traditional notion that only the teacher is responsible for classroom dynamics. Indeed, the teacher will always be more responsible because the larger institutional structures will always ensure that accountability for what happens in the classroom rests with the teacher. It is rare that any teacher, no matter how eloquent a lecturer, can generate through his or her actions enough excitement to create an exciting classroom. Excitement is created through collective effort (Hooks, 1994).

Hatano (1993), in a commentary on the status of research involving contexts by Griffin et al., states that the authors claim "the most effective social interaction is one in which joint problem solving occurs" (p. 158). The authors view interaction in a specific, concrete setting as the "locus and carrier of learning" (p. 255). There must be "extended opportunity for discussion and problem solving in the context of shared activities, in which meaning and action are collaboratively constructed and negotiated" (Hatano, 1993, p. 158). The more students are isolated in their own learning at their own school, the less is their opportunity to become disequilibrated and to move to more sophisticated levels of thinking.

Inspired by Vygotskian general theorizing, Cobb et al. (1993) subscribe to learning as an active construction to resolve experientially based problems. They admit that students' initiative, interaction with peers, and adult guidance are all indispensable. They also claim that children's search for meaning and significance should be incorporated as a critical component in creating the student's appropriate, comfortable, but challenging learning level or what Vygotsky (Moll & Whitmore in Forman et al., 1993) labels the "zone of proximal development" (p. 19). This view is in contrast to the conventional characterization of learning as the transfer or transmission of culturally developed modes or products of thinking from those who know to those who do not (Forman, Minick, & Stone, 1993).

In our efforts to involve students in creating, listening, and performing music, we have in our curriculums transcended the transmission model of teaching. Students are actively and socially constructing and negotiating in these activities. Current theory, however, guides us to consider reflective dialogue or metacognition as an equally important component in the learning process. Students of all ages can become aware of their potential for metacognitive thinking within the framework of each of these musical behaviors (Pogonowski, 1989b).

As Bruner (1996) recently noted, "Modern pedagogy is moving increasingly to the view that the child should be aware of her own thought processes and that it is crucial for the pedagogical theorist and teacher alike to help her to become more metacognitive to be as aware of how she goes about her learning and thinking as she is about the subject matter she is studying. Achieving skill and accumulating knowledge are not enough. The learner can be helped to achieve full mastery by reflecting as well upon how she is going about her job and how her approach can be improved" (p. 64). Regarding the concept of creating communities of learners, Bruner (1996) affirms that, on the basis of what we have learned in recent years about human learning, "it is best when it is participatory, proactive, communal, collaborative, and given over to constructing meanings rather than receiving them" (p. 84). Or, as Thomas (1971) would say, the logic of discovery is far more exciting than the logic of the discovered. The meaning of music is in the interaction, not the fragmentation, of musical elements and factors.

With its emphasis on group work in musical improvisation, composition, performance, listening, and analysis, the Manhattanville Music Curriculum Program (MMCP) is a good example of the social importance of learning. An implicit assumption underlying MMCP is the importance of social interaction in learning music. Strategies that help students construct meaning with musical materials are the modus operandi in this curriculum. Among the three categories of artistic and personal relevance that Thomas (1971) describes, it is the relevance that deals with the relationship of the educational experience to the social environment (the total milieu in which the student lives) that is pertinent here. This concern for social relevance in all learning experience does not diminish the significance of the history of the art. Rather, it demands that learning be in focus with the times and that all factors, whether historical or contemporary, be considered in phase with the realities of contemporary life. The curriculum must deal with music as it relates to the student's culture, his or her environment, and the exigencies of life that shape his or her frame of reference.

The demand for social relevance influences the practices of MMCP in yet another way. In curriculum development, it has forced an awareness of the nature of change and the unpredictability of the directions or uses of music in the years ahead. No one can say what values will be preserved or what the future manifestations of the art will be. This curriculum, therefore, reflects the concern that the learner be allowed to remain sensitive to the viability of music in a changing society. In doing so, music classes can be dynamic, intellectually intriguing, and personal. As the curriculum bestows power on the learner, the details also become more important and memorable.

Borko and Putnam (1998) acknowledge that the educational research community has seen a renewed interest in how learning in schools might be better contextualized or situated in meaningful settings so that the resultant knowledge is indeed more accessible and useful to students when they leave school. Much of this discussion about context is intertwined with terms such as situated cognition (crafting learning opportunities that respond to particular contexts), authentic activities (employing strategies that have potential use in out-of-school life), distributed cognition (sharing information so that one person is not responsible for all of it), and communities of practice, the latter of which Bruner (1996) refers to. Borko and Putnam (1998) raise the important question of how can we create contexts and experiences that will empower students to be continual learners and problem solvers throughout their lives, especially in a rapidly changing society where the needed skills are certain to change before students reach adulthood?

In my own history, learning to use a typewriter facilitated the production of graduate school papers, publications, and grant proposals, but also my inevitable work at the computer. For me, it was an important skill to develop. Today, if I choose to, I can dictate to the computer, and it will provide a hard copy of what I have said. Are the typing skills I devoted time to developing in high school necessary in a technologically sophisticated age? They are for me, but if I were just beginning high school, maybe not. I raise the question because this is what we will have to confront as it relates to every aspect of the music curriculum: What is really important?

The arduous effort and the amount of time it takes for us to teach notational skills needs revisiting. Very often these skills are taught separately and mechanistically from the personal context of music making and consequently are not remembered from year to year as students ascend the public school ladder. More recently, researchers have come to believe that cognition is a much more complex activity than once thought. Knowledge and learning are considered to be situated in particular physical and social contexts, challenging the view that knowledge exists in the mind of the individual and independent of the context of its acquisition and use (Borko & Putnam, 1998). Cognition is viewed not solely as a property of individuals, but as distributed or "stretched over" (Lave, 1988) the individual, other persons, and various artifacts such as physical and symbolic tools (Salomon, 1993).

What Is Context?

A context is a determined place and time, either real or simulated. Contexts are designed to engage students in music making that describes real-life situations as closely as possible. Throughout history, composers have written and will continue to write music in the context of literature as in operas, cantatas, oratorios, and song cycles. They commemorate the contexts of special occasions as, for example, Handel's *Water Music,* Tchaikovsky's *1812 Overture*, and Penderecki's *To the Victims of Hiroshima.* Composers have written music to evoke moods as in Debussy's *La Mer* or his *Nocturnes.* As seen through the eyes of composers, music has always been sensitive to these contemporary conditions and social structures of the time of its creation. As seen through the eyes of children, music can make sense in school only if it has validity in the here and now. This is the spirit of how context is viewed in this discussion.

During the decades of the twentieth century, children's contexts changed dramatically as social, cultural, economic, and technological factors modified the tools and resources in their lives (Graue & Walsh, 1998). In my own life, I revel at the ease at which I am now writing at my computer and deplore the "dis-ease" I experienced every time I had to redo a page of my dissertation on my typewriter. Hours are saved searching the Internet, as opposed to traveling to libraries in remote places. For the children of today, different relationships are available now compared to previous generations. For the computer savvy, there are downloadable teaching aids for completing homework assignments. Access to e-mail facilitates peer interaction. There are Internet teachers on the Education Channel to answer questions about myriad issues. As Graue and Walsh (1998) attest, children cannot possibly remain untouched by their contexts. Just as their contexts are shaped by their presence, children and their contexts mutually constitute each other.

To try to think about children without considering their life situations is to strip children and their actions of meaning.

Though I was making a point about the importance of experience in learning music and learning about life in general, I could have been writing about the importance of context with the following questions:

How would we describe the ocean if we had never been tugged and drawn by its current or felt the panic of its unexpected waves? Could we understand buoyancy without the experience of being held by water? Experience is probably the best foundation for learning. Once we have tasted the salt and felt the water's power, we can expand what we know through numerous sources. If we have never experienced the ocean, we could read about it, but we would not remember the information in quite the same way. Such information takes on more meaning for the individual when generated by experience (Pogonowski, 1987).

This above example, of course, is an ideal experiential background for studying the ocean. The author acknowledges, however, that it is not as practical for a Midwesterner to have this real experience with the ocean as it would be for someone who lives on the coast. The point is that whenever possible, we should root our lessons as close to primary resources as our environment permits. Some things, no doubt, must be left to the imagination. With video and other multimedia, it is possible to set up more than a passive, vicarious encounter with the ocean.

Digesting and reflecting upon information based on experience results in the use of higher-order thinking skills such as analysis, synthesis, and evaluation or what are commonly referred to as critical-thinking skills. Critical thinking occurs when experiences allow us to formulate impressions based on the cognitive and emotional issues present within them.

The combination of the analytical and experiential is a richer way of knowing (Hooks, 1994). When students speak from the perspective of their immediate experiences, something new is created in the classroom for students, sometimes for the very first time. Focusing on experience allows students to claim a knowledge base from which they can speak (Hooks, 1994).

Contextual teaching and learning begin with experience. Experience is always the beginning, but it is only the beginning. According to Levy (1999) we do not learn strictly from experience; we learn from experience followed by reflection. Said another way, we learn by engaging in metacognitive thinking as it relates to our personal encounters. Without the experience, there is little to reflect about. We can study tides, sandbars, and ocean currents, but the facts just don't connect to anything real within ourselves without the experience with which to refer to.

Metacognition in the study of music involves skills associated with individual awareness and personal thinking. Students begin to see themselves as designers of their own learning rather than viewing musical information as something to be gleaned strictly from a teacher or a textbook (Pogonowski, 1989b). By leading students to think about their thinking, we take them beyond the cognitive level to a metacognitive level where they can achieve deeper understanding by examining what they know, how they know it, and the feelings associated with the quality of their knowing. For the interested reader, a more extensive discussion of metacognition and musical thinking can be found in *Dimensions of Musical Thinking* (Boardman, 1989, pp. 9–19).

Social interaction and the social contexts in which learning takes place are receiving more and more recognition in educational and psychological literature. Psychologists and educators are recognizing that the role of others in the learning process goes beyond providing stimulation and encouragement for individual construction of knowledge (Resnick, 1987a). Rather, interactions with the people in one's environment are considered major determinants of what is learned and how learning takes place.

Soltis (1981) describes this social perspective of learning as sociocentric. From this sociocentric perspective, what we take as musical knowledge and how we think and express musical ideas are the products of the musical and verbal interactions of groups of people over time. Sociocentricity supports the development of metacognitive thinking. When we weigh our musical understandings, values, beliefs, and hunches against those held by members of our discourse community, we reflect and evaluate our own musical thinking in the process. Collective or distributed metacognition may be brought about as a consequence of sharing ideas, both musical and verbal. As musical thoughts and opinions launch into action in music classes at any level, they emerge as the impetus for metacognitive thinking by others in the class. When musical compositions by groups of students are tape-recorded for playback, analysis, and reflective discussion, a proliferation of ideas stimulates each person's capacity to engage in metacognition as it relates to one's perception of meaning in music (Pogonowski, 1989b).

Research in the last decade is pointing a finger at the need for teachers to put on a psychological lens to understand students' motivation in order to understand how they learn, what tasks they choose, and why they may display eagerness and invested interest, or, conversely, apathy and avoidance. Borko and Putnam (1998) as well as Paris and Winograd (1998) agree that to understand knowledge and learning we need to better understand the importance of contexts, social relationships, collaboration, and cooperation.

Understanding the implications of self-regulation is important for teachers because the art of teaching requires continuous problem solving and invention. There are no formulae or magic potions to purge the numbness produced by static methodologies.

In preparing new teachers, we face the challenge of how best to inculcate self-regulation skills, or what I often refer to as developing a disciplined ego. Since beginning teachers face problems that are complex and not very often straightforward, it takes much more than a lecture or a discussion of a single point of view to help them grow in their understanding. As Schön (1991) points out, teaching teachers facts and rigid decision-making models is less effective than nurturing within teachers the capacity and skills to deal with the difficult problems of the real world of teaching. Paris and Winograd (1998) note, "It is ironic that teachers are often taught with pedagogical methods that are contrary to the principles that they are being taught, for example, using direct instruction to teach problem-based learning or cooperative learning" (p. 196). Why not give beginning teachers the same contexts, challenges, and choices that help them to become self-regulated learners so that they are able to model this behavior in the music class?

What Is Self-Regulated Learning?

Jones, Valdez, Nowakowski, and Rasmussen (1995) provide a description of engaged learners that captures key aspects of self-regulated learning. Engaged learners are responsible for their own learning. They take charge and are self-regulated. They define learning goals and problems that are meaningful to them, have a big picture of how specific activities relate to those goals, develop standards of excellence, and evaluate how well they achieve their goals. They have alternative routes or strategies for attaining goals and some strategies for correcting errors and redirecting themselves when their plans do not work. They know their own strengths and weaknesses and how to deal with them productively and constructively. Engaged learners are able to shape and manage change.

Paris and Winograd adopt the view that metacognition involves knowledge and control of self (cited in Pogonowski, 1989b). They point out three aspects of self-regulation that need to be controlled and monitored for metacognitive thinking to occur: commitment, attitude, and attention. The authors believe that students can choose to be committed to a task, can elect to have positive attitudes about the task, and can determine to be attentive to issues regarding the task. The wisdom that grows out of classroom teaching experience, however, suggests that in order for this to happen, there is much to be facilitated by the teacher.

A person may forever perceive a bass drum as an instrument that is pounded in time at the end of a parade. Yet when the person investigates the potential for the bass drum for creating music about the characters in a book he or she is reading, he or she is apt to develop a broader and deeper understanding of not only the bass drum, but also of the characters in the story. To musically depict the coming of a thunderstorm, the influences of tension on heartbeats of men in war, the barrenness of lands destroyed by fire, or the development of lava in a volcano is to digest these issues in ways that not only engage the mind, but the heart as well, and each is stronger as a result of the other.

Making music for an intended context motivates the person to listen, analyze, synthesize, read with purpose, share insights with classmates, and become acutely aware of all the parameters of his or her learning experience. The processes by which he or she acquires heightened self-awareness as a learner serves as a motivating force for learning as other contexts are integrated and interpreted through music. The fourth- or seventh-grader, the high school sophomore, and the graduate student immerse themselves in the context in ways that build upon their multiple capacities for learning.

As a profession, we need to think about integrating real-life issues with music so that teaching and learning become contextual and relevant to our students' lives and provide tools for ongoing lifelong learning. If our experiences in music were mainly illustrative and superficial when we were students, we need to know music at the expressive levels of creating, performing, listening, and analyzing to internalize its richness and values. If our point of departure is much like the concept of the bass drum in the parade and is our only exposure to a bass drum, it stands to reason that we have only one way to view it. If we are never challenged to think about, for example, (1) the alternative functions of an instrument, (2) various shapes a mode can take for depicting sacred medieval events, or (3) the same mode used to illustrate the disparate issues surrounding a dramatic twentieth-century occurrence, our repertoire for teaching and learning skills is wanting.

What do we want students to learn about themselves because of our teaching and their learning music? The answer to this question is an important beginning in establishing what kind of teachers we are or are becoming. The following observations, paraphrased from children's own voices, suggest some of the issues raised by the research in contextualized learning, and they also reflect some of my values about what I want my students to know about themselves because of our relationship in music:

- "How do I know me? Let me count the ways ..."
- "I can listen to and create music to express my deepest thoughts ...

thoughts about anyone … anything … anyplace … in my world … both in and out of school."

- "I can create music with my classmates in honor of our moms and dads … practice it carefully, … perform and tape record it … give it to them on their special days."
- "I can think and talk with my friends about the meaning of General Putnam's command at the Battle of Bunker Hill, 'Don't fire until you can see the whites of their eyes.'"
- "I can feel the tension the colonial troops must have felt in anticipation of seeing the British soldiers at such a close distance … and create music that tells the story."
- "I can practice the rhythms for the march we created to help give the troops courage as they march into battle … actually, … it's more fun to practice when you have a vision in your head."
- "I can learn how to learn … because … I know my best learning takes place when I have a chance to talk through musical ideas with my friends and my music teacher … try them out on instruments … find different ways of expressing the ideas … and perform them for the class … and maybe … even the principal of our school."

Addendum

I was invited to attend a conference titled "Preparing Teachers to Use Contextual Teaching and Learning Strategies to Enhance Student Success in and beyond School" during May 1998. The conference, held on the campus of the Ohio State University, was jointly sponsored by the Ohio State University and Bowling Green State University Colleges of Education. Funding was provided by the U. S. Department of Education's Office of Vocational and Adult Education and the National School-to-Work Office.

A definition of contextual teaching and learning was developed for the conference. It states that contextual teaching and learning is a conception of teaching and learning that helps teachers relate subject matter content to real-world situations and motivates students to make connections between knowledge and its applications to their lives as family members, citizens, and workers engaged in the hard work that learning requires. Contextual teaching and learning strategies:

- emphasize problem-solving
- recognize the need for teaching and learning to occur in a variety of contexts such as home, community, and work sites

- teach students to monitor and direct their own learning so they become self-regulated learners
- anchor teaching in students diverse life-contexts
- encourage students to learn from each other and together
- employ authentic assessment.

For more information on the conference proceedings, the reader is directed to its web site, www.contextual.org, with the key words "contextual teaching" and "learning."

References

Boardman, E. (Ed.). (1989). *Dimensions of musical thinking.* Reston, VA: MENC.

Bandura, A. (1997). *Self-efficacy: The exercise of control.* New York: W. H. Freeman.

Borko, H., & Putnam, R. T. (1998). The role of context in teacher learning and teacher education. www.contextual.org.

Brooks, J. G., & Brooks, M. G. (1993). *In search of understanding: The case for constructivist classrooms.* Alexandria, VA: Association for Supervision and Curriculum Development.

Bruner, J. (1996). *The culture of education.* Cambridge, MA: Harvard University Press.

Caine, R. N., & Caine, G. (1997a). *Education on the edge of possibility.* Alexandria, VA: Association for Supervision and Curriculum Development Yearbook.

Caine, R. N., & Caine, G. (1997b). *Unleashing the Power of Perceptual Change.* Alexandria, VA: Association for Supervision and Curriculum Development.

Cobb, P. (1994). Where is the mind? Constructivist and sociocultural perspectives on mathematical development. *Educational Researcher, 23* (7), 13–19.

Cobb, P. , Wood, T., & Yankel, E. (1993). Discourse, mathematical thinking, and classroom practice. In E. Forman and C. Stone (Eds.), *Contexts for learning*. (pp. 91–199). New York: Oxford University Press.

Crawford, M., & Witte, M. (1999). Strategies for mathematics: Teaching in context. *Educational Leadership, 57* (3), 34–38.

Dewey, J. (1916). *Democracy in education*. New York: Macmillan.

Driver, R. A. H., Leach, J., Mortimer, E., & Scott, P. (1994). Constructing scientific knowledge in the classroom. *Educational Researcher, 23* (7), 5–12.

Forman, E. A., Minick, N., & Stone, C. A. (Eds.). (1993). *Contexts for learning*. New York: Oxford University Press.

Graue, E. M., & Walsh, D. J. (1998). *Studying children in context: Theories, methods, and ethics*. Thousand Oaks, CA: Sage Publications, Inc.

Hatano, G. (1993). Time to merge Vygotskian and constructivist concepts of knowledge acquisition. In Forman, E. A., Minick, N., & Stone, C. A., *Contexts for learning* (pp. 153–66). New York: Oxford University Press.

Hooks, B. (1994). *Teaching to transgress: Education as the practice of freedom*. New York: Routledge.

Jones, B., Nowakowski, J., & Rasmussen, C. (1995). *Plugging in: Choosing and using educational technology*. Washington, DC: Council for Educational Development and Research; North Brook, IL: Northcentral Regional Educational Laboratory. (ERIC Document Reproduction Service No. ED 415 837).

Lave, J. (1988). *Cognition in practice: Mind, mathematics and culture in everyday life*. Cambridge, England: Cambridge University Press.
Levy, S. 1999. To see the world in a grain of sand. *Educational Leadership, 57* (3), 70–75.

Moll, L. C., & Whitmore, K. F. (1993). Vygotsky in classroom practice. In Forman, E. A., Minick, N., & Stone, C. A., *Contexts for learning* (pp. 19–42). New York: Oxford University Press.

Paris, S. G., & Winograd, P. (1998). The role of self-regulated learning in contextual teaching: Principles and practices for teacher preparation. www.contextual.org.

Piaget, J. (1985). *The equilibration of cognitive structures.* (T. Brown & K. J. Thampy, Trans.). Chicago: University of Chicago Press.

Pogonowski, L. (1989a). Critical thinking and music listening. *Music Educators Journal, 76* (1), 35–38.

Pogonowski, L. (1989b). Metacognition: A dimension of musical thinking. In E. Boardman (Ed.), *Dimensions of musical thinking.* Reston, VA: MENC.

Pogonowski, L. (1987). Developing skills in critical thinking and problem solving. *Music Educators Journal, 73* (6), 37–41.

Resnick, L. B. (1987). Learning in school and out. *Educational Researcher 16*, no. 9: 13–20.

Salomon, G. (Ed.). (1993). *Distributed cognitions: Psychological and educational considerations.* Cambridge, England: Cambridge University Press.

Schoenfeld, A. H. (1992). Learning to think mathematically: Problem solving metacognition and sense making in mathematics. In D. Grouws (Ed.), *Handbook of research on mathematics teaching and learning* (pp. 334–70). New York: Macmillan.

Schön, D. (1991). *The reflective task: Case studies in and on educational practice.* New York: Teachers College Press.

Soltis, J. F. (1981). Education and the concept of knowledge. In J. F. Soltis (Ed.), *Philosophy and Education* (pp. 95–113). Chicago: National Society for the Study of Education.

Thomas, R. B. (1971). *Manhattanville music curriculum program synthesis: A structure for music education.* Clifton Park, NY: Media Materials, Inc.

Thorndike, E. L. (1922). *The psychology of arithmetic.* www.contextual.org.

Whitehead, A. N. (1929). *The aims of education.* In H. Borko, & R. T. Putnam, (1998). The role of context in teacher learning and teacher education. www.contextual.org.

Lenore Pogonowski is professor of music education and music at Teachers College at Columbia University in New York, New York.

3

CRITICAL AND CREATIVE THINKING

MARK S. DETURK

Critical and creative thinking are often referred as higher-order thinking skills. While there are similarities between the two types of thinking that can make them quite complementary, beginning with the assumption that there exists a task to be accomplished by such thinking, the differences between the two are pronounced, and they shall be treated separately within this chapter.

Defining each term raises important questions, and different definitions lead different scholars to alternative opinions. Critical thinking is typically referred to as a convergent task, while creative thinking is more likely to be the product of divergent efforts. Some authors seem to confuse the two by referring to composers who think critically about their creative work, while others mention the possibility of critiquing creatively. This kind of cross-referencing can lead to tremendous confusion. Critical thinking really represents aspects of what is better known as metacognition—being self-conscious (aware) about one's own thought processes. For the sake of clarity, critical thinking will refer here to the process of constructing an evaluation of either a musical performance or a musical composition. The music critic is the model. Creative thinking will refer to a musician's efforts to improvise or compose new music.

Musical Critical Thinking

Music criticism has enjoyed a cherished position in musical history and as a profession. Evaluation is the primary task of critical thinking, and music is evaluated in cognitive and affective ways that are informed by experience. "Critical thinking is the result of experiential learning that embraces the learner's affective and cognitive domains" (Pogonowski, 1987, p. 38).

Music students may critically evaluate a performance with attention to technical and expressive detail, or they may evaluate the musical work itself with attention to the ways in which the elements of music combine to form that work. Performance criticism seems to get far more attention in music classrooms than criticism of composition. Indeed, the entire venture of evaluating a musical work seems foreign to most school musicians.

Hudgins and Edelman (1986) define a good critical thinker as one with "the disposition to provide evidence in supporting one's conclusions and to request evidence from others before accepting their conclusions" (p. 333). Good critical thinkers about music rely upon conceptual musical evidence as the basis for their evaluations. They critically evaluate a particular work or performance by understanding the music and the merits of its parts and its totality. In this way, evaluation is derived from musical evidence rather than from peer pressure, whim, or fashion.

To define critical thinking, Whitaker (1996) draws upon John Dewey's term "reflective thinking" as "active, persistent, and careful consideration of any belief or supposed form of knowledge in the light of the grounds that support it and the further conclusions to which it tends" (p. 2). Introducing a new term to represent another, in this case "reflective" to represent "critical," creates confusion, but the shared emphasis on the search for grounds that support evaluation is consistent: Finding evidence on which evaluations can be based, as opposed to accepting impulse or the suggestion of others, is the benchmark of good critical thinking.

The good critical thinker must be equipped in at least three ways: first, with a conceptual knowledge of music and an understanding of the elements of music; second, with a storehouse of high quality musical experience that serves as a yardstick against which other music is measured both affectively and cognitively; and third, with a metacognitive strategy or "disposition" (Ennis, 1987, p. 10) to seek musical evidence as the basis for musical evaluation. The critical thinker must wish, and know how, to make an informed decision.

The mechanism by which the thinker arrives at evaluation is not well understood. Richardson (1996) has introduced the idea of the process or processes used by musical "connoisseurs" as one or more processes to be emulated. Studies of both professionals and children reveal a complex process.

Critical Thinking in the Music Curriculum

The capability to employ critical or evaluative thinking has been consistently listed as an important educational goal (Bloom et al., 1956). Likewise, higher-level thinking has long been stated as a broadly held goal in music education. The Resolution on the Creative Arts adopted by the American Association of School Administration in 1959 proclaimed, "It is important that pupils, as a part of general education, learn to appreciate, to understand, to create, and to criticize with discrimination those products of the mind, the voice, the hand, and the body which give dignity to the person and exalt the spirit of man" (Ernst & Gary, 1965, p. 1).

Over the past forty years, teachers have been urged to prepare their students to do the following:

1. "Compare musical styles ranging from serious masterworks to jazz classics. They should also prize quality renditions of music" (Leonhard & House, 1959, p. 184).
2. "Discriminate with respect to music" (Ernst & Gary, 1965, p. 11).
3. "Examine the criteria employed in making value judgments about music" (Schwadron, 1967, p. 79).
4. Perform "acts of decision making, judging, or selecting based on a given set of criteria. As an example, using specific criteria other than emotional inclination, the music learner evaluates a musical composition new to him" (Sidnell, 1973, pp. 70–71).
5. "Make judgments about music, and value the personal worth of music" (First National Assessment of Educational Progress, 1970, p. 16).
6. Develop "aesthetic judgment and aesthetic value ... [necessary] in formulating judgments regarding the use and quality of music" (Abeles, Klotman, & Hoffer, 1984, p. 95).
7. "Listen to, analyze, and describe music," as well as "Evaluate music and

music performances" (Consortium of National Arts Education Associations, 1994).

Teaching Critical Thinking about Music

Instruction must prepare the student for each of three requirements of musical critical thinking. First, the critical thinker must understand the elements of music. Attention should be devoted to acquiring and relating the basic concepts of music and its performance. Students need to understand the cognitively low-level concepts of timbre, tempo, dynamics, and simple melody and rhythm, as well as the middle and higher level relational concepts of complex melody and rhythm, harmony, tonality, form, texture, and expression. They also need to comprehend various levels of performance concepts with regard to tone quality, accuracy of pitch and rhythm, ensemble, and personal sensitivity. Well-taught students know these concepts and the labels that make them useful and retrievable. These same students display their conceptual knowledge as they perform, describe, and create music.

Students must be able to employ the elements of music and of quality performance as the basis for evaluation. At every level, the curriculum should include some attention to each. Elementary general music instruction might include the performance concepts of good tone quality, intonation, ensemble, and expression, along with the traditional emphasis on the elements of music.

Secondary school performance teachers might continue teaching the elements of music because they become the basis for describing, creating, performing, and critiquing music.

Second, the critical thinker must have high quality resources available for comparison. Through experience with a rich resource of music of all kinds, students acquire a personal storehouse of music that serves as a background against which evaluation can be performed. Music classes should provide ever deeper and broader musical experiences that students can make their own.

Two concerns are obvious. One is that the music taught in class needs to be of high quality if it is to serve effectively for the purpose of comparison. The importance of quality literature as the vehicle of study and experience cannot be overemphasized. General music and performance teachers should constantly ascertain if their selections meet this requirement. The demands of entertaining general music students or performance-group audiences often tempt teachers to devote time to music of lesser value. Teachers need to defend the selection of literature as a primary issue in curriculum decision making.

Another concern is that the most noteworthy elements of the high quality music studied need to be labeled and have attention drawn to them. Without labeling, much of the musical material stored in memory may be irretrievable. For example, students can be directed to sections of works by name rather than by rehearsal number. "Let's begin at the second theme, please" involves a great deal more conceptual learning than "Let's begin at measure thirty-seven." Likewise, tonalities can be called minor, not sad; pitches are out of tune, not sour.

The third requirement of critical musical thinking is that the thinker must wish, and know how, to make an informed decision. The habit of relying upon concept knowledge and stored musical experience as the basis for musical evaluation must be established. Transfer of learning cannot be assumed. Students need to hear unfamiliar music and be encouraged to discuss it in elemental musical terms and to compare it to other works on those terms, as well as on affective terms. Teachers might begin conversations about pieces by asking students first to describe those instruments or voices involved. This may be followed by accurately representing themes (melody), motivic rhythm and other rhythm characteristics, and tempo. Finally, attention may be paid to group considerations of key (harmony), form, and style. Only after music can be accurately described can it be convincingly evaluated. Comparison with other known works and discussion of a composer's intent represent still higher levels of critical thinking.

Students can be exposed to the critical thinking of others and asked to respond to it in a way that will make them sensitive to the need for supportive conceptual evidence as the basis for criticism. The understanding of how connoisseurs think could be a real help. Students can be asked to argue for and against the merits of particular pieces or performances, orally or in writing. Asking students to evaluate the quality of some other person's critical thoughts provides a valuable detached view of the process, just as editing someone else's writing provides a detached view of the composition process.

Evaluating Critical Thinking about Music

Evaluating higher-level thinking skills has always been a problem for teachers. It is a difficult task that seems to defy efficient group solutions. This may be one reason that so much teaching is directed instead at lower level learning—it is easy to test. Music teachers, however, are especially familiar with the argument that something can be worth teaching and learning even if it is difficult to test. Like the subject of music itself, critical thinking about music is worth teaching, though evaluating it can be elusive.

The evaluation of critical thinking skills is best accomplished by confronting students with evaluation tasks and observing the process. In this sense, the teaching procedure and the evaluation procedure are similar. Further, evaluation of students' critical thinking serves to continually redirect the teaching effort toward lower-level learning objectives. Critical-thinking evaluations almost always point up areas of conceptual weakness, sending the teacher off to strengthen the students in these areas and then reevaluate their thinking process.

Critical thinking is not easily evaluated by traditional short-answer examinations. In a thinking evaluation, supplying a correct answer is not the real assignment for the student. Instead, the goal for students (as clearly communicated by the teacher) should be to display their thought processes. Students can do this through some form of "self-report" using written essays or personal interviews. This allows for an evaluation of the process itself. According to Hudgins (1966), "Directions which many teachers give to their pupils to 'show your work' or to 'explain why you chose' a particular alternative seem well advised. Such explanations provide the teacher with information which bears directly upon the pupils' processes of thinking" (p. 11).

Even when essay tests have successfully elicited from students the thought processes that they employed, there has always been the problem of finding a reliable method for assessing those essays. One rubric with some proven success (DeTurk, 1988a) involves the rating of student thinking via the SOLO Taxonomy (Biggs & Collis, 1982). It is the accuracy and sophistication of the thinking process, not the correctness of any final conclusion, that is evaluated.

According to this procedure, students are asked to write an essay in which they describe, analyze, and evaluate in musical terms a composition heard or performed. Those essays are then assigned to one of five categories based upon their content and structure. These categories represent increasingly sophisticated levels of critical thinking reflecting conceptual knowledge and its structure. They are described below with illustrative excerpts from sample student essays.

1. Prestructural essays display no structured learning of the subject and typically avoid, deny, or simply fail to respond accurately to the assignment. (Notice that evaluations based on nonmusical concepts fall within this category.) Example: "The first piece of music makes me feel dominant, triumphant. ... The second piece makes me feel carefree like taking a trip to an exotic island. ... The evil in the first song and the happiness in the second song is why they are different" (no musical concept cited).

2. Unistructural essays rely upon a single lower level musical concept or fact (simple rhythm, tempo, dynamics, or performance medium) as the basis for unsophisticated conclusions reached hastily. Example: "The first piece of music had a very heavy, strong beat. ... The second piece had a much lighter beat with a more positive attitude. ... I don't think one is any better than the other" (single music concept cited: rhythmic stress).
3. Multistructural essays employ several unrelated musical concepts or facts of the same type as unistructural essays. They seek multiple evidence but do not present a unified argument. Example: "The first piece starts out loud and gets softer right away. There are people singing in it. ... It sounds like the music is being played by string instruments. ... The second piece starts out with real slow music played by string instruments. As it goes on it gets faster and a flute is heard. ... Both pieces have a lot of different instruments in them. The first piece goes from loud to soft a lot, but the second one stays pretty much the same" (three music concepts cited: dynamics, instrumentation, and tempo).
4. Relational essays display both a grasp of higher level concepts (such as form, orchestration, or style) and present unified arguments that successfully incorporate evidence from several concepts into convincing answers that deal with the assignments as narrowly defined. Example: "The second piece is more contemporary than the first. The choir leads the first piece, in comparison to just one singer leading the second piece. Instrumentally, they were also different. The first had more of an orchestra sound to it. The second had more of a jazzy band sound to it. ... The first began loud and harsh, the second began with a warm and flowing tone. Both pieces had different sections or forms within them. I thought the quality of both pieces was very good. I tend to like the second piece better because of the more contemporary sound" (four lower music concepts cited: instrumentation, medium, dynamics, and timbre; two higher music concepts cited: form and historical style period).
5. Extended abstract essays demonstrate very sophisticated levels of critical thinking. For example, "The first piece has three sections. The first section is a full orchestra playing long, full chords, is forte and has a minor sound. ... The second piece has two sections. The first is gentle and relaxed; the second is jazzier and more upbeat. The sax, bass and drums provide a happy dancing beat. ... These two pieces each have a different purpose. ... For this reason, they are hard to compare. Each completes its mission" (three lower music concepts cited: medium,

dynamics, and tempo; three higher music concepts cited: form, tonality, and musical function; discussion of musical purpose [function] exceeds the bounds of the assignment).

The reliability of the SOLO Taxonomy across subject disciplines has proven to be quite high (Biggs & Collis, 1982). In a study of 279 critical essays about music written by high school juniors and rated by three different readers, the reliability was 0.89. For only fourteen (5 per cent) of the essays were those readers unable to reach agreement as to what level rating was appropriate. Each judge felt the ratings were valid in representing the students' abilities to think critically about music. One reader altered her approach to teaching as a result of the insight gained from this evaluation procedure (DeTurk, 1988b).

Musical Creative Thinking

Like critical thinking, creative thinking is higher-level thinking with a specialized purpose—the production of new music. The focus on "output" separates creative thinking from problem solving, another advanced thinking skill. For instance, problem solving might lead to the conclusion that creative thought was necessary for some purpose.

Eisner (1964) quotes Morris Stein's definition of a creative product as "a novel work that is considered useful, tenable, or satisfying by some group at some point in time" (p. 10). Creative musical thinking most often involves the unique, personal manipulation of the materials of music as currently understood by the creative thinker. For serious art works, such manipulation is generally thought to be both original and expressive in nature.

The authors of *Dimensions of Thinking* (Marzano et al., 1988) outlined five aspects of creative thinking that are reviewed here with respect to music.

1. Creativity takes place in conjunction with intense desire and preparation. Motivation to create must be strong enough to see students through to the completion of the task. Persistence, often used as a measure of motivation, is a prerequisite for and one indicator of creative thinking. Students are most persistent at creative thinking projects that they value themselves. An assignment like composing a four-part chorale for piano may not motivate every student.

2. Creativity involves working at the edge rather than at the center of one's capacity. Creative thinkers often test their abilities and seek new knowledge in the process of creating. By accepting a creative task, they subject themselves to an endeavor whose demands are not entirely known to them in advance. They are, therefore, risk takers in pursuit of

their objective. For some students, the risk itself motivates. For others, it provides an excuse for failure. For most, it is an element that must be monitored and controlled.

3. Creativity requires an internal rather than external locus of evaluation. Working to personal standards in pursuit of a personal product serves to isolate the creative thinker from peer pressure and possibly even teacher evaluation. This can be threatening to the classroom teacher who feels accountable to the schools and parents for the nature and quality of student work. Yet everything we know about creative individuals points to their own individual, intrinsic set of values.
4. Creativity involves reframing ideas. There are many similar terms for this reframing process. Divergent, fluid, flexible, metaphoric, and lateral thinking all share a focus on developing alternative approaches. These terms imply the creation of new schemas or thought patterns that lead to original paradigms, style practices, musical genres, and theories. Such thinking requires tremendous time and concentration and probably is not realistic as a limited classroom objective.
5. Creativity can sometimes be facilitated by getting away from intensive engagement for a while to permit free-flowing thought. Whatever the mechanism is for the "Oh, my gosh!" experience in which a revelation is received, its implications for the classroom teacher are limited. If students need time away from projects to allow for "thought fermentation," it might be suggested that their work be given a due date and then returned for improvements at a later time. Meeting a due date is, after all, a professional creativity requirement of the first magnitude.

Webster (1988) and Kratus (1988) have spearheaded a movement to understand the teaching and learning involved in creative music making. Webster (1988) comments on the scarcity of effort to teach composition to students by saying, "It is ironic that arts educators, particularly music educators, are the most guilty of avoiding and even discouraging creative thinking" (p. 33). He too finds five characteristics common to the creative thinking mechanism: "a problem-solving context, convergent and divergent thinking skills, stages in the thinking process, some aspect of novelty in the process, and usefulness of the result" (Webster, 1988, p. 34).

Creative Thinking in the Music Curriculum

It is strangely true that few music courses include teaching creative thinking. Creativity is rarely encouraged in this subject, the most abstract of the creative arts. Nonetheless, teaching creative thinking in the creative arts has been espoused regularly as both natural and appropriate. Further, recent increases in the concern for teaching thinking in all subjects might benefit music in particular.

Leonhard and House (1959) urge the music teacher to "*emphasize* creativity in all music instruction" (p. 260). Hoffer (1973) feels that "musical learning should not be confined to the recreation of what others have done. At a level consistent with their musical sophistication, students should engage in creating music through composition or improvisation, or both" (p. 58). Abeles, Hoffer, and Klotman (1984) write that "creative activities are undertaken because the act of creating is itself of value to the students" (p. 152).

While these and similar sentiments from reputable music educators abound, there seems to be less consensus about teaching creative thinking than there is about teaching critical thinking. This is true for other subjects as well as for music education in particular. In the past, students have been encouraged to understand creative thinking rather than taught to do it. Studies of the thinking of master composers have been common. During this century, articles and books reporting the thought processes of respected musical creators, such as Leonard Bernstein, Aaron Copland, Roger Sessions, and Igor Stravinsky, have been very popular. Recognition and appreciation of creative thinking in others can be strengthened, however, by doing it.

At the least, an effort should be made to structure music courses so as not to block creative efforts. The curriculum ought to contain the flexibility to allow for creative exploration. Music classes, especially at the secondary level, often appear to be among the most rigidly structured in the schools. That very structure may discourage the learner who has a creative objective to pursue. Further, the extreme demands of many performance classes simply prohibit students from devoting attention and energy to the creation of music. Should it surprise us to find that, for these and other reasons, the most musically creative students in our schools may avoid music classes?

Teaching Creative Musical Thinking

While music may be called one of the creative arts, school teachers seem to avoid teaching the creative aspect of our art form. "We may well find that the mathematics or science teacher is much more effective at getting children to think creatively about their subjects than the music teacher" (Webster, 1988, p. 33).

Methodology for the teaching of creativity is controversial. A variety of opinions can be found about such basic issues as at what age to begin, how much structure to build into the experience, and even what it means to teach creative thinking. As pointed out in *Dimensions of Thinking,* (Marzano et al., 1988) however, creative and critical thinking are similar processes and might be expected to benefit from a similar progression of instruction. Some components of teaching creative musical thinking include:

1. The creative thinker must understand the elements of music. Like critical thinking, creative thinking requires a knowledge of and curiosity about the elements of music. The circular nature of this relationship means that creative work should send the student back to further understand the concepts of music, thus reinforcing and expanding earlier learning. Curricula such as the Manhattanville Music Curriculum Project (Thomas, 1970) are constructed upon this reciprocal relationship between basic knowledge and creativity.

2. The creative thinker must have high quality resources available for comparison. Creative thinking often operates like a metaphor. The thinker may wonder, "Can I do something like the piece I heard yesterday?" This kind of thought requires a resource of musical works with which to draw parallels. Teachers who teach high quality music to their students prepare them to think creatively. By labeling the musical elements and forms of those works studied, the teacher makes them even more available to students.

3. The creative thinker must wish to, and know how to, carry out the process of production. Though established composers and improvisers may cite an internal need to express themselves, the disposition to create may not be apparent in every school child. Students need motivation in the form of encouragement, modeling, and valuing of the creative effort from their teachers. Room must be made in the daily musical life for discussion of, and attempts at, creativity. Finally, teachers must make available to their students assistance with the craft of musical creation.

Evaluating Creative Thinking about Music

The fact that creators usually work with reference to their own evaluative criteria does not preclude a teacher from making informed assessments of a student's creative thinking efforts. The personal nature of creative thinking almost dictates that assessment be made on an individual basis. The time-consuming nature of this kind of evaluation may be one of the reasons that instruction in creativity is not more common.

Studies often mention three different aspects of creativity: process, product, and characteristics of the individual. Only the first two aspects are appropriate for evaluation in the schools, since the third does not vary as a result of instruction. The product (the composition) is worthy of evaluation since good process (creative thinking) normally bears a commensurate product. Information about the process employed is most valuable for the design of further instruction and requires regular individual consultation with the student.

Kratus (1988) presents a series of evaluation scales, checklists, and data collection techniques for assessing the processes and products of creative thinking rather than the traits of the creative thinker. He defends their validity, reliability, and reasonableness as methods of use to teachers. "By focusing on process or product instead of person, measurement can more directly measure a music lesson's objectives or a music program's goals in terms of student behavior in specific activities" (Kratus, 1988, p. 13). He emphasizes procedures and grading scales that evaluate both the musical characteristics and the creative characteristics of creative processes and products.

Implications

Raising concern about musical thinking skills has several implications for the teaching of music that might cause educators to reflect upon their own teaching, their own student experiences, and how research informs them about music learning. Some of these implications are discussed below.

1. Musical thinking skills are included among the objectives listed in most books and articles written about music education during the past century. An examination of these materials reveals a priority placed upon the development of thinking skills useful in adult life for choosing, evaluating, and creating music to perform or hear. Teaching students higher order thinking skills is not a new or temporary concern.

2. Performing ensembles perform in a superior fashion if their curriculum includes attention to broad musical learning beyond rehearsal. Studies have shown that ratings of both listening skills and group festival performances improve for groups and the individual students involved who are taught to think about music rather than just rehearse it.

3. The public is critical of school music education for not teaching the subject of music at a level useful for adults. The ongoing need to defend teaching music in school may be the result of the general public's memory of music instruction that developed little-used performance skills, but failed to prepare it to think in a sophisticated manner about music.

4. When asked to list those musical topics about which they were curious, students frequently mention composition, orchestration, and improvisa-

tion. Student desire for advanced instruction of this type is often ignored by teachers. There appears to be a student population with the interests and abilities to pursue such subjects, which require higher level musical thinking.

5. What is good for the best is good for the rest. Current education thinking holds that if we can identify elements of the curriculum that are beneficial for the most advanced students, we ought to ask sincerely if these elements should not be taught to all students. If higher level thinking is a valuable skill to foster and encourage for some, then perhaps it should be a part of every student's course of study. Following such a line of thought relieves teachers of the arbitrary task of identifying particular students as especially deserving of such instruction.
6. Teachers need to be able to assume different roles. Some discomfort may arise from the need to serve as maestro for students when they are rehearsing, virtuoso when teaching an instrument or voice to them, and coach when encouraging them toward higher level thinking. Especially when thinking creatively, students may have valid thoughts quite different from our own. Here, as elsewhere, exists the possibility of finding students more skillful than ourselves. Good teachers recognize and encourage those students without feeling threatened.

References

Abeles, H. F., Hoffer, C. R., & Klotman, R. H. (1984). *Foundations of music education.* New York: Schirmer Books.

Biggs, J. B., & Collis, K. F. (1982). *Evaluating the quality of learning: The SOLO taxonomy.* New York: Academic Press.

Bloom, B. S., Englehart, M. D., Furst, E. J., Hill, W. H., & Krathwohl, D. R. (Eds.). (1956). *Taxonomy of educational objectives, Handbook I: Cognitive domain.* New York: David McKay.

Consortium of National Arts Education Associations. (1994). *National standards for arts education: What every young American should know and be able to do in the arts.* Reston, VA: MENC.

DeTurk, M. S. (1988a). Evaluating music concept learning with the SOLO taxonomy. In J. A. Braswell, (Ed.), *Proceedings of the 1988 Southeastern Music Education Symposium* (pp. 162–71). Athens, GA: Center for Continuing Education, University of Georgia.

DeTurk, M. S. (1988b). *The relationship between experience in the performing music class and critical thinking about music.* (Doctoral dissertation, University of Wisconsin-Madison, 1988). *Dissertation Abstracts International,* 49(06) 1398.

Eisner, E. W. (1964). *Think with me about creativity: 10 essays on creativity.* Danville, NY: F. A. Owen Publishing.

Ernst, K. D., & Gary, C. L. (1965). *Music in general education.* Washington, D.C.: MENC.

Hoffer, C. R. (1973). *Teaching music in the secondary schools* (2nd ed.). Belmont, CA: Wadsworth.

Hudgins, B.B. (1966). *Problem solving in the classroom.* New York: Macmillan.

Hudgins, B.B., & Edelman, S. (1986). Teaching critical thinking skills to fourth and fifth graders through teacher-led small group discussions. *Journal of Educational Research, 79,* 333–42.

Kratus, J. (1988). Evaluating children's creative processes and products in music. In J. A. Braswell, (Ed.), *Proceedings of the 1988 Southeastern Music Education Symposium* (pp. 10–22). Athens: Georgia Center for Continuing Education, University of Georgia.

Leonhard, C., & House, R. (1959). *Foundations and principles of music education.* (2nd ed.). New York: McGraw-Hill.

Marzano, R. J., Brandt, R. S., Hughes, C. S., Jones, B. F., Presseisen, B. Z., Rankin, S. C., & Suhor, C. (1988). *Dimensions of thinking: A framework for curriculum and instruction.* Alexandria, VA: Association for Supervision and Curriculum Development.

National Assessment of Educational Progress. (1970). *Music objectives.* Ann Arbor, MI: National Assessment of Educational Progress.

Pogonowski, L. (1987). Developing skills in critical thinking and problem solving. *Music Educators Journal, 73* (7), 37–41.

Richardson, C. P. (1996). A theoretical model of the connoisseur's musical thought. *Bulletin of the Council for Research in Music Education,* no. 128, 15–24. Urbana, IL: University of Illinois at Urbana–Champaign.

Schwadron, A. A. (1967). *Aesthetics: Dimensions for music education.* Washington, D.C.: MENC.

Sidnell, R. (1973). *Building instructional programs in music education.* Englewood Cliffs, NJ: Prentice-Hall.

Thomas, R. B. (1970). Rethinking the curriculum. *Music Educators Journal, 56* (6), 68–70.

Webster, P. R. (1988). Creative thinking and music education. *Design for Arts in Education, 89,* (5), 33–37.

Whitaker, N. L. (1996). A theoretical model of the musical problem solving and decision making of performers, arrangers, conductors and composers. *Bulletin of the Council for Research in Music Education,* no. 128, 1–14. Urbana, IL: University of Illinois at Urbana–Champaign.

Mark S. DeTurk is associate professor of music at the University of New Hampshire in Durham, New Hampshire.

4

THINKING PROCESSES IN A DIFFERENT KIND OF CLASSROOM

THOMAS PRIEST

Musicians express their ideas and beliefs through an elaborate symbol system of sound, image, and movement. They share their understanding as listeners, composers, and performers of a particular world view that is generated and perpetuated within a cultural context. Since we seem to learn best by engaging in these various musical behaviors, this chapter will discuss how learners may think creatively and critically while functioning as listeners, composers, and performers.

It is fascinating to discover the tremendous diversity of musicians upon our planet. In some cultures, virtually every individual is considered an active participant, and everyone shares a common music with an equal level of fluency. In others, there are varying degrees of specialization. In the Euro-American tradition, specialization has become extreme. Individuals are allowed to become passive musicians, taking little if any responsibility for musical production; people become clearly labeled as "musicians" or "nonmusicians," and we have musical specialists who make their living through their specialized skills. We even have musicians who focus upon teaching music. This high degree of specialization, of course, reflects how other aspects of our lives are systematically managed and maintained. For example, we do not simply have one healer who takes care of all that ails us, but instead we have a variety of healers who care for each particular malady. Depending on our particular concern, these individuals might include a minister, a chiropractor, a psychiatrist, a podiatrist, a music therapist, or a musician, and we might contact these individuals in person or through various forms of media. Music educators function within a formalized educational setting that is designed to prepare individuals to function within a society that values and produces specialists in a tremendous number of professions or domains of understanding. Since our society tends to foster specialization, it often seems natural for music teachers to focus upon one or more musicianly roles. Therefore, music educators develop and create musical specialties; these include areas of performance, history, composition, theory, analysis, improvisation, cognition, and psychology.

Engaging in certain musical behaviors may identify a specialist, but it would be incorrect to suggest that any specialist would or should engage only in a certain musical behavior. A performer, for example, is better prepared to perform if he or she possesses a thorough knowledge of musical context, for the past and present knowledge of music in a culture significantly shapes each musical setting. Each performance is situated in a specific time and place, and the performer's comprehensive knowledge of music in culture, as understood through the areas of specialization mentioned above, influences each creation or recreation of a musical event. Although novice performers may proceed without a thorough understanding of how their works offer meaning, a broader understanding of the music they choose to share often proves more rewarding for the performers as well as for their audiences. Therefore, music specialists successfully function to the degree that they understand how their specialty is integrally related to a broader understanding of music in culture.

When we consider what constitutes an appropriate music education for the general public, musical specialization may fail us. From what we know about learning, instruction focused on large interdisciplinary curricular themes is the most effective way to promote understanding (Marzano, 1992). Comparatively, a musical education that draws upon many aspects of musical knowledge will more likely prepare individuals for the variety of roles in which they will choose to participate. Therefore, it behooves us to consider how music learning might take into account a broader understanding of music in culture.

Creative and Critical Thinking

Since most rationales for teaching and learning music suggest that it is a vehicle for nurturing creativity, it is appropriate to recognize how individuals may function creatively, as well as critically, within various music-learning environments. Although we naturally see composition as a creative act, we are becoming more and more aware of the creative nature of performance and listening. Because individuals may respond creatively to problems of analysis, of performance, and of composition, Webster (1990) called for the profession to turn its attention to creative thinking rather than creativity. Creative thinking, however, is integrally related to critical thinking, and one of these modes may subsume the other, depending on the particular focus of the musician and the nature of the problem to be solved. Musicians create, critically examine their products, and assess their value within a cultural framework. In some contexts, musicians attempt to solve problems of production in which the standards or goals are clear, and they attempt to recreate or reproduce a musical event within certain guidelines. In this kind of work, critical-thinking skills tend to dominate. In other contexts, however, musicians attempt to solve problems for which the standards or goals are unclear or nonexistent. This is where creative-thinking skills emerge, and musicians are able to establish new standards or create new frameworks for musical activity.

In *Dimensions of Thinking: A Framework for Curriculum and Instruction* (Marzano et al., 1988), the authors state that it is virtually impossible to think creatively without thinking critically. When we solve a problem, we do it more or less creatively and more or less critically. These cognitive constructs resonate with the oscillatory nature of divergent and convergent thinking processes discussed by Guilford (1959). Divergent thinking is characterized by the generation of many possible solutions to a given problem, and convergent thinking involves the assessment of possible solutions and convergence upon the best possible answer. Divergent processes tend to be more aligned with creative thinking, and convergent processes tend to be more aligned with critical thinking. Like critical and creative thinking, they are interdependent.

In their examination of thinking processes, Swartz and Perkins (1989) recognize that the classic challenge for creative thinking is "breaking set" or seeing a situation in a new way. When thinking tends to be dominated by old patterns and routines, it is easy to overlook novel but effective approaches. Swartz and Perkins (1989) also cite problem finding as a more recent focus of creative thinking. Correspondingly, Getzels and Csikszentmihalyi (1976) assert that creative thinking is not simply a matter of finding novel resolutions to old problems and questions, but it also includes actively finding and formulating new problems and new questions.

Lipman (1991), providing a philosophical perspective, suggests that creative and critical thinking naturally fuse into what he calls higher-order thinking. This is "particularly evident when the critical and creative aspects support and reinforce each other, as when the critical thinker invents new premises or new criteria or when the creative thinker gives a new twist to an artistic tradition or convention" (Lipman, 1991, p. 20). Lipman (1991) also suggests that the two thinking processes do not change, but the purposes and intentions may change. He contends that when we examine judgments, we can most easily see a shift from critical thinking to creative thinking. A judgment is always a decision, but the intentions or purposes of that decision may oscillate. When criteria have been established and are considered reliable, critical judgment may determine whether a given product or response does or does not meet the established criteria. But when the criteria themselves are questioned or are nonexistent, there tends to be a loss of boundaries. This shift of intention allows us to move from actual into possible worlds (Lipman, 1991).

In music, we live in worlds that transcend the boundaries of language. We think creatively and critically within structures of sound. Although we may construct meaning about music and culture through spoken or written language, music essentially allows us to learn and effectively communicate knowledge that cannot be conveyed with language. Recognizing that different domains of understanding call for different modes of thinking, it would seem that McPeck (1981), a proponent of informal logic, would readily acknowledge the nonverbal thought processes that take place while an individual is thinking musically. He argues that critical thinking always manifests itself in connection with some identifiable activity or subject area and never in isolation. He is adamant that critical thinking must be connected with a certain discipline, activity, or subject. Music educators, therefore, may notice that thinking strategies, primarily designed to foster learning that is expressed through language, may prove an ill fit for music-thinking processes.

In an examination of the historical, social, and theoretical contexts of goals and practices in art and music education, May (1989) attempts to define critical thinking. She, however, quickly acknowledges that any verbal definition of critical thinking may miss important aspects of thinking in music or art since decisions about line, shape, color, texture, contour, form, and other elements may be made without the use of spoken or written language. The learner-artist, for example, often responds to intrinsic qualities of the art form that are beyond the constraints of the linearity or spatial-temporal order of language.

While music allows us to learn and share knowledge outside the bounds of language, Marzano (1992) recognizes the need to broaden our abilities to use and understand language. By using metaphors, he proposes that we can open our eyes to new ways of seeing, prompting us to explore options that we might not have pursued otherwise. Therefore, he proposes that metaphors are an appropriate tool for nurturing creative or divergent thinking. Since music offers us an infinite pool of metaphors, it can also open our ears, as well as our eyes, to new ways of hearing and seeing. As Marzano calls for the broadening of our abilities to use and understand language, we must also broaden our abilities to use and understand music.

Despite our tendencies to function as musical specialists, it is worthwhile to critically examine the basic roles of listener, performer, and composer. Although we develop patterns of action associated with certain musical professions, we ultimately maintain and nurture our abilities to use these three basic musical behaviors. Active listening may be neglected, however, since by default in the Euro-American tradition we too often nurture the role of passive observer-listener. There are, however, different qualities or levels of listening, and many musicians have testified to becoming cognizant of musical events of which they were previously unaware. For this reason, music educators have often preferred to use language that supports and nurtures comprehensive forms of listening. In music curriculums based on standards of achievement, we use the terms "describe" or "analyze" in an attempt to nurture higher qualities of listening. As we look at the primary roles of listener, performer, and composer, we will see how these behaviors are distinct yet interdependent. Bruner (1960) asserts that intellectual activity is the same for professionals as it is for all learners; the difference is in degree, not in the kind of activity. Therefore, as teachers develop curriculum, they should carefully examine the behaviors of music professionals. These behaviors may be used as models to develop experiences that fluently and flexibly allow students to function in a variety of music-related roles throughout their lives. In the following sections, the *Five Dimensions of Learning* (Marzano, 1992) will be used as a guide to analyze and describe the roles of composer, performer, and listener. Through these descriptions, we may gain a better understanding of how to guide students through a learning process by acknowledging the distinct yet interdependent nature of these three basic roles.

The Thinking Composer

Although there may be as many compositional strategies as there are composers, it is worthwhile to develop a composite profile of a hypothetical composer that could be used to guide teachers and students as they develop their own compositional strategies. The following description does not suggest that all composers function in this manner, but instead offers one exemplar of behaviors that could be used to guide the development of instructional strategies.

Existing within a cultural context, a hypothetical composer is naturally affected by surrounding sights and sounds. Directly inspired by music of the past and the present, this composer may actively draw upon sound structures that he or she finds useful or attractive. As a listener, the composer compares and classifies music from genres or styles that he or she finds interesting or meaningful. Each piece selected for analysis offers a number of musical problems. The composer searches for questions to explore musical structure: "What is the form?" "What does it sound like?" "What forces do the musicians use to create this structure?" These kinds of analytical questions may be answered verbally, but they are most definitely answered aurally. The composer, for example, may hear a fascinating texture and carefully listen again and again to determine how the effect is achieved. Perhaps some sketching or graphing takes place to analyze and code the sound structure for later recall. ("Coding" is a procedure for extending and refining a musical experience that helps to classify and compare various musics for later recall and examination.) If possible, the composer may consult the score to gain a better understanding of how the effect is achieved. Predictions are made and tested as he or she attempts to re-create the effect. In the process, however, new effects emerge. The original texture begins to yield other possibilities. Some of these are coded for later recall, and others are discarded. As the composer converges upon the desired texture, a melody begins to emerge. Perhaps this melody was pulled from an internal melodic catalogue or from an external notebook of melodic materials; perhaps something new emerged from the evolving texture.

Similar to the development of the texture, a series of improvisations may be used as experiments to develop a fertile pool of melodic material. These improvisations are assessed for their usefulness; some are retained, and some are discarded. Similar divergent and convergent processes surge and ebb as the composer pursues his or her creative endeavor.

Although composers are naturally curious about musical structure, many are also greatly influenced by social and political forces. Recognizing that the arts are metaphors for any given historical or cultural context, the composer may actively ask questions and draw attention to various social or political themes. Therefore, upon hearing a piece of music, the composer may ask questions about its context: "When and where was this music created?" "Who performs, listens, or dances to it?" "Why and for whom was it created?" "How is this music transmitted?" "What was the creator trying to express?" "What were the performers trying to express?" and "What significance does it have for various individuals or groups?" (Barrett, McCoy, & Veblen, 1997). Since the influence of culture is profound, composers are more influenced by cultural factors than they generally would care to acknowledge. As they attempt to express their thoughts, pervasive cultural forces essentially influence them, consciously or subconsciously. Therefore, the composer-learner produces music that is a means to personally express a view significantly influenced by past and present musical styles, as well as a particular historical and cultural context.

As teachers construct frameworks for learning, they should actively seek out ways students may participate in various learning modes. The hypothetical composer offers a useful model for cycling students through diverse musical behaviors designed to develop compositional products. Although the course of action was designed to develop compositions, it becomes apparent that the composer is also engaged in performing and purposeful listening. Notice that the compositions developed could become crucial artifacts of the educational process, as well as the improvisations, the sketches, the notes, and the performances of student composers.

We may see that this composer represents not only an individual student, but also small or large groups of students. The teacher also may choose to take on the role of the composer, guiding his or her students through the experiences described above. Such an activity with a large group could provide students with an important model for pursuing their own compositional abilities within small groups or as individuals. Students who learn to think as composers are better prepared to function in a variety of roles.

The Thinking Performer

As composers explore musical structures through improvisation, they often function as performers in order to evaluate their emerging works. As a composition develops, the composer must be able to continually hear, make judgments, and revise his or her thinking. These divergent processes offer an excellent model of creative thinking. Creative thinkers who prolong their perception of how a final product will look or sound are more likely to produce products that will be deemed original (Getzels & Csikszentmihalyi, 1976). Therefore, we may conclude that performers who engage in divergent thinking will be more likely to produce varied and more original performances, and they will be better prepared to function within a variety of genres and styles.

In preparing for a performance, musicians naturally engage in musical analysis, and they begin to develop strategies for overcoming performance problems. The performer might study the score and listen to many performances—live or recorded—in order to examine expressive or technical problems posed by a given composition. Say, for example, a given composition poses tremendous articulation problems. The performer recognizes the dilemma and begins to develop strategies to overcome these difficulties. The performer may practice the passage at different tempos but soon recognizes that the articulation problem demands a high degree of flexibility. Perhaps the performer will begin to develop études based on the rhythmic and articulation elements employed by the composer. Or the performer may begin to improvise upon a variety of rhythms and articulations suggested by the composition. By improvising upon the same elements used in the composition, the performer is able to surpass the technical demands needed to perform the composition and may confidently enter the performance arena. This scenario is a good example of using knowledge meaningfully by extending and refining, in this case, the given problem of articulation. In this situation, the performer-learner is able to effectively use musical ideas afforded by the composition to construct an improvisation or composition that has both personal and practical significance.

Similar to the composer, the performer also benefits from an in-depth examination of music and its cultural context. An examination of structure may provide the performer with an understanding of form, climax, harmonic rhythm, and other technical devices that the composer uses to convey his or her intent. When the performer has a better understanding of various structural elements, he or she is better prepared to create a performance that accentuates various structural qualities. For example, when a performer recreates a Baroque sonata, it is stylistically correct to improvise ornamentation upon the melody, and as sections of the melody recur, it is appropriate to again alter the ornamentation. By recognizing the repetition and contrast of the melodic structure, the performer is better prepared to produce an effective and original performance.

By realizing a Baroque composition, the performer is confronted with questions that may be posed about any musical context (see the questions presented in the previous section). The performer may also ask how this music and its meaning have changed through different interpretations or versions. These and other questions provide the performer with the ability to pursue different viewpoints and hear other voices.

Using the performer as a model for learning, the teacher should have students engage in a variety of musical behaviors. When confronted with problems of performance, it is natural for the performer to listen to how other musicians have solved various performance problems. The teacher should be proactive in guiding students towards recordings or live performances that provide meaningful solutions and be prepared to give aural examples through singing or playing to suggest how a given problem might be solved.

Although many teachers do create or borrow études for solving technical problems, they often are reluctant to think of these études as "real music." This is very unfortunate because études may not only be used to solve a performance problem, but they may simultaneously be used to develop students' musical imaginations. A teacher modeling how and why an étude was developed provides a fertile framework for students to develop their own études for solving problems of performance. Teachers may actively ask students to develop études for solving specific performance problems. In a group setting, études developed by individuals may be shared with others. When students create their own études and learn to enjoy this process of development and practice, they are more likely to want to continue to find and solve problems of musical performance.

The Thinking Listener

Since we have seen how the composer and performer actively engage in purposeful listening, it becomes apparent that listening is the most fundamental skill for musical development. Whether one is functioning as a composer or as a performer, listening skills are of paramount importance. Since listening skills are usually not overtly examined outside of music learning environments, listeners are far less hindered by cultural norms. For this reason, listening may be considered the most creative musical behavior. The knowledgeable listener may structure and restructure a listening experience so that each time a given selection is examined, the experience may be assimilated in a different way.

Upon initially hearing a composition, a listener might respond in a holistic fashion. The sounds may summon a myriad of feelings, and the piece may be compared with what was heard in previous musical models. The listener constructs meaning based on past experiences and begins to code the experience for later recall and reflection. He or she classifies the selection by comparing it with an internal catalogue of previously experienced music.

Although individuals may speak of emotions embodied in music, this is reasonably questionable. It seems more accurate to say that humans create or respond to music that suggests various emotions. Music evokes feelings or emotional responses from humans, but these constructs are essentially human, not musical. McMurray (1991) makes a useful distinction between feelings and emotions, suggesting an infinite array of responses not symbolized by language. However, broad categories of feelings can be classified into emotions that may be symbolized through language using terms such as frustration, love, sorrow, or joy. According to McMurray, these specifically named emotions each represent a body of feelings resulting from experiencing a certain kind of event, and they may be characterized by the properties of a narrative. Within the human condition, listeners expect a series of beginnings, developments, and conclusions. Music experienced, for example, at the funeral of a young leader will likely suggest sorrow. Because such an event may be described using language, the mourners may tend to code the music with the same language that describes the event. The term "sorrow," however, inadequately describes the countless feelings experienced as the music is heard. This is another example that supports May's (1989) position that language inadequately describes the ability to think in and through the arts. McMurray (1991) states that although feelings not verbally classified are vague and often indescribable, they are not less important than those feelings that have been verbally classified. It is perhaps more honest to suggest that the music heard at a funeral helps individuals to reconcile, code, and construct meaning from the experience.

Depending on the individual's purpose, listening takes many forms. The performer may listen in order to compare and contrast technical skills or analyze errors, but he or she is also interested in the expressiveness of the entire composition and how it functions within its cultural or historical context. As discussed previously, the composer is naturally drawn towards understanding and examining musical structure, but is also concerned with social or political underpinnings. As a connoisseur, the listener is free to respond to holistic or structural elements. In order to explore different kinds of listening, he or she may ask the same questions asked by the composer and performer. Each listening experience is coded in relationship to previous listening experiences, and listeners may choose to analyze and describe these experiences through movement, drawing, writing, graphing, or by examining musical notation. All of these actions may help the listener construct meaning from the experience.

Knowledge of the cultural and historical context can only enhance the listening experience. As one listens to a piece, it is worthwhile to ponder the composition's origin. In addition to the previously cited questions, it is also worthwhile to ask what significance a particular musical selection has for today's audience. By examining the many facets of a composition, individuals are better prepared to flexibly organize a variety of listening experiences.

As teachers prepare to engage students in listening experiences, they may search for questions about a particular musical context. Because the intentions of the listener greatly affect how and what the listener attends to during a listening episode, the teacher should consider what the purposes of the listening experience might or could be. As students listen, they should be encouraged to code the experience through various processes. Humans often code musical experiences through movement in the form of clapping or dance, but teachers may also choose to seek out other forms of movement to help students describe the nature of a given musical event. Coding may also take place through drawing, graphing, or verbal descriptions. All of these forms offer students a vast pool of resources for comparing, classifying, abstracting, and constructing meaning from musical phenomena. Since listening is perhaps the most creative musical activity, it is essential that teachers embrace and celebrate the diversity of responses students may use to code their listening experiences. Invented notational systems, as well as traditional notation, also offer effective forms of demonstrating musical understanding. If students create unique processes for demonstrating their musical understanding, teachers need to be prepared to accept these forms as viable artifacts of music learning.

Summary

If, as Marzano (1992) suggests, the most effective way to promote learning is to focus upon large interdisciplinary themes, then the fragmentation of knowledge into discrete subject areas is clearly counterproductive. Intuitively, we must also recognize that the isolation of musical behaviors is also counterproductive to developing musical understanding in the broadest sense. Music educators must seek to build alliances to help individuals understand music's role in society, and we must continue to broaden our understanding of musical knowledge by engaging our students in a variety of musical behaviors.

Finding agreement with Bruner (1960) that intellectual activity is the same for professionals as it is for all learners, this chapter proposes that music educators look to professional musicians for developing models of music learning. Assessment of music learning should focus on students' use of knowledge and complex reasoning rather than on the recall of low-level information (Marzano, 1992). This chapter provides realistic examples of how musicians attempt to understand music in the broadest sense. Engaging students in a more holistic experience of music making and learning will better prepare them to function flexibly and fluently in a multifaceted world. Assessment strategies should provide students with opportunities to demonstrate their understanding through a variety of musical behaviors that emulate how professionals learn and master their disciplines.

References

Barrett, J., McCoy, C., & Veblen, K. (1997). *Sound ways of knowing.* New York: Schirmer.

Bruner, J. (1960). *The process of education.* Cambridge, MA: Harvard University.

Getzels, J. W., & Csikszentmihalyi, M. (1976). *The creative vision: A longitudinal study of problem finding in art.* New York: Wiley.

Guilford, J. P. (1959). Traits of creativity. In H. H. Anderson (Ed.), *Creativity and its cultivation* (pp. 142–61). New York: Harper and Row.

Lipman, M. (1991). *Thinking in education.* New York: Cambridge University.

Marzano, R. J. (1992). *A different kind of classroom: Teaching with dimensions of learning.* Alexandria, VA: Association for Supervision and Curriculum Development.

Marzano, R. J., Brandt, R. S., Hughes, C. S., Jones, B. F., Presseisen, B. Z., Rankin, S. C., & Suhor, C. (1988). *Dimensions of thinking: A framework for curriculum and instruction.* Alexandria, VA: Association for Supervision and Curriculum Development.

May, W. (1989). *Understanding and critical thinking in elementary art and music.* East Lansing, MI: Institute for Research on Teaching, College of Education, Michigan State University. (ERIC Document Reproduction Service No. ED 308 982).

McMurray, F. (1991). Pragmatism in music education. In R. J. Colwell (Ed.), *Basic concepts in music education II* (pp. 27–53). Niwot, CO: University Press of Colorado.

McPeck, J. E. (1981) *Critical thinking and education*. Oxford: Martin Robertson.

Swartz, R. J., & Perkins, D. N. (1989). *Teaching thinking: Issues and approaches*. Pacific Grove, CA: Midwest.

Webster, P. R. (1990). Creativity as creative thinking. *Music Educators Journal, 76* (9), 21–28.

Thomas Priest is assistant professor of music and education at Weber State University in Ogden, Utah.

5

STRUCTURING LEARNING IN A DIFFERENT KIND OF CLASSROOM

BETH ANN MILLER

Music specialists, like all educators, worry about what their students are truly learning. They wonder if little Suzie really understands the organization of essential elements of music or simply has memorized enough to sing her alto part in the next concert. Teaching many students on a limited time schedule, music educators ponder how to teach their students so that they will have the musical insight necessary to pursue music independently as adults.

Many music programs look good on the surface. The public performances are well rehearsed and enthusiastically attended; the music room is well supplied and graced with attractive posters; the music teacher works very hard to enrich the program through the use of many experiences, ranging from using multiple classroom instruments to engaging guest artists. However, the ultimate goal of the music education program is to ensure that all students understand the essence of music—not just that a whole note equals two half notes or that Bach lived in the Baroque period, but the deeper structure of music determined and explained by the manner in which basic elements are combined to create a cohesive whole. This concern addresses the difference between memorizing facts or perfecting the technical skills of performing on one hand and constructing mental schemata that represent essential musical concepts on the other.

Of course, we hope that eventually many of our music students will intuit these mental concepts as a result of the musical experiences they engage in within our classrooms. But how can we raise the percentage of students who succeed in that construction? Perkins (1991) expresses the problem like this:

> We grasp pretty well what it is for someone to know something: he or she has information in storage and can retrieve it on call. However, for someone to understand something ... what must he or she be able to do? Certainly just knowing ... will not do. Whatever understanding is, it plainly goes beyond stored information.

Perkins (1991) goes on to suggest that deep learning is recognized when a student can use the information in a personal and novel way: explaining concepts in his or her own words, showing, generalizing, or drawing inferences or analogies (p. 4).

Clearly, the acquisition of lower-level thinking skills such as recalling and encoding information cannot be the end result of our music education programs. If students are to reach the level of understanding toward which we strive, they must move beyond these low-level skills to the ability to make use of higher-level thinking processes. Many agree (Barrett, in Boardman, 1989; Marzano, 1992; Perkins, 1991; and Resnick, 1987) that providing opportunities for higher-order thinking should be inherent in content-specific course work. Marzano (1988, 1992) has outlined three thinking skills that might describe the cognitive processes drawn on by our students: skills of knowledge acquisition, skills of processing, and skills of transfer and application. (Marzano's work provides the scaffolding for much of this chapter.)

How can practicing music specialists teach their students to use higher-order thinking skills? It is not enough to add a quick Monday-morning "thinking activity" picked up in a Saturday workshop titled "Creative Thinking Strategies for Your Classroom." The task for music specialists is to find ways to provide a consistent climate of questioning, problem solving, analyzing, and active construction of knowledge by all students. This chapter will suggest some ways that teachers can facilitate student use of higher-order thinking in music classes. Each skill is presented in an "if-then" order.

The cognitive processes associated with each skill are listed first, and then suggestions for how teachers can provide opportunities for students to develop higher-order thinking skills are presented in a discussion of each bulleted item listed under "*then*."

Skills of Knowledge Acquisition

Knowledge acquisition skills help a student to acquire and integrate knowledge using the thinking processes of focusing, gathering information, and remembering. *If* students are to focus, gather information, and remember by

- discerning a need, a discrepancy, or a puzzle
- setting goals
- recalling known information
- formulating questions
- observing
- obtaining information
- encoding information,

then teachers must

- ascertain known skills or knowledge
- provide a need, a question, or a puzzle
- guide the search for meaning
- guide progress from the known to the newly known by sequencing learning and ideas in a developmentally appropriate order
- provide experiences supporting varied learning styles
- model thinking processes
- guide concept formation
- provide practice time.

Teachers must ascertain known skills or knowledge. "Cognitive psychologists view learning as a highly interactive process of constructing personal meaning from the information available in a learning situation and then integrating that information with what we already know to create new knowledge" (Marzano, 1992, p. 5). So, if students are to acquire new knowledge, teachers must first ascertain what it is that students already know. Despite the obvious logic in this rule, it is a step sometimes overlooked by busy educators. The result of this oversight is that students may be either confused or underchallenged. One way to become accustomed to considering the "known" is to begin a lesson plan by noting what information the students have already acquired that will make the new information understandable to them. For example, a written lesson plan might begin with:

> *Known:* Longer "boom whackers" [plastic tubes] produce lower pitches; shorter boom whackers produce higher pitches.
> *Lesson Goal:* The students will apply their knowledge of the relationship of size versus pitch on boom whackers to the various sizes of recorders in a recorder consort.

Starting from a familiar point also gives the students a sense of security, which brain researchers believe is crucial to learning (Sprenger, 1999; Jensen, 1998; Tomlinson & Kalbfleisch, 1988).

Teachers must provide a need, a question, or a puzzle. If students are to be motivated to think, teachers must quit doing their thinking for them. Instead of lecturing and telling, teachers must frame questions and plan situations that require the students to construct their own understanding. Brooks and Brooks (1993) call this "posing problems of emerging relevance to students" (pp. 35–36). They describe a worthwhile problem as one that

(a) demands a testable prediction

(b) requires inexpensive equipment

(c) is complex enough to elicit more than one problem-solving approach

(d) benefits from group effort

(e) is a relevant problem.

Brooks and Brooks (1993) note that relevancy may not necessarily be pre-existing, but may be initiated by teacher behavior. These five stipulations are demonstrated in the following classroom episode:

> *Known:* Rule for a D.C. al fine
> *Lesson goal:* Rule for a D.S. al fine

> Ms. Miles planned to teach her third graders a song from their music text that used a "D.S. al fine" (a relevant problem). She knew that the students had previously used repeat signs and "D.C. al fine" to determine how to perform a complete piece. Rather than explaining the procedure for going back to the sign, she created a puzzle by asking the students to follow the music as she

> played the new song (inexpensive equipment). When the recorded performers reached the end of the page, singing, "Yes, it's a …" Ms. Miles abruptly pushed the pause button and assumed a very perplexed expression. Making a face, she exclaimed, "That's a really weird ending!" Some students mirrored her facial expression and others turned the page to see if the song continued on the next page, but Sally thought only a moment before raising her hand. "I know, Ms. Miles, we go back to the beginning and stop when we get to the fine!"
>
> "Oh, we've done that before, haven't we? Do you all think that will work?" asked the apparently still confused Ms. Miles. "Let's try it" (a testable prediction). Remembering that the students need to experience the whole, Ms. Miles started the song from the beginning, but this time continued from the D.S. to the beginning, as Sally had suggested. The students frowned and shook their heads.
>
> "That didn't make sense," protested Bill. "We need to go back to someplace that says 'beautiful day' so the sentence makes sense, like 'Yes, it's a beautiful day'" (more than one approach). Soon the class noticed the funny-looking sign above one of the "beautiful day" lines (group effort). Of course, trying that sign as they listened again to the recording worked well, and everyone was not only satisfied, but ready to listen to Ms. Miles' brief explanation of the term "dal segno al fine."

Solving Ms. Miles' puzzle took more time than simply explaining to the class how to proceed through the piece and lecturing on the meaning of the new term. Grappling with the possibilities, however, engaged all the students in searching for a workable solution. Brooks and Brooks (1993) would agree with Ms. Miles' approach:

> When posing problems for students to consider and study, it's crucial to avoid isolating the variables for the students, to avoid giving them more information than they need or want, and to avoid simplifying the complexity of the problem too early. Complexity often serves to generate relevance and, therefore, interest. It is oversimplification that students find confusing.

Teachers guide the search for meaning. The children in Ms. Miles' third grade truly needed to know about the "D.S. al fine" in order to be able to finish their new song. If learning is to be meaningful, then what we do in the classroom must be relevant, holistic, and authentic. Newmann and Wehlage (1993) suggest five hallmarks of authentic instruction:

(a) higher order thinking

(b) depth of knowledge

(c) connectedness to the world beyond the classroom

(d) substantive conversation

(e) social support for students achievement.

The teacher journal excerpt below illustrates a unit that fulfilled all five points:

> By now, all the kids have finished making and reporting on their own invented instruments that they had constructed at their homes (connectedness). So today we organized our own version of Britten's *Young Person's Guide to the Orchestra,* which we had studied in detail at the beginning of this unit (depth of knowledge). First, they arranged themselves and their instruments into categories (higher order thinking): winds, strings, unpitched percussion, and pitched percussion. Then the students in each category brainstormed an improvisation to perform during their section (conversation). Finally, we videotaped their Britten-like performance in families, then individually in family categories, and then all together to show to their classroom teacher and other students (social support). Fun! (B. Miller, personal journal, January 2, 1997).

Teachers guide progress from known to new known by sequencing learning and ideas in a developmentally appropriate order. To some extent, this order is more or less common or generic, because it is age-dependent, experience-dependent, and reflected in the curricular guidelines found in current music series books. However, this order is also site specific, since it is subject to variables such as class size, number, and length of music lessons per week, available materials, socioeconomic factors, and administrative and public support. Despite teacher aspirations, curricular requirements, music textbook assumptions, and test score results, students must start from where they are—from what they know. The most effective teachers remember to look at students and classes on a case-by-case basis and make judgments each day about what students know and what they can logically learn next.

Despite this individual nature of learning, there are some valuable guideposts in our search for developmentally appropriate sequencing. The theories that best account for the site variables just mentioned, in my opinion, are those of Bruner (1966), applied to the specific field of music education by Bergethon, Boardman, and Montgomery (1997). Many youngsters arrive at kindergarten with limited music experience and with vaguely formed concepts about how the basic elements interact to produce the total musical sound. Yet Bruner (1977) proposes that "any subject can be taught effectively in some intellectually honest form to any child at any stage of development" (p. 33). He suggests that "the task of teaching a subject to a child at any particular age is one of representing the structure of that subject in terms of the child's way of viewing things" (p. 33)—we must provide musical experiences that match the operational stages of the students.

Learning a new operation, according to Bruner (1966), involves first understanding the form of the idea—getting the "feel" of something without necessarily having the ability to explain it formally. This early understanding might be represented through an enactive model, such as demonstration. Thus, an appropriate approach for the music teacher is to model how the music sounds through physical movement. As the students watch and mimic the actions, they begin to develop a physical feel for the music's characteristics. They associate, for example, a descending melodic passage with descending body movement and an ascending melodic passage with an upward motion. At some point, the teacher can assess the students' success in internalizing the concept by asking, "Can you show me how this music moves?" without first providing a model.

Once satisfied that the student understands the concept well enough to demonstrate it enactively, the teacher may begin to model ways to represent the music visually. The ability to hold a mental representation of the concept in one's mind and thus represent the music with a visual that looks like the music sounds could be called the "iconic" stage of representation. Again, students require strong models and extensive practice at this stage before they have internalized the music's properties.

This iconic stage seems to be the part of the process that usually gets short-changed in our desire to hurry students into reading the symbolic notation required for admittance to performing groups. It may be that, while music teachers do a good job of providing enactive experiences with the youngest students, we tend to leap too quickly into symbolic notation. This practice encourages the student to learn music simply by rote, mimicking the teacher or memorizing information without real understanding. Since basic concepts can be grasped more easily through iconic representations than through abstract symbolic notation (for example, "**– – —**" is much more descriptive for the novice musician than ♩♩𝅗𝅥), there is no pressing need to rush the learning process. In fact, it seems to me that traditional notation is easier for my students to grasp when they already have a clear understanding of music concepts and have described, performed, and created music using both enactive and iconic representations.

Finally, those students who are mature enough to think in abstract terms and symbols and who are experienced enough to represent music through iconic representation may be able to go on to the third stage. At this point, they can use abstract symbols, such as traditional music notation or technical vocabulary, in verbal explanations to represent what they hear in the music.

If we accept this three-stage theory, we should organize our teaching in a spiral curriculum, so that the basic structure of music may be addressed each year in ever-increasing depth. Indeed, the two most widely used music textbook series (*The Music Connection,* 1995; *Share the Music,* 1995) reflect a spiral system. Going one step further, I believe that effective teaching also involves planning each lesson episode or unit to reflect a spiral-learning progression. This in-depth planning allows for exploration and representation of concepts in developmentally appropriate ways, as shown in the lesson plan in Figures 1 and 1a, Example of spiral-learning lesson plan.

Teachers provide experiences supporting varied learning styles. Samples (1992) has suggested that Bruner's three ways of knowing—enactive, iconic, and symbolic—might be considered descriptive of learning modalities. According to Samples (1992), iconic knowing is linked to the ways of knowing central to the visual and spatial arts. Enactive knowing frames the wisdom of movement, kinesthetic action, and dance. Symbolic knowing—the realm of reason and reductive logic—is primarily carried out through coded symbols—letters, numbers, and abstract codes.

Many educators in addition to Samples (Cutietta, 1990; Ellison, 1992; Ellsworth & Sindt, 1994; Hoerr, 1992) have expressed the belief that teachers should encourage learning by providing children opportunities to experience material through several learning modalities. As Samples (1992) writes: "It is clear that the human brain processes experience differently depending upon which sensory or processing system is engaged. We discovered that these diverse ways of processing could be orchestrated intentionally by virtue of how and what assignments were given" (p. 63).

Recent research on brain function also bears out the soundness of such an approach, verifying that learning takes place as an individual uses various sensory pathways to interact with materials (Lowery, 1998; Wolfe & Brandt, 1998; Jensen, 1998). Incorporating various learning modalities—auditory, tactile, kinesthetic, and visual—may help students to construct their own understanding of musical concepts instead of simply memorizing discrete facts.

As an example of the use of learning modalities, consider Armstrong's (1994) suggestion that "The human body provides a convenient pedagogical tool when transformed into a reference point or 'map' for specific knowledge domains" (p. 76). In music, an example of a similar kinesthetic strategy might be a "body scale" (Bergethon, Boardman, & Montgomery, 1997, p. 159), in which students touch their knees for "1," touch their thighs for "2," their hips for "3," and so on, moving higher on the body as the pitch rises.

Using various learning modalities allows classes to work longer on one piece of music, giving students time and opportunity for deep learning to occur. In fact, it may be that truly effective lessons, especially in the primary grades, must cycle through all the modalities to allow students to meet the music in many ways, as illustrated in the previous lesson about "The North Wind" (shown in Figures 1 and 1a). Hands-on means everybody. Another important benefit of using many modalities is that it ensures engagement by every student, not just the few with their hands up or the verbal skills to talk about what they hear. In the lesson presented in Figure 2, every child demonstrates ABA form in four modalities.

The constructivist agenda accepts the view that teachers can facilitate learning only by giving students materials, time, and direction. It honors the individual students' need to pose and solve questions through use of manipulative, interactive, and concrete materials (Brooks & Brooks, 1993; Lowery, 1998). Furnishing the students with as many different pathways of learning as possible seems sensible to ensure that each child has the opportunity to work in his or her preferred learning mode.

Teachers model thinking processes. An important job of today's constructivist teacher is to help children learn the needed thinking process by modeling his or her own progress while seeking to solve a problem. This entails such actions as

(a) talking out loud about his or her thinking or the thinking of other experts (such as more capable students)

(b) consistently expecting more than just a right answer

(c) probing for more information (Rosenshine & Meister, 1992).

When teachers model thinking processes themselves and call upon students to do the same by asking "How-did-you-figure-this-out" questions, they help their students in several ways. First, they encourage metacognitive thinking, defined in Marzano (1988) as "being aware of our thinking as we perform specific tasks and then using this awareness to control what we are

Grade: Kindergarten
Known: Children have sung upward and downward melodic contour demonstrated with both enactive and iconic representations.
Main music concept: A melody may move upward or downward by steps.
Lesson goal: Children will use their bodies, streamers, and bells to represent upward and downward melodic contour. They will order icons to match the sound.
Materials needed:

1. plastic streamers for each child
2. arrows showing the "oo—oo's" of the North Wind
3. poster map of the song
4. individual maps of the song
5. xylophones for half of the class

Context	Content	Behavior	Mode	Cognitive Skill
"North Wind"	melody	describe	enactive	focus/encode

"The other night I heard a sound outside my house that went up and down like this: 'oo—oo.' What do you think it was? Listen for the wind sound in this song." "Listen again to see what that North Wind did to my house." Continue by asking other questions so they have a need to hear the song several times.[aural]

Context	Content	Behavior	Mode	Cognitive Skill
"North Wind"	melody	describe	enactive	represent

"Sometimes the North Wind blows us, too. Find enough space for yourself that you can wave your arms in the wind without touching someone else, and pretend the wind is blowing you around." "Can we see the wind? No, of course not, but we can see how it makes things move and flap around." [distribute plastic streamers] "Can you think of some things that the wind could blow?"
"When I sing the song this time, let's show how the wind blows on the oo—oo's." [the teacher sings and models the upward and downward movements of the melody = enactive representation of the melodic contour][kinesthetic]

Context	Content	Behavior	Mode	Cognitive Skill
"North Wind"	melody	describe	iconic	analyze

"I wanted to make some pictures to show how the wind sound might look, but first I had to figure out how many oo—oo's there are in the song." [sing while children count.]

continued on next page

Figure 1. Example of spiral-learning lesson plan

"Here are some pictures [upward/downward arrows] I drew of the wind sounds. Let's see if we can put them in the right order to match the song." [sing and compare throughout the song.][visual]
Note: In actual practice, this lesson may cover more than one lesson, so by this time, the students are able to sing the song themselves.

"Here are maps of the song for each of you [see Figure 1a]. Touch each picture as we sing. [iconic representation] [tactile]

Context	Content	Behavior	Mode	Cognitive Skill
"North Wind"	melody	perform	iconic	transfer

Guide children to play the upward and downward patterns on xylophones. Review small=high; large=low relationships on the bell bars and have partners hold the xylophone vertically with the high bells up. [multimodal]

Figure 1 continued

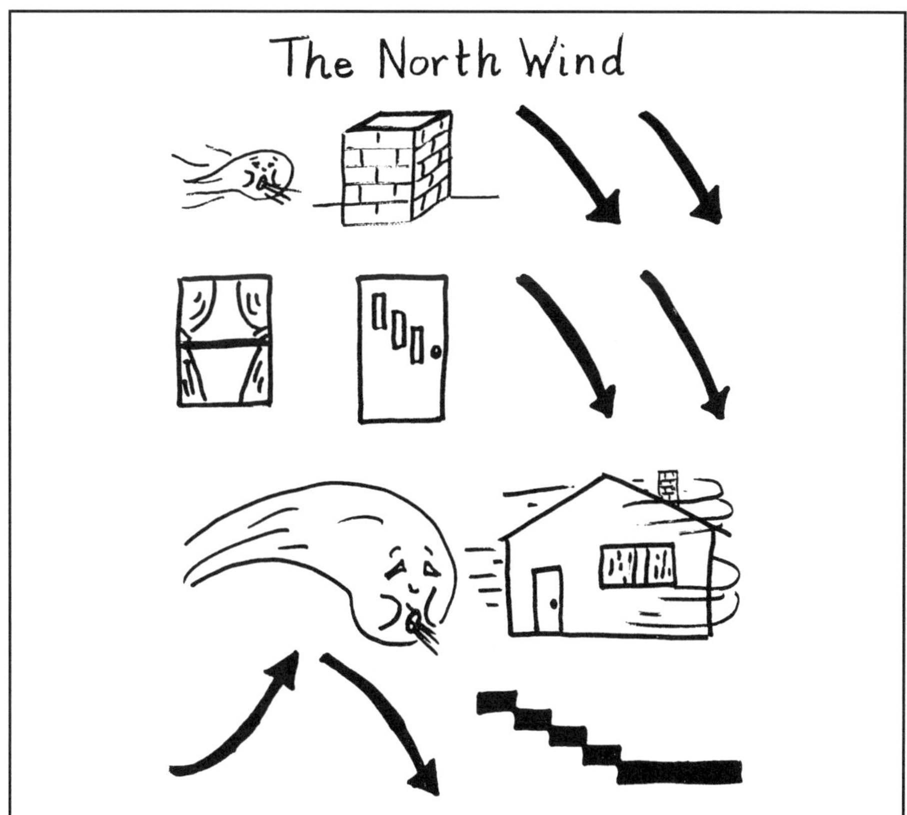

Figure 1a. "North Wind" map

doing" (p. 9). Resnick (1987) agrees, observing that "various forms of social interaction are used ... to make visible normally covert aspects of the problem-solving process and to increase students' self-conscious monitoring and management of their thought processes" (p. 20).

Second, in stressing process over correct answers, teachers help to break the prevalent situation found in many classrooms of a few students answering all the questions while the rest feel unable or unwilling to participate. In contrast, when the teacher says, "You're right, but tell us how you got that answer, so that others will know the next time I ask," the message is given that all students are as important as the one with the correct answer or the confidence to volunteer.

Third, a student may supply the correct answer for wrong or inadequate reasons. For example, consider the following questions and students' answers:

"Yes, that note is a G. How did you know?"

- Sam told me.
- There's a G above it. [a chord symbol]
- It looks like the G on the other page.
- It's on the second line up ... you know, the one the treble clef circles around.
- It has a stick ... on it.
- I said the sentence. [mnemonic]
- I just know—I take piano [lessons].
- I guessed.

Probing for reasons gives the teacher the opportunity to sort out real understanding from lucky guesses and misguided thinking. When children's reasons are not adequate or correct, the teacher has the perfect window of opportunity to clarify, re-teach, or even expand. "Sam-told-me" answers can be redirected to Sam himself, who now has a chance to explain his answer. "There's-a-G-above-it" types of answers provide the opportunity to review or introduce new information, such as chord symbols. "It-looks-like-the-G-on-the-other-page" sorts of answers give the teacher a chance to compliment the student on finding a way to solve the problem and at the same time, to ask, "But what if that other page wasn't there?" Students taking private lessons need to know that "I-just-know" answers don't help the other students learn to read notes aloud, so are considered incomplete answers. Accepting

Grade: First

Known: The children worked with AB and ABA form in kindergarten.

Main music concept: A musical whole may be made up of same, varied, or contrasting segments [form].

Lesson goal: The children will show they understand ABA form through aural, visual, kinesthetic, and tactile modes.

Materials needed:

1. baggies of paper circles, squares, and triangles, each in a different color
2. stations containing:
   a. paper
   b. pencil
   c. two each of three rhythm instruments

Context	Content	Behavior	Mode	Cognitive Skill
"Who Took My Roosters and My Hens?"	form	perform	enactive	recall

"Last week we sang a song about some chickens that got lost." Sing and review the ABA form. **[aural]**

Context	Content	Behavior	Mode	Cognitive Skill
"Hey, Betty Martin"	form	perform	enactive	apply

"Do you remember this song?" Sing to **help children** recall. "Let's dance like the song says." **[aural/kinesthetic]**

Context	Content	Behavior	Mode	Cognitive Skill
"Hey, Betty Martin"	form	describe	iconic	expand

"Here are some shapes. Please use them to show the pattern of this Betty Martin song." **[tactile/visual]**

Context	Content	Behavior	Mode	Cognitive Skill
original compositions	form	create	iconic	translate

"Around the room are several stations containing sets of instruments. Please choose a station with two other children. Then the three of you make a piece of music that has the ABA pattern. Write your music down on the paper, so you can show us how it looks." **[multimodal]**

Figure 2. Example of lesson plan using modalities

all reasons with a positive attitude before probing further gives a sense of comfort to reticent students.

This kind of Socratic questioning is discussed further in Paul (1990), who lists six types of questions:

(a) questions of clarification

(b) questions that probe assumptions

(c) questions that probe reasons and evidence

(d) questions about viewpoints on perspectives

(e) questions that probe implications and consequences

(f) questions about the question.

Teachers with thinking students may be the teachers who constantly demand thinking by requiring higher-order reasoning, by probing for more information, and by valuing process over product. In the following series of lessons, a teacher sets up scenarios that force her students to work on process tasks requiring higher-level thinking and to defend their reasoning:

> A class of fourth graders has been playing soprano recorders for only two weeks when their teacher leads a study of Glière's "Russian Sailors Dance," a piece consisting of twelve repetitions of a main theme. The students compose twelve rhythmic variations on the one note (A) they have learned to finger and then play along with the orchestra.
>
> Later, when they know three notes, the students write an original class composition. As they work together, their teacher verbalizes options facing all composers:
>
> "Sometimes a composer will end the first phrase on a note that is not the tonic ... but not always. What would you like to do?"
>
> "Often the second phrase balances the first phrase in length ... but not always. Can someone suggest a second phrase for our melody?"
>
> "Wow! I see you have a sequence here. Can you study what you have written and figure out what I mean by 'sequence'?"
>
> Another day, the teacher writes a short melody on large poster paper, cuts it into phrases, and hangs it on the chalkboard. "We have a new tune to play with our five notes, but I'm afraid it's all mixed up. Let's see if we can arrange it in some logical way." As the students begin to study the parts, suggest an order, and play their arrangements, the teacher constantly questions:

> "Why do you think that phrase should go next?"
> "What makes that a logical choice?"
> "If you put it this way, do you think it will make a balanced piece?"
> "I see you've discovered the similarity between these two very short phrases; what do you think the composer had in mind with them?"
> Soon the students have constructed their new piece in a musically satisfying way, practiced the piece many times during the puzzling process, and experienced the opportunity to think as composers think.

Teachers guide concept formation. Students come into our classrooms with a wide variety of past experiences, varying ability levels, an assortment of discrete facts, and different levels of conceptualization. Instead of trying to meet all their various musical and intellectual needs by teaching facts, we need to focus on the most powerful elements of music: rhythm, melody, harmony, dynamics, timbre, form, and expressive qualities. Teaching for conceptual understanding is more likely to be appropriate for all students.

Launching curriculum from key concepts and principles ensures that struggling learners focus on what is most important and powerful in the curriculum. This approach invites advanced learners to extend their understanding in a way that is meaning-rich instead of either repeating the known or engaging in often tangential or trivial enrichment (Tomlinson & Kalbfleisch, 1998).

Concept formation may require direct instruction (Marzano, 1988). While some music concepts may be gained through undirected contact with music, such as informal singing or listening, deliberate instruction usually is more effective. One research study (Miller, 1995) showed that daily sing-along sessions in one first-grade class did not result in any more growth in conceptual understanding than similar first-grade classes that did not have daily sing-along sessions. Such findings may indicate that exposure to music, even with daily practice and performance, does not by itself impart an understanding of the key musical concepts that produces lifelong, independent musicians. These findings may suggest that teachers should not presume students understanding, but overtly state principles concerning the basic elements of music. For example, the teacher in the previous lesson on ABA form might review aloud several times during the lesson, "Music sometimes has sections that sound the same or different; this piece sounds like 'same-different-same.'" The teacher of the "North Wind" lesson should not presume that all students will understand the concept fully as a result of the lesson's activities and discoveries, but should openly state the basic rule: "Music may go up or down by steps."

Marzano (1988) contends that there is an important relationship between correct vocabulary and concept-formation—that "concept knowledge and word knowledge seem inexorably linked in the thought and language of a given culture" (p. 35). While it is important for music teachers to use the accepted language of the subject domain, it is also true that often young children demonstrate a clear understanding of a particular element without accompanying verbal competency. Such was the case with Rosemary, who consistently surprised her teachers with her ability to show what she knew without the "inconvenience" of speech. The following is an excerpt from Rosemary's music teacher's journal:

> I had arranged the magnetic strips on the chalkboard to represent the rhythm of "Fuzzy Wuzzy," but all in one long line instead of organizing it according to the rhythm of the three stanzas. When I started class, I asked if anyone had noticed the strips. Several raised their hands and shouted, "Fuzzy Wuzzy." I asked, "How did you know?" One little guy jumped up and said, "because it goes ..." and pointed with his finger as he chanted the long and short sounds of "Fuzzy Wuzzy."
>
> After reviewing the rhythm together, I taught the students my newly-composed melody using the body scale. Then I exclaimed, "I'm afraid that these magnets don't really look like this song sounds." Before I had really gotten out the question, "Why?" several children were saying, "It doesn't go up and down." I really didn't mean to choose Rosemary again, since she had been picked last week, but she looked so determined that I found myself asking her if she wanted to fix the magnets. Well! She astounded me! Not only could she fix them, but she could do it with almost no assistance. When she got to the top of the scale, I thought I might choose someone to finish the song. While I looked around at the class, however, Rosemary began slapping on the magnets with an amazing assurance—down the scale with one magnet to each pitch! I thought [for] sure whoever did the arrangement would try to go down with double pitches like it went up. When she got to the bottom, she arranged the last three all on *do,* looked at me questioningly, watched me sing the last three notes with the body scale, and fixed them to reflect *do-re-do*! I said, "May I give you a hug?!"
>
> Rosemary, according to Mrs. T., rarely speaks and then with great difficulty and slowness. To most people with average verbal

> skills and expectations, she would seem dull-witted. But she is anything but dull! She is extremely bright, if she can represent her thoughts that clearly through nonverbal means! We teachers are so verbally oriented that we often forget to provide the opportunities for alternate learning modalities. When Rosemary first came to the front, I made the mistake (for any child of this age, but especially for Rosemary) of asking her to verbalize in some way. Immediately I realized my mistake, because the dismayed look on Rosemary's face told me she couldn't verbalize anything! But she certainly understood, perceived auditorily, made the cognitive leap from her listening to the iconic representation, and manipulated the magnets successfully to show how the melody of the song sounded!! (B. Miller, personal journal, September 24, 1993)

Yet, at other times, young children can be very clear about communicating what they know through a combination of words and icons. John, in the same first grade class as Rosemary, had little trouble verbalizing his thoughts. Another entry in their music teacher's journal reads:

> I took out a wooden teddy bear, and we noticed that it had no hair—which led into the "Fuzzy Wuzzy" chant. We kept the underlying beat, found the long sounds, and played the short and long sounds on rhythm instruments—sand blocks, guiro, wood blocks, and slotted rhythm sticks. There was a lot of time left, so I asked if we could do it differently. John suggested that we could do it soft, medium, and loud and conduct it by using little, medium, and large circles [icons representing dynamic levels] "like we did last year." I said I didn't bring the posters of the circles, since I didn't know we would need them, but that he could draw them on the board. He and the other first graders took the class away from me, drawing various sized circles on the chalkboard and singing "Fuzzy Wuzzy" with dynamic levels that matched their own drawings. It was just what I desire: independent musicians making their own musical decisions by constructing their own experience using what they remembered from prior learning! (B. Miller, personal journal, September 7, 1993)

Teachers provide practice time. Hanging on my office wall is Bigge's (1982) assertion: "Any subject matter worth confronting students with is worth careful, penetrating, thorough study. If it is not worth this kind of study, it is not worth inclusion in the curriculum. Typically, we try to teach too many items—which remain nothing more than items—quickly to be forgotten" (p. 304).

As I began to understand and align myself with constructivist thought and teaching practice, this quote was an important influence. For many years, I had faithfully "taught" the main elements of music in my K–5 general music classes, but in a manner more resembling a survey course than a laboratory for deep learning. My lessons were filled with good music examples illustrating the musical element being stressed in the unit and enriched with activities in varied learning modes, but I rarely stayed on one piece of music long enough for the students to learn it well. I rarely gave them time enough to practice a hands-on skill to mastery. I was in such a hurry for coverage that not every child got to play the tone bells in the example and not every child got to track the listening map on the poster. Students left my room having had an enjoyable experience, but without any tune learned well enough to hum it in their homes. Even worse, they often left without the deep understanding necessary for applying the lesson's concepts to a new situation.

Studying constructivist theory made me understand that I could teach more effectively by exploring one piece more deeply over a longer period of time. Now xylophones are available for each child to practice, and time is devoted to free exploration, as well as for more guided work. Posters of music maps now have been reproduced in smaller versions so every student can "feel" the shape of the music. These days, it is common for a parent to remark that his or her son or daughter has been singing a certain song at home. Additionally, my assessments show overall musical growth much improved and concepts being applied in new contexts. In the following vignette, a youngster with barely average ability and background profited by personal involvement and extended time working with "duration," as proved by his ability to retain and apply the concept in a subsequent situation:

> Brian's kindergarten class had been working with the conceptual notion of "duration." They had used their fingers to feel the long strands of gold Christmas tree garland and cut-outs of short shiny ornaments meandering down a large poster, as shown in Figure 3, Christmas garland map. As they traced the decorations, the class performed various long and short sounds to render the representation, always adding a loud "crash" at the bottom where the broken ornament lay in fragments. There seemed to be no end to their ideas—mouth noises, singing sounds, long and short words, and instrument sounds. At last, they were given individual black-and-white replicas of the poster and time to practice their own choice of sounds with a partner.
>
> After the next week's review, Brian and his class were challenged to score their own long and short composition. They were each

given a piece of green construction paper showing the outline of a stylized Christmas tree, five colored self-stick circles, and a box of crayons. Following the teacher's model, they set to work producing long-short compositions as shown in Figure 4, Christmas tree composition.

Some weeks later, a different teacher asked the class to "draw something containing circles." When Brian produced his drawing (shown in Figure 5, Brian's composition), the teacher was puzzled, "What have you drawn, Brian?" Brian, slightly exasperated at her ignorance, replied, "Why, it's music, of course." Despite the new situation and the considerable span of time since the music lesson, Brian accurately performed his composition for her, proving that the care originally spent on fully developing the concept and providing practice time for the students paid off in deep understanding.

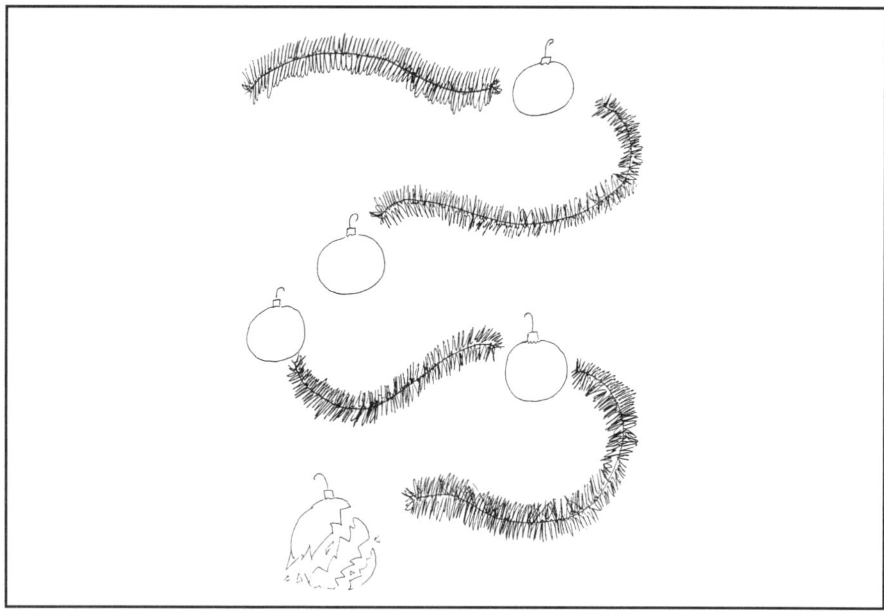

Figure 3. Christmas garland map

Skills of Processing

Processing skills are used to extend and refine acquired knowledge. *If* students are to organize and analyze information by

- comparing
- classifying
- ordering
- representing
- identifying attributes, relationships, main ideas, and errors,

then teachers must

- provide activities and time for students to organize and analyze information
- provide opportunity to use higher-order thinking, metacognitive thinking, and problem-solving skills
- teach learning and organizing strategies
- generalize skills involved in organizing and analyzing for future use by students.

Teachers provide activities and time for students to organize and analyze information. If students are to acquire the ability to analyze by drawing on the skills listed above, teachers must provide opportunities and guidance. Such thinking skills, like the acquisition of concepts, may not form incidentally, but may require explicit instruction and guided practice (Marzano,

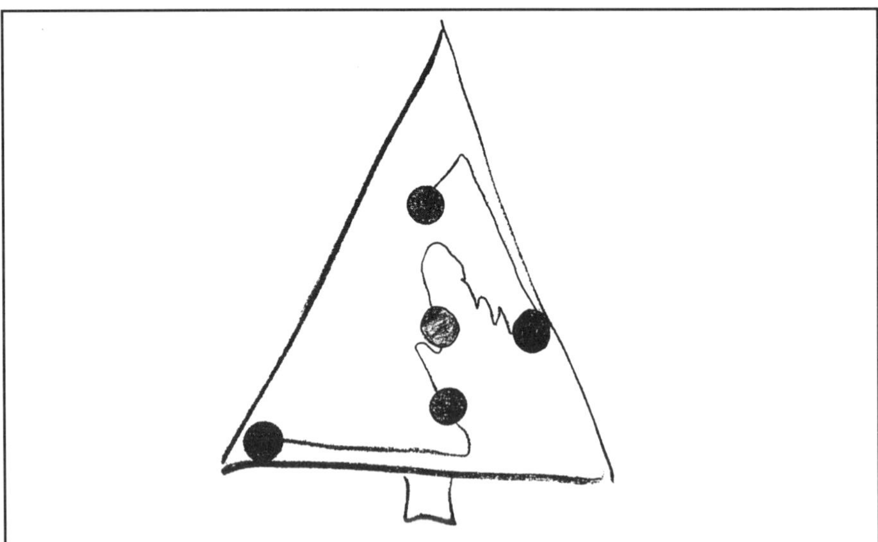

Figure 4. Christmas tree composition

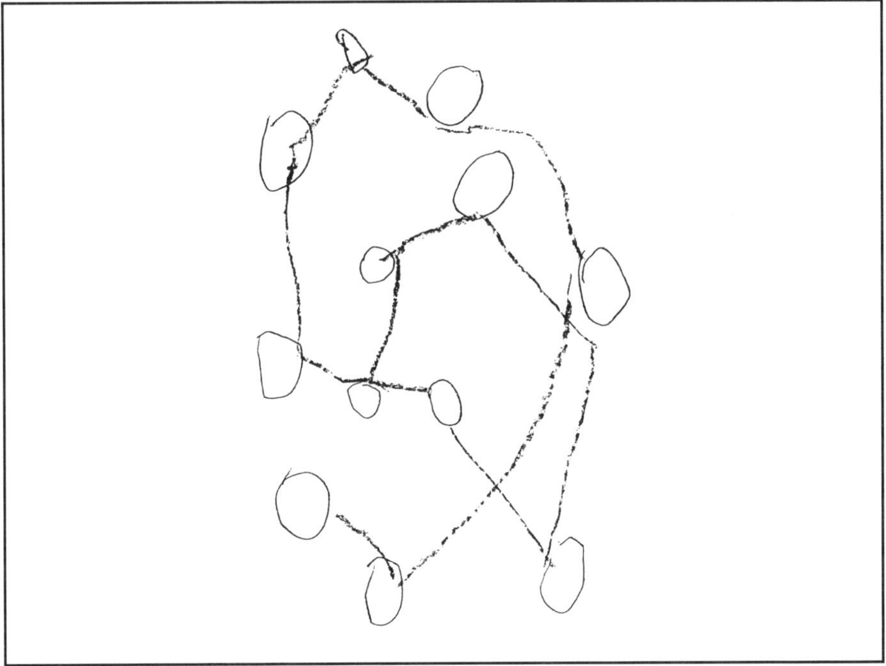

Figure 5. Brian's composition

1988). Activities that demand analysis can be engaging for the students while still focusing primarily on the basis music elements, as demonstrated in this lesson:

> Primary-school children categorized "found sounds" (wooden chopsticks, pie tins, boxes of macaroni, plastic garbage cans, etc.) into tapping, ringing, shaking, and booming groups. Then they repeated the categorization process using classroom percussion instruments. Questions and discussion pointed out common characteristics within each group ("Wow, look! All the ringing instruments are made of metal!") that may assist concept formation. Finally, the students arranged themselves in groups according to the categories and performed as an "orchestra" under the leadership of a student conductor.

It took some time and patience for the teacher in the above example to allow each student to play a found sound and an instrument, compare it to the other sounds in the activity, and decide on the appropriate category. Still, the students thoroughly enjoyed themselves, and every child was completely engaged in this classifying process. By subsequently using the categories for the orchestra performance, the students were not simply classifying as an exercise in thinking, but were using the information in a context-bound situation to learn more about how instruments are grouped in the world at large.

Older students in performance groups may gain from comparing two or more recorded versions of a piece from their current repertoire by responding to the following questions:

"Which version is played at the faster tempo? Which tempo do you like best? Why?"

"How do the two versions treat the fermata at the end of the A section? Which treatment seems more expressive to you?"

"In which version do the trombones bring out their countermelody? Do you want our trombone section to play it like that, or does it detract from the melody?"

"Compared to the two professional recordings, what do you think our own version needs? Are we performance-ready?"

Such listening, comparison, and discussion may provide a sense of ownership to performing groups that can spark individual practice more than conductor- or teacher-owned decisions. It may also result in performers who listen more to their own part in relation to the whole group sound.

The activities described next required attentive listening and analytic thinking that simply playing one's part or singing along with the teacher does not always induce.

> Some of the intermediate-age students had begun the school year with a careful study of the basic elements of music, focusing on how composers manipulated those elements to create sounds in nature. For example, "How did Saint-Saëns manipulate the elements to make 'The Aviary' sound so birdlike?" This in-depth listening and analyzing exercise was followed with group assignments requiring the students to add found sounds and/or traditional music to poems about nature and to be able to identify the musical elements involved in their composition. For example, "When we got to the part about the frog, we scraped the guiro. That added a new tone color to our composition and also a particular rhythm pattern and a louder dynamic level."

The verbalizing apparent in all three of the above examples is also important. Many musicians agree with Langer (1977), who observed that music expresses what cannot adequately be described in words, and we saw earlier how Rosemary represented the music without speech. Nevertheless, there is a common vocabulary that helps musicians think about, describe, and communicate intentions and ideas. Learning this esoteric music vocabulary allows us to talk about music the way musicians do, to more fully communicate our own notions, and to better understand the basic conceptual ideas in the field. For teachers, hearing students independently talk about music using "musicianly" vocabulary is a way of assessing—an indication that the student is becoming able to represent music at the symbolic level. Activities like the ones in this section give teachers the opportunity to overtly present conceptual ideas without lecturing. Since concept formation is not a quick or easy process, many such activities must be experienced over the span of a student's formative years.

Teachers provide opportunity to use higher-order thinking, metacognitive thinking, and problem-solving skills. Marzano (1992) suggests that teachers should actually teach higher-order thinking: "The K–12 curriculum should include explicit teaching of high level attitudes and perceptions and mental habits that facilitate learning" (p. ix). But, of course, this can, and perhaps should, be done within the context of a certain discipline—in our case, music. In fact, Marzano (1992) warns against separating thinking skills instruction from content-area instruction, calling such a separation a "false dichotomy between teaching thinking processes and teaching content- or domain-specific knowledge" (p. 31).

An obvious way, then, to teach higher-order thinking is simply to engage students in activities that utilize certain thinking strategies. For example, one way to help students analyze music is to represent sound in a visual way. Since most students are more used to "thinking with their eyes" than engaging in careful, detailed listening, visual maps (such as "The North Wind" map shown in Figure 1a) often clarify for them what they are hearing with their ears. Hyerle (1996) writes, "Seeing is one modality for perceiving, though for most of us it is our primary modality. Visual perceptions balance with auditory and kinesthetic access to knowing" (p. 10). Even for those students who are particularly adept at organizing what they hear in music, it would seem logical that visual aids other than notation would strengthen their mental schemata even more.

A particularly valuable visual tool for comparing musical versions is the Venn diagram. The easiest way to set it up is in columns, with each outside column representing unique characteristics of one of the variations and the middle column representing commonalities between the two versions (see Figure 6, Venn diagram using "Aiken drum" example).

This selection was used in a second-grade class after the students knew their own textbook version quite well. Since some of the terms were new to the children, each child was given a magnetized strip of construction paper on which was written one characteristic that he or she was to place on the board in the correct column. If a child did not know in which column it needed to be placed, the class would help by discussing the problem.

"Aiken Drum"

Unique to textbook version	Present in both versions	Unique to King'singers' version
• children's voices	• introduction	• mens' voices
• always unison	• coda	• vocal harmony
• each verse different	• strong beat	• singers hum
• tambourine	• flute	• varied dynamics

Figure 6. Venn diagram using "Aiken drum" example

The exercise required the students to listen to both versions many times in order to verify their answers. It also fostered a need to know the definitions of some of the items, which gave the teacher a chance to provide information in a more authentic situation than overt lecturing. Additionally, it fostered development of the musical vocabulary that Marzano (1988) suggests is necessary for individuals to be able to function at the symbolic level.

Teachers should "talk the talk." Another way to encourage and inform higher-order thinking is for teachers to use the language of thinking (Astington, 1998). Teachers should talk about their own new information, their own mistaken ideas, and their own struggle to find the answers to questions. They can even use advanced metacognitive terminology. For example, instead of asking students, "What do you think will happen next?" the teacher might ask, "What do you predict will happen next?" Even very young students will understand the question from the context and, at the same time, learn that to "predict" is to hazard a guess about the outcome of a particular situation based upon known information or perceptions.

Teachers teach learning and organizing strategies. The Venn diagrams mentioned earlier are only one of many visual tools appropriate for use in organizing material (see Hyerle, 1996, for more information). Rather than trying many such strategies, however, it may be more valuable to choose a few to practice on several occasions. Perhaps, in that way, students will become familiar enough with the skills to adopt them for their own private use. Indeed, the ultimate goal is the habitual use of these thinking skills by students in future practice.

Using the visual tools already being used in one's school in other disciplines is one way to integrate music instruction with the total school experience. According to Hyerle (1996), "The difference between an add-on thinking skills program and one that creates long-term effects may be found in the degree to which these processes transfer into different content areas" (p. 73).

Graphic organizers do not have to be complex. As Hyerle (1996) reminds us, "Even the most basic level of organization of information is inherently conceptual" (p. 52). Presume, for example, that my main goal for my fifth graders is that they know the basic elements of music and understand that changing the nature of any single element affects the total sound of the music. I might arrange those primary elements as "slices" in a visual pie, showing that, together, these slices represent the whole of music. Going back to the visual pie with each new unit throughout the year provides the students with a tangible picture that they can use for organizing thought and discussion as we study various styles of music throughout the school year. Eventually, they can mentally conjure up those elements with no paper pie in sight.

Teachers help students generalize the skills involved in organizing and analyzing for future use. Teachers can verbalize outright, "When you need to compare two things in the future, this is a way you can do it." With younger students, we can generalize for them:

"If we know one part is the same as something we've already played, it makes it easier for us to learn the music, doesn't it?"

With more mature students, teachers can ask:

"What method do you think we should use to solve this problem?" or "What did you find out about how to solve this problem because we took time to analyze it?"

Teachers can also assist students to transfer information by taking time to plan for numerous activities that are similar, but not exactly the same. Lowery (1998) writes:

> Rehearsal ... [differentiated here from repetitive practice] takes place when people do something again in a similar but not identical way to reinforce what they have learned while adding something new. New additions increase the likelihood that the knowledge they are learning is not task-specific. Nontask-specific experiences increase the likelihood that the knowledge will be transferable and useful in a variety of ways (pp. 28–29).

Time for this type of rehearsal takes commitment from music teachers who may already worry about coverage in classes that meet only once or twice a week. Still, infrequent meetings make such rehearsals even more necessary if students are going to retain information. It behooves teachers to carefully select fewer, but more powerful, topics and materials so that students can spend more time with the "grand ideas" of music (paraphrased from Lowery, 1998, p. 29).

Skills of Transfer and Application

These cognitive skills enable the student to generate, integrate, and evaluate knowledge meaningfully. *If* students are to integrate, evaluate, and generate by

- predicting
- inferring
- elaborating
- summarizing
- establishing criteria
- verifying
- evaluating
- creating,

then teachers must

- guide their integrating skills, such as predicting, inferring, elaborating, and summarizing
- provide activities for establishing criteria, verifying, and evaluating
- provide time and support for creating.

Teachers guide students' integrating skills, such as predicting, inferring, elaborating, and summarizing. Hynes and Kukuk (1988) remind us that, although convergent questions are necessary in every classroom for assessing student acquisition and processing straightforward facts, it is the divergent questions that initiate the thoughtful, creative answers. Exploring concepts through divergent questions and activities gives students the opportunity to extend and refine information more fully. Some examples of questions that might engender divergent thinking are the following:

- Predictive: "What do you think will happen next?"
- Inferential: "What do you make of that?"
- Elaborative: "What are some things that might have happened instead?"

"Where else might you find this idea?"

- Summarizing: "Can you make some rules about this?" "How could you explain the whole idea?"

In the following vignette, the teacher's predictive, inferential, elaborative, and summarizing questions guide the listening experience for a class of nine-year-olds:

> Now you know the main theme that Glière wrote for his composition, "Russian Sailors' Dance." Pretty great melody, isn't it? I'd love to hear the whole composition, but first let me ask you: how many variations do you think that Glière can have the orchestra play without boring us? [predict] Let's listen …
>
> He played it twelve times! Wow! Were you bored? No? Why not? [infer] If you wanted to make it even longer, can you think of any more ways you could play the melody? [elaborate]
>
> So, what can we expect to hear the next time we listen to music with a "theme and variation" form? [summarize]

Divergent responses may be encouraged by giving substantial wait time for answers and even by acknowledging the merits of wrong answers. For example: "I'm glad you said that, because I'm sure a lot of students were thinking the same thing and now I can clear up that idea. Thanks!"

Various cultures exhibit thinking process in different ways. That is, in some cultures thinking seems to be displayed as effortful pondering, while in other cultures, thinking seems to be only an inward process with no visible signs (Bruner et al., 1996). A study by Flavell et al. (1995) showed that many American children believe thinking is an effortful, deliberate process, so perhaps teachers of young children should even model thinking with their own posture and facial expressions, saying, "Let's think about that problem for a minute."

Encouraging teachers reserve judgment on an answer until the student has given his or her reasons, and acknowledge a novel solution. Frequently, more students are willing to participate when they are allowed to brainstorm in small groups prior to large-group discussion, as the teacher's directions illustrate in the following example:

> How many different measures of 4/4 time do you think you could come up with? Today, we're going to play a game I call "Musical Boggle." With your partner, use your fraction fringes to write down as many different measures as you can that contain four beats. Let's see who can come up with the most in the next ten minutes. We'll check them and cross off any that two or more

> groups have. The winners will be the partners who have the most measures left that are one of a kind.

Kirby and Kuykendall (1991) suggest that order may be more valued in our schools than creativity and that creative students and teachers may be viewed as a bit too unconventional to fit in. Yet divergent thinking requires a willingness to stray from the rigid norm and explore the unusual. The teacher in the next description has decided to introduce the soprano recorder in a curious and playful manner, allowing the students to explore the instrument in a visual, tactile, and imaginative way before the first "real" lesson:

> Today we're going to play "Third Rock from the Sun." We are going to pretend that we are aliens from another planet and have found this unidentified object. [She displays a soprano recorder.] We have no idea what it is, but we will touch it and look at it until we figure out some things about it and some possible uses. The only problem is that we have no mouths (since we're from another planet!), so the only thing we cannot do is put it into our mouths. Use the next ten minutes or so to make as long a list as you can about this thing's parts and possible uses, and then the whole class will share ideas.

Teachers looking for divergent thinking also help students elaborate by pointing out how music is a constructivist rather than a reductionist study, that is, how music is interconnected with so much else in life. These teachers take the time to discuss similarities among the disciplines, to use analogies to other subject areas, and to plan activities that exhibit those connections. In the lesson episode below, the teacher helps first graders draw a connection between familiar literature and the musical form they are studying:

> And here at the end of the piece is the A section again. Composers know that one way to please listeners is to end the way they began. Some stories work the same way, don't they? Remember when we told the story of "The Three Billy Goats Gruff"? In the beginning, the goats were happily munching grass and pink clover. Then in the middle of the story they had that problem with the mean old troll. And at the end, they were happily munching grass and pink clover again. Can you think of any more stories in an ABA form?

In the last example, the music teacher and the math teacher have collaborated to help their students see the connection between their current math unit on fractions and note values:

> Today we're each going to make two fraction fringes [as shown in Figure 7, Fraction fringe]—one to help you in your new fraction unit in math and one to put in your music folder for some of our music problems. They will look almost alike, because notes have the same names and relationships as math fractions.

Elaborative activities and discussions, such as the ones reflected in the previous examples, help students make mental connections among their various subject domains. Perhaps more importantly, they provide the memorable episodes (novel and changing teaching strategies) that Jensen (1998) contends lead to better recall.

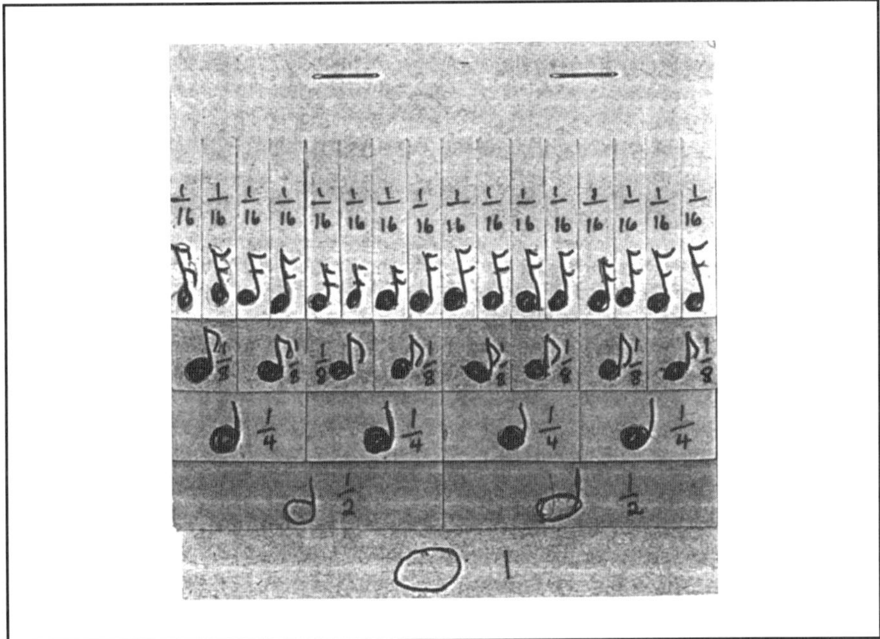

Figure 7. Fraction fringe

Teachers provide activities for establishing criteria, verifying, and evaluating. Marzano (1988) suggests that many students, especially younger ones, are poor at judging whether they have learned specific material. Therefore, an important job of the teacher is to help students establish criteria for process and evaluation in a manner that will help them eventually become self-monitoring. One way to achieve this is to list on a poster the steps that must be followed to solve a problem or to complete a particular process. The corollary to setting criteria is subsequent verification or disproving of a theory or conclusion. Here's a classroom example:

> The fifth-grade students have been studying the twelve-bar blues thirty-five minutes a week for two months. At first the listening examples have strictly followed all the "rules" of traditional blues, and, by comparing those selections, the students have constructed a list of criteria to describe the genre. After the students have many experiences in listening, singing, improvising riffs, playing the blues chord patterns on Autoharps, and making up original words, the teacher begins to introduce music that differs slightly from the students' list of "rules." Class discussion then centers around questions like, "What about this piece matches your rules and what doesn't?" or "How many rules can be 'broken' before it is no longer 'blues'?"

Using what they have learned in previous lessons consisting of analyzing, criteria-setting, and evaluating, performing groups may judge their own personal and group achievement, as exemplified here: "There! We played the whole piece. How did we sound, compared to the recorded versions we heard at our last practice? Did we make mistakes? Did we sound musical? How can we improve our performance?"

Teachers provide time and support for creating. It is a given that the most powerful reason for learning something is a need or desire to use that knowledge or skill in a useful or personally engaging endeavor (Bruner, 1996). Yet, students sometimes seem to perceive work done in school as having no purpose. One way to situate musical learning in a meaningful context is through composition, as in the following example:

> A class of intermediate students was a diverse group, and most students had only a rudimentary understanding of music notation. Despite their limited prior experience, their assigned task was relatively complex:
>
> (1) Choose a published poem.
>
> (2) Mark the words with long or short lines to establish a rhythm.
>
> (3) Convert the long and short lines to traditional rhythmic notation.
>
> (4) Use a keyboard to make up a melody for the rhythm.
>
> (5) Write the melody under the rhythmic notation using alphabet letters.
>
> (6) Convert the melody to traditional notation.
>
> Students progressed through the steps at their own speed, asking for help, when necessary, from another student or the teacher. The

> freedom of choice and self-direction inherent in the assignment seemed to motivate them to focus more than in previous assignments, for they worked diligently for extended periods of time over several weeks.
>
> When their music teacher perceived that several students were having similar problems, she stopped the entire class for a mini-lesson pertaining to the difficulty at hand. Since all the students needed that mini-lesson in order to complete their own tasks, they attended to the short lecture carefully.
>
> Eventually, all the students completed an original setting of their chosen poem, which was then recorded on audiotape for them to keep. Finally, the class shared their compositions in concert.

Most teachers want their students to reach the level of thinking required to apply their knowledge in generating their own work. Improvisation or original composition, as the ultimate in musical creative thinking, can be encouraged in even the youngest students. The next example illustrates the kind of modeling and scaffolding that supports creativity in the very young:

> A class of first graders had categorized various classroom instruments according to dynamic levels by placing them on mats showing iconic representations of soft, medium, and loud sounds. There had been time for discussion about various ways to play certain instruments and about how to produce changes in volume. Then the instruments were set aside while they heard *Listen to the Rain* (Martin, 1988), a picture book describing the progression of a summer storm from the first soft sprinkles to the windy, thunderous climax and the final intermittent drops from the trees.
>
> Working as a class, the children then composed an accompaniment for the book using the instruments already categorized and at hand. As they made suggestions, their music teacher superimposed icons such as light raindrops or jagged lightning onto a large poster on which was drawn a long crescendo followed by a long diminuendo sign. Their first performance included the words of the book, but in the second performance the music stood alone. In other words, the words of the book functioned as the scaffolding for the students' composition as they worked, but were not a necessary part of their final creation (B. Miller, unpublished paper, June, 1999).

In the above excerpt, there were several instances of scaffolding, or conditions that supported student achievement. As mentioned, the text and illustrations of the book provided the main direction for the creative process. In addition, the categorizing of possible instruments allowed the students to know in advance how they all sounded, and the teacher encouraged investigation into alternate sounds for the instruments with such questions as:

"How would it sound if you tapped the tambourine instead of shaking it?" (timbre)

"Could you also play that cymbal softly?"(dynamics)

Another support provided to the first graders was the iconic representation of the music drawn by the teacher as they brainstormed what they thought should happen in the composition. Finally, working as a whole class in response to the teacher's facilitating comments also provided modeling and direction to their work, as, for example: "So, Jim, you think the finger cymbal should only be played at the end for a coda, right? How many agree that would sound nice?"

As students mature and gain more experience with music composition, some of the scaffolding can be removed, but it is still important to provide enough information for the students to be comfortable with the process. In the next example, second-grade students are no longer working as a whole class under the direction of the teacher, but are still provided a complete model and the security of a partner. They are working without the support of the illustrations and text of a book such as the one that informed the *Listen to the Rain* composition. Furthermore, these more experienced students are asked to create their own icons to represent the music instead of relying on teacher-invented icons.

Henry Cowell's "The Banshee" in *The Music Connection* (Silver Burdett Ginn, 1995, grade two) provided the second graders with a delightfully spooky listening experience and the opportunity to try playing the inside of the piano as Cowell had done.

> The children practiced following the listening map of the piece, giving them experience with an iconic model for their own subsequent work. Then they studied the key or legend that described Cowell's various techniques while they talked about the way the icons matched and represented the sounds. Their teacher modeled the assignment with one student before they began following this set of directions:
>
> 1. Choose only one of the four instruments at your station. (In allowing each set of partners to choose one instrument from four possibilities, they gain the personal freedom to be creative but experience some of the constraints placed upon any composer when choosing timbre and structure.)
> 2. Draw a picture of the sound of that instrument in your key box similar to the map for Mr. Cowell's piece.

3. Compose your piece with your partner.
4. Draw a map of your piece using the signs that you put in your key.
5. Add a title and the composers' names.
6. Practice for your performance (B. Miller, unpublished paper, June, 1999).

Conclusion

If we believe that learning is an interactive process in which an individual constructs new and meaningful knowledge by integrating current information with prior understanding, then we must let that viewpoint guide our decisions and actions in the classroom. In order to help our students become independent musicians and be capable of the kind of higher-order thinking described in this chapter, we must provide opportunities for each individual to interact with the music personally, to practice various kinds of thinking skills, and to use his or her knowledge in meaningful ways.

References

Armstrong, T. (1994). *Multiple intelligences in the classroom.* Alexandria, VA: Association for Supervision and Curriculum Development.

Astington, J. W. (1998). Theory of mind goes to school. *Educational Leadership, 56* (3), 46–48.

Bergethon, B., Boardman, E., and Montgomery, J. (1997). *Musical growth in the elementary schools.* Fort Worth, TX: Harcourt Brace College Publishers.

Boardman, E., Ed. (1989). *Dimensions of musical thinking.* Reston, VA: MENC.

Brooks, J. G., & Brooks, M. G. (1993). *In search of understanding: The case for constructivist classrooms.* Alexandria, VA: Association for Supervision and Curriculum Development.

Bruner, J., Oliver, R. R., Greenfield, P. M. et al. (1966). *Studies in cognitive growth: A collaboration at the Center for Cognitive Studies.* NY: John Wiley and Sons.

Bruner, J. (1977). *The process of education.* Cambridge, MA: Harvard University Press.

Cutietta, R. A. (1990). Adapt your teaching style to your students. *Music Educators Journal, 76* (6), 31–36.

Ellison, L. (1992). Using multiple intelligences to set goals. *Educational Leadership, 50* (2), 69–72.

Ellsworth, P. C., & Sindt, V. G. (1994). Helping "aha" to happen: The contributions of Irving Sigel. *Educational Leadership 51,* (5), 40–44.

Flavell, J. H., Green, F. L., & Flavell, E. R. (1995). Young children's knowledge about thinking. *Monographs of the Society for Research in Child Development, 60* (1), Serial No. 243.

Hoerr, T. R. (1992). How our school applied multiple intelligences theory. *Educational Leadership, 50* (2), 61–67.

Hyerle, D. (1996). *Visual tools for constructing knowledge.* Alexandria, VA: Association for Supervision and Curriculum Development.

Hynes, G., & Kukuk, J. W. (1988). The art of questioning. In *Readings in general music.* (pp. 12–15). Reston, VA: MENC.

Jensen, E. (1998). *Teaching with the brain in mind.* Alexandria, VA: Association for Supervision and Curriculum Development.

Kirby, D., & Kuykendall, C. (1991). *Mind matters: Teaching for thinking.* Portsmouth, NH: Boynton/Cook Publishers.

Langer, S. (1977). *Feeling and form.* New York: Prentice-Hall.

Lowery, L. (1998). How new science curriculums reflect brain research. *Educational Leadership, 56* (3), 26–30.

Martin, B. (1988). *Listen to the rain.* New York: Henry Holt.

Marzano, R. J. (1988). *Dimensions of thinking: A framework for curriculum and instruction.* Alexandria, VA: Association for Supervision and Curriculum Development.

Marzano, R. J. (1992). *A different kind of classroom: Teaching with dimensions of learning*. Alexandria, VA: Association for Supervision and Curriculum Development.

Miller, B. A. (1995). Integrating elementary music instruction with a whole language first grade classroom (Doctoral dissertation, University of Illinois, 1995). *Dissertation Abstracts International*, 57 (04) 1535A.

The Music Connection. (1995). Morristown, NJ: Silver Burdett Ginn.

Newmann, F. M., & Wehlage, G. G. (1993). "Five standards of authentic instruction," *Educational Leadership, 50* (7), 8–12.

Paul, R. (1990). *Critical thinking: What every person needs to survive in a rapidly changing world*. Rohnert Park, CA: Center for Critical Thinking and Moral Critique.

Perkins, D. N. (1991). Educating for insight. *Educational Leadership, 49* (2), 4–8.

Resnick, L. B. (1987). *Education and learning to think*. Washington, DC: National Academy Press.

Rosenshine, B., & Meister, C. (1992). The use of scaffolds for teaching high level cognitive strategies. *Educational Leadership, 49* (7), 26–33.

Samples, B. (1992). Using learning modalities to celebrate intelligence. *Educational Leadership, 50* (2), 62–66.

Share the Music. (1995). New York: Macmillan/McGraw-Hill Publishing Co.

Sprenger, M. (1999). *Learning and memory: The brain in action*. Alexandria, VA: Association for Supervision and Curriculum Development.

Tomlinson, C. A., & Kalbfleisch, M. L. (1998). Teach me, teach my brain: A call for differentiated classrooms. *Educational Leadership, 56* (3), 52–55.

Wolfe, P., & Brandt, R. (1998). What do we know from brain research? *Educational Leadership 56,* (3), 8–13.

Beth Ann Miller is a music specialist for Maine School Administrative District #1 in Presque Isle, Maine.

6

MUSICAL THINKING AND TECHNOLOGY

BRIAN MOORE

When we think about the twenty-first century and reflect upon our society, we cannot help but be struck by the pervasive changes that we have all experienced. These changes have been both positive and negative, many seemingly working at cross purposes. Great opportunities for personal choice have gone hand in hand with outrageous acts of personal expression, some even violent. Much of our "global village" is comprised of faceless individuals who hide in chat rooms behind e-mail pseudonyms. Now more than ever, "We are drowning in information but starved for knowledge" (Naisbitt, 1984, pp. 16–17). Technology has been a catalyst for many of these changes as, for example, the breadth and depth of personal choice through on-line Internet shopping. For other changes, technology has been both cause and effect—the global village is a result of mass communication and global transportation opportunities.

Our society's technology has also impacted education. Increases in children's access to computers have driven change in teachers' preservice and inservice activities. Of concern to music educators is the need for multiple ways of thinking that parallel the multiple uses and applications of technology. Technology as both tool and topic provides the framework and blueprint for "thinking about thinking."

These multiple uses and applications of technology reveal several themes or ideas that relate to the topic of thinking. These themes do not exist in isolation, but rather, as in a great symphony, they interact in various ways. As the modulation of a musical theme involves shifts in its tonal center, so the themes presented here are best understood as shifts in interconnected relationships rather than as isolated changes. Each of the following four themes will be considered in light of its implications for thinking, concluding with implications for music education:

- The shift from an industrial to an information society
- Shifts in time and space (the ways and places in which technology affects us)
- The shift from "technology-assisted" to "technology-required"
- The shift from "technically simple/user complex" to "technically complex/user simple."

Where we are going is shaped by our understanding of where we have been, and how we will move into the future is influenced in part by how we got to the present. "That which has been is that which will be, and that which has been done is that which will be done" (Ecclesiastes 1:9). While we all have the ability to think, to perceive, to react, to reason, and to abstract, the degree to which higher and more complex levels of thinking are required has increased. Examining the shifts related to technology can reveal areas needing attention, as well as provide encouragement about what is working.

The Shift from an Industrial to an Information Society

The industrial society of the early twentieth century was characterized by manufacturing. Structural and procedural problems could be articulated and defined. Solutions were best achieved by hiring efficiency experts to analyze a task and break it into small, manageable components. Efficiency was achieved by minimizing the time required to perform a specific task with little consideration for other aspects of a job.

Because problems could often be clearly articulated and defined, solutions were often viewed as singular. The thinking was that one solution existed because there was one best way to solve any given problem. This approach to problem solving frequently involved analysis, and the assembly line became a metaphor of the industrial age. For example, to solve the problem of how to mass-produce cars quickly and efficiently, the manufacturing process was analyzed and broken down into a series of discrete and sequential steps and tasks, each of which could be repeatedly performed by one worker. The assembly line was a linear approach to solving problems. Even language was affected; a worker was "on the line," success was measured by the "bottom line," and so forth.

No one individual worker had a complete picture of the whole, but viewed his or her efforts only in relation to the adjacent individuals on the assembly line. The assembly line was a singular solution for multiple industrial situations as it solved the problem of not only manufacturing cars, but also cereal, clothing, and myriad other goods as well. Because of the success achieved using this approach, such solutions were often viewed as long term and expected to last perhaps as long as twenty to thirty years (see Figure 1, Characteristics of an industrial society compared to an information society).

The evolution of the industrial society into an information society has seen the provision of services and acquisition of data as commodities, in addition to the manufacture of durable goods. The proliferation of dot-com corporations reveals an industry based on bits and bytes—invisible digital information. Accumulating and distributing knowledge as a product, these companies have become a new manufacturing industry.

The assembly line (workers with specific tasks functioning in a strict linear sequence) has given way to the team (workers with broader skills and responsibilities working in consort with others). Linear thinking and linear approaches to accomplishing tasks have developed into intricate, and often complex, webs and networks of interactivity.

Solving problems when knowledge is a commodity becomes much more ambiguous. Problems can seldom be clearly defined, perhaps due in part to the fact that the commodity cannot be directly seen. Solutions can be fuzzy, and multiple approaches may appear necessary. Today's solutions are also viewed as short term at best, because no sooner is a solution put in place than a new problem arises. Questions and problems spring into view that simply did not exist three to five years ago. Who could have imagined in the 1930s and 1940s that everyday business in the twenty-first century would require a computer next to every phone and a delivery system called the Internet?

Industrial Society	Information Society
Problems clearly defined	Problems with "fuzzy" parameters and unknown aspects
Problems required solutions	Problems require approaches
Analysis	Thinking "outside the box"
Multiple problems all with a single solution	Multiple problems each requiring multiple solutions
Linear solutions	Multidimensional approaches
Micro-view	Global perspectives
Long-term solutions	Short-term "fixes"

Figure 1. Characteristics of an industrial society compared to an information society

Implications for thinking. It is interesting that the language of the assembly line has been carried over to the communications mode of the twenty-first century as we speak of being "on line." But the implications are quite different—we are "on line" over "the Web"—which consists of linear points connected multidimensionally. While the Web is a tremendous source of information, it is also overwhelming and at times even seemingly impossible to navigate. Matters are even more complicated when we realize that product and process are intertwined. The digital product is the Web, yet the process used to access and retrieve is the Web itself—the library and the card catalogue are one and the same!

The ability to acquire and retain data was fundamental to being able to think in an industrial era. Memorization was critical, as foundational knowledge was important. Knowledge was stored only in print and through oral tradition; thus, to be truly literate was to "know things." The encyclopedia is an interesting metaphor for this perspective. In an encyclopedia, information is readily available, but it is organized alphabetically rather than conceptually. In other words, information is stored in isolation in an "assembly line" sequence with topic "A" having nothing to do with topic "B" other than its starting letter.

As mentioned earlier, problem solving was typically accomplished through analytical and convergent thinking in search of a single solution.

Creative, critical, and high level industrial-era thinking was exemplified by the inventor (e.g., Thomas Edison) and was viewed as belonging to the realm of genius. This type of thinking was considered unnecessary and certainly not the norm for everyday living and working.

In contrast, today's information society routinely requires divergent thinking, creative problem solving, and higher levels of thinking. Information is stored and retrieved by conceptual and topical groupings. A Web site consists of a collection of similar types of information that often point to other sites containing related material. The emphasis on data acquisition and memorization of facts as tools for problem solving has shifted to emphasis on data selection and information evaluation.

Since the information age views knowledge and data as commodities, the tools required to work with these "products" become critical. If the manufacturing of goods required expertise and experience in physical work, mechanical inventiveness, and task analysis, the distribution of information as product requires mental work, digital creativity, and the synthesis of disparate concepts and topics.

Shifts in Time and Space

In the 1950s and 1960s, futurists predicted an increase in leisure time since technology was expected to simplify our lives and allow us to be more efficient and effective. Many predicted that the forty-hour, five-day-a-week work schedule would be drastically reduced. What has actually transpired is that the workday has expanded and now lasts virtually twenty-four hours a day. With the use of e-mail and the Internet, work can be carried out across time zones and continents. The definition of the "work day" is no longer measured by an eight-to-five time frame (see Figure 2, Shifts in perceptions of time and space).

Another shift in the way time is used is "synchronized" vs. "asynchronized" communication. Personal, face-to-face conversation is an example of information flowing in a synchronized manner between sender and receiver. The telephone is also a synchronized medium, as information flows back and forth in real time. But the phenomenon of electronic mail has created a new, asynchronized flow of data as the sender and receiver deal with information "out of synch." This type of communication is a digital version of pen-pal writing, whereby individuals share information not in real time, but with indeterminate lapses between communiques.

An example in education of this shift in time is distance learning. Not only does the place for learning take on new meaning, but the term "class time" has an entirely new definition. Asynchronized instruction offers learning on demand, with content and pedagogy available when the students choose to acquire it, rather than when the teacher is scheduled to provide it.

The work environment has also seen dramatic changes. A specific infrastructure is required when a society focuses primarily on manufacturing. This results in a physical place where work is carried out. When information manipulation becomes the product and the process, the product may be located in a virtual work space rather than a physical setting. An individual may have no single place of work, but multiple locations, one of which may be his or her home. The same is true for the learner, as the "classroom" can be virtually anywhere. As wireless technology continues to develop and become the norm, the ability to teach and learn at any time and from any place may become a standard form of education.

Time	Space
The "8 hour work day" vs. the virtual workday (twenty-four hours a day, seven days a week)	A set physical location for one's work vs. a "virtual" location (the virtual office or distance-education classroom—"work" able to occur at virtually any location)
Work occurring in real time (synchronized) vs. work and learning on-demand (asynchronized)	Set group of individuals brought together by the setting (the office, the classroom) vs. changing teams/workgroups

Figure 2. Shifts in perceptions of time and space

In an industrial society, a worker is often identified by his or her workplace. The assembly line worker, the teacher, and the musician all have traditional and readily acknowledged places for work, be it the factory, the classroom, or the concert hall. In an information society, a worker can not be as easily identified by his or her environment. The office worker may operate out of a home. The distributed company may have no office at all since employees work out of whatever setting they desire as they collaborate via phone, fax, and the Internet. Hence, the work setting comes to be replaced by the work group as a defining characteristic of work.

Implications for thinking. With the possible exception of the inspiration component of creative thinking, the kinds of thinking discussed in the chapters of this book require time—time to perceive, to process, to reflect, and to think. At their heart, many aspects of technology thwart these reflective aspects of thinking. Because technology, especially computer-based technology, is measured by speed, the user is expected to work more quickly, adapt sooner, and achieve results at an ever-increasing pace. Creative thinking, due perhaps to inspiration (i.e., ideas that come to mind with seemingly little time required to generate them), receives a lot of attention in the information age. Many futurists have noted that this emerging need for new ways of thinking has resulted in the three "R's" (reading, 'riting, and 'rithmetic) being replaced by the three "C's" (communication, collaboration, and creativity).

Critical thinking, creative thinking, metacognition, and other aspects of thinking, however, require time. If our efforts in the teaching and developing of thinking are to be successful, our curricula, pedagogy, and approach will need to counter the "shrinking" of time that technology creates in order to develop desired higher levels of thinking. It is possible that technology may actually provide a solution to its own problem. Time to think, to reflect, and to allow for incubation can be achieved in part via the distance-education delivery system. The teacher can provide content, and the student can receive this information at whatever pace seems appropriate. The decisions to be made are ones of "best fit"—what means of delivery are the most expedient for the curricula at hand.

The Shift from "Technology-Assisted" to "Technology-Required"

Most technology has been created to fulfill a need. Technology used as a tool to accomplish a specific task, to solve a certain problem, or to streamline a process has been the impetus for its advancement. When the personal computer became affordable in school situations in the late 1970s, the resulting software was a menu-driven approach to computer-assisted instruction. The teaching/learning process could be accomplished via other means, and in many instances actually required such other means. As an example, computer-assisted drill-and-practice did not actually teach, but it did provide opportunities to reinforce and practice what had already been learned (see Figure 3, Technology-assisted compared to technology-required resources).

The educational environment in an information society requires technology in order for teaching and learning to happen. Technology-based instruction cannot occur unless the hardware and software resources are available.

This environment for education creates new challenges for teacher and learner alike. The fundamental techniques of each kind of technology have to be articulated, addressed, and mastered by the teacher. Only then can the art of teaching be applied to the science of technology. To move beyond the basics requires highly developed ability in the use of the hardware and software, as well as the ability to adapt these resources creatively in order to effect greater learning.

Technology-Assisted	Technology-Required
Technology as resource	Technology as requirement
Reinforcement as primary learning/teaching approach (e.g., drill and practice)	Presentation, delivery, practice, and assessment all empowered and driven by the technology

Figure 3. "Technology-assisted" compared to "technically required" resources

Implications for Thinking. In the way that new learning environments require specific technologies, so will new learning experiences require different ways of thinking. Thinking skills do not happen in isolation, but are part of a content, that is, subject matter. The environment, or context, in which these skills are used helps shape thinking as well, and so thinking becomes part of subject matter. For example, music critical thinking in a music theory setting/environment is different from that required of an ensemble in a rehearsal room. Music educators need to reexamine curricula and pedagogy in terms of the thinking skills required. These skills must be viewed as complex combinations in order to be realistic. As an example, the composition of music is both inspiration and perspiration. The thinking skills of divergent thinking (inspiration) and convergent thinking (perspiration) are examples drawn from critical thinking. The creative thinking skills inherent in inspiration are part of a thinking scheme that includes problem-solving and content-based skills. The manner in which these skills are combined by the requirements of the compositional tasks at hand provides teachers a pedagogical and curricular view of the teachable aspects of composition. "We may be a society with far fewer learning-disabled children and far more teaching-disabled environments than currently perceived. The computer changes this by making us more able to reach children with different learning and cognitive styles" (Negroponte, 1995, p. 198).

The Shift from "Technically Simple/User Complex" to "Technically Complex/User Simple"

Technology has grown and will continue to grow in its sophistication, power, complexity, and prevalence. Component stereos, personal computers, and even automobiles have become more and more technically complicated while at the same time easier to use. New developments such as one-touch programming on VCRs and self-diagnostics for cars are intended to create a simpler user environment. But such simplicity is achieved only through the use of more complicated technology. Increased catalog and Internet shopping is also an example of businesses conducting commerce in ways that make it easier for the consumer. Orders can be placed twenty-four hours a day, seven days a week, from virtually anywhere in the world. Again, this convenience is possible only because of the technically sophisticated resources available (see Figure 4, Shift from "technically simple/user complex" to "technically complex/user simple").

In education, gone are the days when a single teacher working independently could program a simple application for a particular learning situation (examples of such programming languages and environments were BASIC, LOGO, and HyperCard). While some of these environments still exist and have even been more fully developed, modern computing operating systems are very complicated entities, with commercial-strength application development requiring teams of programmers. All of this is reflective of the greater complexity of technology that strives to create a simple user-experience.

Implications for thinking. Critical thinking and evaluation skills are important abilities that today's student will need in order to cope with tomorrow's world. As technology grows in complexity, influential decisions need to be made as to whether the end results actually are "simpler." After all, despite all of their features, there still are a lot of VCRs still flashing "12:00 a.m."

Simple technology yielding a complex and sometimes difficult experience by end user	Ease of use achieved via complex and sophisticated technology
Software (especially educational software) developed by individuals	Software production requiring teams of writers and developers

Figure 4. Shift from "technically simple/user complex" to "technically complex/user simple"

Implications for Music and Music Educators

In discussing the four shifts related to technology and their implications for thinking, issues emerge for music and music educators:

Industrial and Information Society. In the industrial age, music was primarily available via live performance and, as such, was a focal point of a family's and community's culture. With the advent of technology such as the phonograph and radio, music could be had on demand. The information age adds an aspect of personal selection and choice via technology that allows the recording of music through tape media (cassette, video), digital (recordable CDs), and the Internet (MP3 files and hard disk-based recording). Because one no longer needs to be at a live performance in order to hear music, the issue has become not one of production of music in the performance sense, but the selection of music in a personal sense.

Music education needs not only to develop future generations of performers to create both live performances and recordings, but also to instill heightened perceptual and critical abilities in future generations of music consumers. The informed listener is one who can make intelligent decisions based upon personal needs, likes, and desires. He or she must be able to discern, evaluate, and judge not only the inherent quality of a product, but also assess its "fit" in meeting a specific need. Such skills are part of the composition and improvisation process. Given the ability for personal music recordings that technology provides, being a "consumer" of music will also mean being a producer of music. Music as information thus requires abilities in composition, improvisation, and critical thinking.

Time and space. Music is a temporal art. Time is the canvas, and sound is the medium. The concept of communication that is out of synch appears to be at odds with the performance of music. And yet it is the sharing of musical performance in asynchronous ways that has actually increased access to music. From the invention of the phonograph, the cassette recorder, the compact disc, and now the MP3 format and MIDI files, music performance has a continued history of being able to be "saved" for performance at the demand of the listener. This phenomenon is not solely in the domain of popular music. Classical musicians and ensembles currently use Internet-based technology such as MP3 to provide their music in asynchronous ways in order to increase its exposure to the public (Shannon, 2000).

For music educators, teaching and learning a temporal art in terms of compressed and extended time will be challenging. The best example of the shift to the twenty-four hour workday is the concept of distance education. Learners are able to gain skills and knowledge at their own pace and in their own time frame. While the technology exists to deliver practically any musical content, the questions of curricular integrity and instructional efficiency still need to be addressed. Music education must be able to continue the traditions of pedagogy and curricula that have worked, while at the same time provide cutting-edge instructional strategies that will facilitate distance education opportunities.

The environment for music and music teaching has always had a strong identity, especially for music programs in this country. Students are known by their ensemble, their home room, and their school. The technological advances of the information age require music educators to recognize that other ensembles have already emerged alongside the traditions of bands, orchestras, and choirs. Internet jam sessions (all done in real time), the young composer/arranger working in his or her own virtual studio, and the tremendous access to music of other cultures yielding nontraditional acoustic ensembles (e.g., keyboard ensembles and steel-drum bands) are all viable, important music work places for today's musicians. Technology has created new ensembles and instruments such as MIDI synthesizers that, for many students, have replaced acoustic instruments. The same technology that enabled music to be personal has also made it portable (by means of radio, cassette tape player, tiny compact disc players, MP3 players, and personal electronics). Therefore, schools may no longer be the primary time and place for a student's musical work to take place. "Technology and media may present us with our greatest challenge: The more prevalent the arts and media become in our society, the tougher it will be to justify the study of the arts in our schools" (Kimpton, 2000, pp. 34–35).

To meet this challenge will require that the music education community, especially school-based music education, provide the experiences, tools, and curricula that enable and empower students to use this music technology in settings and purposes that go beyond performance. For example, the identity of the ensemble characterizes the performer and conductor, as we are known as choir directors or orchestra conductors. Technology environments, especially those in home and other nonschool settings, create studio identity (e.g., computer, synth, hard-disk recording software, and a software-based mixing console). This studio identity stresses the composer. The medium is now a compact disc recording, a Web site, or an MP3 file. The emergence of the student as composer creates an obvious need for a working understanding of the compositional processes and the types of thinking that each process requires.

Music educators find themselves at an important crossroads. The potential for many young musicians to find their outlet for musical creativity and expression lies outside the school environment. The concepts of critical thinking, creative thinking, convergent and divergent problem-solving, and others addressed here all need to be part of the twenty-first century music curriculum. This may require teaching/learning experiences beyond the resources of the local school, like distance teaching as well as distance learning. This could include the use of Web sites with content information from experts or video and audio streaming (access to off-site sound and video in real time via the Internet). School-based experiences could also be presented in which homework takes on a new meaning, for example, assignments to solve musical problems with technology resources found at home.

Technology-assisted and technology required. Instrumental music is an excellent example of a technology-based discipline that existed long before the information age. The instruments of the modern orchestra are very sophisticated examples of technology. Without the technology of the oboe, the trumpet, or the violin, the orchestra would not exist. In order for the orchestra to exist, so must its requisite technology. As music teachers, instrumental ensemble directors are generally aware of what is required to teach instrumental music. Learning fundamental techniques that eventually lead to mastery are common-knowledge approaches to the discipline. This awareness provides an excellent paradigm for teaching and learning in computer-based music instruction systems. The instrumental skills classes common in undergraduate music education preparation provide a model for introductory technology courses. The undergraduate student needs foundational skill development in topics such as MIDI, digital audio recording, notation software, and sequencing, and the opportunity to try these skills in teaching scenarios (the pedagogy of music technology). These curricular topics acknowledge that teachers must possess fundamental knowledge concerning conceptual categories of music technology (the skills class models required courses in strings, brass, woodwinds, and percussion where students acquire some performance ability coupled with conceptual approaches to teaching a particular family of instruments).

Musical performance, listening, and composition through technology-based environments provide new sounds and new symbols. MIDI hardware provides electronic timbres and thus can be heard in the electronic medium. This situation is parallel to digital video, where movies and effects are created only with technology. Timbre categories such as pad, synth lead, and SFX (sound effects) are now commonly available collections of electronic-based timbres. Today's composers have incredibly expanded palettes. (It is interesting that when MIDI keyboards and tone generators became affordable and available to the K–12 teacher, the first desired sounds were piano and harpsichord, an effort to use technology to yield acoustic sounds.) The requirement for heightened musical evaluation skills is due in part to this increase in available musical materials and resources.

Teachers also need to develop expert-level skill and master-teaching ability in at least one aspect of music technology, such as sequencing or music notation. This need parallels applied music, where we expect every music major to play a major instrument. If teachers and schools are to provide these unique technology-based learning environments, then teachers must be prepared to use and teach these tools and techniques at both the preservice and in-service levels.

Music software has also given new ways of representing music via notational systems. Virtually every sequencer presents music in three formats: (1) traditional notation, (2) event lists, and (3) piano roll notation. (A sequencer is software that records, edits, and plays back music performance either through MIDI instruments and/or digital audio.)

It is also possible to view and edit analog sound waves. Composers can now directly edit and manipulate sound using filters, copying, pasting, and other techniques. Digital audio recording has placed the potential of a complete recording studio into a home-based computer. The notation of such digital audio is the waveforms presented across time lines.

All of these new methods of representing music emphasize the fact that the art and aesthetic of music are in its hearing, not in its notation. When we go to a performance, the aesthetic exists temporally, not visually. While traditional notation systems are important, it is equally important to realize that with new technologies come new symbols that serve a purpose—the visual transmission of musical information. To work effectively as a composer, a performer, and perhaps even as a listener with new musical environments will require understanding new notations systems for editing and transmitting musical information.

The fantastic depth and breadth of today's music create a sense that music surrounds us and is woven into the fabric of life. Music educators need to instill in their students the realization that such diversity and quantity have levels of sophistication that are a reflection of the technical complexity noted earlier. Having a lot of music available does not mean that it is of high quality. Having the computer resources that make it possible to create original music does not mean that the user will become an expert composer. (Does the availability of a word processor directly create a great author?) The technology that enables us tremendous access to such a wide variety of music also requires a high level of music literacy and sophistication to be an intelligent composer and a listener.

Conclusion

Perhaps the best example of enforced change is technology. The computer purchased today may need to be replaced in just months. Not only is our society reliant upon this technology, but so is the entire world. The global village is connected by communication systems, and the global economy exists because of the speed and presence of the Internet.

As our reliance upon technology continues and increases, so does the rate of change. The change from an industrial society to an information society was a shift in people's perception of time and space. Economies based upon manufacturing and mass production have grown to include information services and data distributions that can happen literally anytime, anyplace. Our perspective that the world is shrinking demonstrates the blurring of time and place. What will be required of us as musicians and educators is the ability to foresee change, maximize its potential, and minimize its negative impact. As music educators, we must be willing to take the lead in teaching and learning music, as well developing new knowledge and skills in music making, music creating, and music enjoyment. We must balance the needs and desires of our students, the nature of teaching/learning environments, our professional abilities in curriculum, and pedagogical development to develop musical thinking for the twenty-first century. The ability to memorize and recite as the sole means of navigating a society generally succeeded in an agricultural era and even to a point in an industrial era. But these thinking skills, while still fundamental, simply are not enough for the person living in an information era. Higher levels of thinking, including creative thinking, critical thinking, and metacognition, need to be developed and applied in all areas of society.

Technology will continue to create wonderful potentials, as well as uncomfortable questions. Advances in biotechnology raise ethical questions concerning genetic engineering. Freedom of expression via the Internet raises concern over inappropriate content, especially where children are involved. Music making, music performance, and music composition that are easily made and freely distributed begs questions of taste, artistry, and expression. We need to develop in our students the thinking abilities that allow them to be productive, creative, musical, and discerning. The technology and our students will allow us to do nothing less.

References

Kimpton, J. (2000). *Arts Education Policy Review, 101,* (3), 34–35.

Naisbitt, J. (1984). *Megatrends: Ten new directions transforming our lives.* New York: Warner Books.

Negropointe, N. (1995). *Being digital.* New York: Alfred A. Knopf, Inc.

Shannon, V. (2000, June 26). "Web pulls strings for classical trio: Online exposure helps to secure chamber group's recording deal." *International Herald Tribune.*

Brian Moore is professor of music education at the University of Nebraska–Lincoln.

7

MUSICAL LEARNING AND TEACHING AND THE YOUNG CHILD

BARBARA J. ALVAREZ AND MARGARET H. BERG

The musical world of the young child is a playground of sounds. The thinking processes of young children are intuitive, imaginative, and based on direct experiences in their physical and social environments. Since the first edition of this book, research has continued to support the notion of the importance and impact of early experiences on brain development (Baker & Martin, 1998). We now know that children are born with the basic wiring that links the brain and the entire nervous system. From birth, children's experiences begin to establish and fortify the complex network of nerve cell connections called synapses. The imaging techniques now available show that children who have the opportunity to interact with environments full of rich sensory experiences and experience meaningful interactions with others show brain development marked by more synaptic connections. According to Diamond and Hopson (1999),

> In the 1990s, researchers ... discovered new ways to foster greater intelligence by nurturing brain growth during its most active phases. Where society once viewed the child's brain as static and unchangeable, experts today see it as a highly dynamic organ that feeds on stimulation and experience and responds with the flourishing of branching, intertwined neural forests. This discovery presents us with a way of helping our children reach their fullest and healthiest mental development. But it has a dark side, as well, if the child's mind is understimulated and underused (p. 1).

Musical experiences are, of course, an essential part of important early childhood experiences. This is not to say that we have all of the research needed to show us how musical development unfolds from infancy on or that we have all the needed studies to help us understand the effects, both musical and nonmusical, that result from music experiences. However, research and writing over the last century on early childhood music have established a good initial understanding of how musical concepts develop in a variety of music learning settings (Alvarez, 1981; Deliège & Sloboda, 1996; Scott-Kassner, 1992; Sims, 1990). In the past ten years, psychologists have taken a greater interest in the study of cognition, particularly focusing on the influence of the environment on children's learning. Even the popular press has avidly followed the discussion and controversies surrounding studies related to musical experience and brain development (Begley, 2000). This chapter's focus on musical thinking and the influence of context on thinking reflects the current thread of interest in the study of child development.

Musical Thinking

Let us first define early childhood and then musical thinking in the early childhood years. The term "early childhood" generally refers to those years from birth through age eight. Our focus is predominantly on musical development in the preschool years, ages two to five; however, some reference will be made to infant and toddler development (from birth to age two).

Ideally, all musical experiences involve musical thinking. But what *is* "musical thinking" in the early childhood years, and how is it unique? While core thinking skills—focusing, information-gathering, remembering, organizing, analyzing, generating, integrating, and evaluating (Marzano et al., 1988)—are applicable to a variety of instructional contexts, musical thinking is distinguished by audiating (Gordon, 1987) or hearing music internally, as well as generating and mentally manipulating imagined sounds (Webster & Richardson, 1993, p. 9). Furthermore, "musical thinking is special because it can represent a powerful blending of cognitive (factual) content with affective (feelingful) content in ways that few other disciplines can. In the West, it is common to think of these as separate entities of the human psyche that have nothing to do with each other. This is far from the truth" (Webster & Richardson, 1993). Early childhood specialists have identified the interdependence of cognitive, affective, and skill development in young children, and we now recognize that a child's affective response to music is also a crucial component of musical thinking.

National Music Standards

Additional developments since the publication of *Dimensions of Musical Thinking* (Boardman, 1989) that influence our discussion of musical thinking include the voluntary National Standards for Music Education (MENC, 1994) and the *MENC Position Statement on Early Childhood Education* (MENC, 1991).

The *Position Statement on Early Childhood Education* was developed by the Early Childhood Task Force, which was a part of MENC's "Future Directions" efforts. The statement was adopted by the MENC National Executive Board in July, 1991. A part of that statement includes ten beliefs about young children and developmentally and individually appropriate musical experiences (Sims, 1995). These beliefs highlight the philosophy of early childhood education on which this chapter is based:

1. All children have musical potential.
2. Children bring their own unique interest and abilities to the music learning environment.
3. Very young children are capable of developing critical thinking skills through musical ideas.
4. Children come to early childhood music experiences from diverse backgrounds.
5. Children should experience exemplary musical sounds, activities, and materials.
6. Children should not be encumbered with the need to meet performance goals.
7. Children's play is their work.
8. Children learn best in pleasant physical and social environments.
9. Diverse learning environments are needed to serve the developmental needs of many individual children.
10. Children need effective adult models. (MENC, 1991)

There are two sets of National Standards for Music Education that impact the discussion of early childhood musical thinking. These are the K–12 Standards and the PreK Standards. The latter will be discussed in this chapter.

The PreK Music Education Standards (ages 2–4) include four content standards with appropriate Achievements Standards intended for age four:

1. *Content Standard:* Singing and Playing Instruments. *Achievement Standard:* Children use their voices expressively as they speak, chant, and sing; sing a variety of simple songs in various keys, meters, and genres, alone and with a group, becoming increasingly accurate in rhythm and pitch; experiment with a variety of instruments and other sound sources; and play simple melodies and accompaniments on instruments.
2. *Content Standard:* Creating music. *Achievement Standard:* Children improvise songs to accompany their play activities; improvise instrumental accompaniments to songs, recorded selections, stories, and poems; create short pieces of music, using voices, instruments, and other sound sources; and invent and use original graphic or symbolic systems to represent vocal and instrumental sounds and musical ideas.
3. *Content Standard:* Responding to music. *Achievement Standard:* Children identify the sources of a wide variety of sounds; respond through movement to music of various tempos, meters, dynamics, modes, genres, and styles to express what they hear; and participate freely in music activities.
4. *Content Standard:* Understanding music. *Achievement Standard:* Children use their own vocabulary and standard music vocabulary to describe voices, instruments, music notation, and music of various genres, styles, and periods from diverse cultures; sing, play instruments, move, or verbalize to demonstrate awareness of the elements of music and changes in their usage; and demonstrate an awareness of music as a part of daily life (MENC, 1994, pp. 11–12).

Musical thinking is manifested in actions. The National Standards suggest a range of activities in which children can be involved in order to develop musical thinking skills. The four early childhood content standards show clearly that, for young children, musical thinking grows through musical experiences.

Theoretical Developments: The Social Context of Musical Thinking and Learning

In the past twenty years, the writings of Vygotsky (1978), Csikszentmihalyi (1988), Gordon (1997), Webster (1993), and Gardner

(1997) point to the impact of the environment on learning. Many contemporary scholars posit that what and how a student learns is situated in the social and physical environment (Brown, Collins, & Duguid, 1989). Piaget's (1952) theory of cognitive development continues to inform our practice and is evident in the use of sensory, action-based, and child-initiated activities. While many scholars agree with Piaget (1952) that children are active knowledge seekers who construct their understanding of the world, they also acknowledge the strong influence of the social and physical environment (Berk, 1991; Egan, 1999; Phillips & Soltis, 1998; Vygotsky, 1978).

Lev Vygotsky (1978), a Russian psychologist and contemporary of Piaget, believed, contrary to Piaget, that learning and more complex thinking originate in social interactions rather than individual problem solving. Children learn how to do challenging tasks from more capable adults or peers. Vygotsky also disagreed with Piaget on the role of language in cognitive development. While Piaget claimed that a child's use of language is egocentric and nonsocial, for Vygotsky (1962) language serves a pivotal function as a catalyst for higher-order thinking through its use by others and the self during problem solving (Berk, 1991). Furthermore, being able to express one's point of view fluently contributes to language literacy. Egan (1999) suggests that "the fullest achievement of literacy requires the fullest achievement of oral capacities as well" (p. 33).

Vygotsky (1978) used the concept of the zone of proximal development (ZPD) to explain how children learn from others. When working cooperatively on a problem, the child is able to work on more complex tasks than when working individually. The child eventually incorporates the language used by the more capable adult or peer into his or her private speech when working on a similar problem alone. As a result of this social interaction, the child is able to solve more challenging problems and therefore think more critically about the subject than if he or she had worked alone.

More recently, researchers have identified features of social interactions that facilitate working in a child's ZPD. First, participants create intersubjectivity or a shared understanding of a task (Rommetveit, 1974; Wertsch, 1985). Adults often try to create intersubjectivity by comparing a previously solved problem to the current one or by using analogies or child-friendly language to help the child view the problem from a different perspective. Second, the adult creates a scaffold (Bruner, 1983; Collins, Brown, & Newman, 1989) or support structure in the form of assistance that is adjusted in type and quantity over the course of instruction.

In addition to learning through direct instruction from an adult or peer, young children also learn through observation and imitation (Bandura, 1970). Often, the young child will work to imitate the musical behavior of a peer several minutes after the observation takes place (Cohen, 1980). When the young child is surrounded by other learners at varying levels of development, he or she is able to learn through legitimate peripheral participation as a member of a larger learning community (Lave & Wegner, 1991).

The degree of challenge provided by the environment is of pivotal importance for Csikszentmihalyi (1988). In his theory of flow, he suggests that we experience a sense of timelessness when engaged in meaningful tasks that provide an adequate amount of challenge (Csikszentmihalyi, 1988). Young children are often engaged in flow as their whole person seems absorbed in the present task.

Several researchers have proposed theories specific to music learning that utilize aspects of the general psychological theories reviewed above. The purpose of the following material is not to provide a comprehensive review of the theories but to draw links between them and the general theories outlined above. In particular, we will highlight how the music-specific theories also point to the strong impact of the environment on music learning. While much research on music thinking in the young child posits links among perception, production, and cognition, more research is needed to better understand the interaction among these three behaviors, as well as developmental patterns (Scott-Kassner, 1992).

Several aspects of Gordon's *Music Learning Theory for Newborn and Young Children* (1997) also take into account the impact of the environment on music learning. Gordon (1997) divides learning into three categories—skill, tonal, and rhythmic—that are further divided into two types—discrimination and inference. Gordon's theory resonates with the concept of scaffolding by which the teacher and parent model musical behavior then gradually shift their roles to function as guides (Walters, 1992).

Additionally, the concept of legitimate peripheral participation, in which a child with less experience and/or skill participates mainly as an observer, corresponds to the first preparatory audiation stage. In the early years, children acculturate to the musical environment through observation and imitation. Gordon and his associates encourage parents and teachers to follow a musical event with silence so that children have an opportunity to make a listening response, which might occur much later in time or by another child in a different part of the room (Valerio et al., 1998). For Gordon, the musical environment is of primary importance. Children learn a variety of tonal and rhythmic patterns, coupled with movement responses.

Webster's (1990) model of creative thinking in music uses research on creative thinking as a foundation for illustrating how enabling skills and conditions influence the thinking processes used to design a musical product. While creative music experiences for young children are more exploratory and less product-oriented than suggested by Webster's model, recognition of the impact of the social and physical environment, particularly one that supports multiple problem solutions, on creative thinking in music has clear connections to situated cognition theory (Cohen, 1980; Flohr, 1985; Kratus, 1985, 1989; Pond, 1981). Certainly, a rich, supportive environment for young children can also help to foster creative production in older children (for a discussion of the assessment of creative thinking in music, including developmental differences in children's improvisations and compositions, see Webster, 1992).

The work of Howard Gardner (1987, 1997) offers a variety of insights with application for early childhood musical experiences. His work has reinforced the notions of the importance of holistic experience (kinesthetic and music), the usefulness of engaging children with musical problems, and the seamless connection between activity and assessment. According to Gardner, music is one of eight intelligences that constitute a person's intellectual profile (Checkley, 1997). Evidence for music as an intelligence includes: (1) the sequential nature of skill building toward competence, (2) evolutionary and biological evidence, and (3) the unique symbol system (musical notation) associated with music. Gardner supports problem-based assessment experiences that are integrated with other classroom activities (Gardner, 1993).

Implications of Theoretical Developments for the Young Child and Music

How can theories such as those discussed above be applied to early childhood music experiences? Based on the connection that contemporary theorists draw among knowledge, activity, and the social and physical environment, music experiences for the young child need to consist of meaningful activities that allow for considerable interaction with peers, as well as the teacher and parent. The implications of this will be discussed in the broad categories of authentic tasks and make-believe experiences, physical environment, social environment, the role of the adult, and modes of instruction and interaction.

Authentic tasks and make-believe experiences. For young children, the best way to learn is through activity. Applicable theoretical developments reinforce what early childhood specialists already know intuitively—that knowledge is not abstract and that teachers need to "embed learning in activity and make deliberate use of the social and physical context" (Brown, Collins, & Duguid, 1989, p. 32). Since thinking often involves solving problems and children can be assisted in problem solving by more capable peers, ample opportunities for make-believe play are needed so that children can learn from each other, as well as try on the role of more competent problem solver (Berk, 1991). Children might pretend to be involved in such authentic music activities as performing an instrument, playing in a band, singing a baby to sleep, or conducting an orchestra.

The physical environment—a rich learning environment. The learning environments of young children should be rich with enticing stimuli and encouraging adults (Alvarez, 1989). These materials need not be store-bought to be effective for learning and motivating children (see Andress, 1998, for ideas on how to make inexpensive instruments and materials). The teacher or parent needs to change the environment periodically, as well as make sure that the materials provide an adequate amount of stimuli so that children are engaged in musical thinking. For young children, being able to make activity choices can address the need to have some control of their own learning.

The social environment—peer interaction. Our definition of the learning community should be enlarged to account for children learning from peers and from the teacher (as well as the teacher learning from the children). An instructional environment that includes free-play/choice time and centers will allow children to explore music and discuss music events. A multiage environment may stimulate increased musical growth as children have the opportunity to observe children with a greater range of musical abilities. Multiage settings also help children feel confident and practice their learnings while mentoring younger children or less proficient peers. Even when playing individually, children may try to re-create and use another child's problem-solving strategy, or they may simply observe fellow peer activity. As a result of peer interaction and observation, the development of individual musical competence can accelerate.

The role of the adult. The theories previously discussed construe the teacher/parent role more broadly than in the past. Beyond providing direct instruction, the adult is responsible for preparing a rich and stimulating environment, asking enticing questions, and adjusting the amount of assistance according to children's needs. The adult should provide for a variety of music experiences, including vocalizing/singing, performing with varied sound sources, moving, and listening, and music materials. In addition, assistance should be provided when children need help gaining initial competence and confidence as they work with new materials and concepts. Often, this assistance will be in the form of making an analogy between the new idea and a well-known event or character from a popular story or cartoon. At the same time, since more advanced students in a class can assist other children, the teacher needs to work toward giving less direction over time and allowing other children to contribute as mentors.

Modes of instruction and interaction. Direct instruction, which consists of teacher-led, whole-group, circle time activities, is the type of early childhood music experience most often offered. Recently, there has been a growth in the number of small-group early childhood music class opportunities. Such experiences are valuable for children's development, as well as for bonding experiences with parents in infant/toddler classes. One should, however, keep in mind that the instructional environment should consist of a wide variety of musical experiences, including individual free play/choice time, paired or small-group activities with and without indirect teacher instruction, and large-group activities such as circle time.

Strategies for Developing Thinking Skills in the Young Child

The following strategies are presented as illustrations for the theories and implications discussed above. This section is not intended as a guide for what to teach in an early childhood music curriculum; however, there are many sources available for such materials (see, for example, Andress, 1998; Feierabend, 2000a & b; Palmer & Sims, 1993; or Stauffer & Davidson, 1996).

Each strategy is described in case-study format in order to highlight the complexity of a rich, early childhood learning environment. Each sequence shows a different view of the previously discussed theories in action. However, all the strategies are written with one principle in mind: young children will readily explore and grow in a rich musical environment that contains stimulating musical models—both peer and adult—and intriguing resources.

Strategy #1: Infant/Toddler, Birth to Age Two

Key Concepts: Observation and imitation; parent/child music play; scaffolding; holistic experience

Environment/Materials: A child-safe play area with blocks and other toys; a comfortable, floor play area; a tape or CD player with recorded music for movement

Scenario: A mother and her child are playing at home. (A similar focus on the interaction between parent and child could also be found in many infant/toddler/parent group music experiences.) The child is playing with blocks, and the mother is observing, encouraging, and occasionally participating. (A nine-month-old infant might be sitting and exploring all properties of the blocks looking, smelling, and especially tasting. A fifteen-month-old toddler might be dropping blocks in a bucket, using a block to tap on the bucket, or beginning to stack the blocks.) The mother follows the child's

continued on following page

lead and begins to play with the blocks, adding an improvised rhyme: "tap-a-tap-a-tap-a" (taps gently on the child), "tap-a-tap-a-toe" (rests block on toe), "tap-a-tap-a-tap-a" (taps gently on the child), and "around and round we go" (puts the block on top of her own head, changing the final resting place each time the rhyme is repeated). The rhyme and game are repeated a number of times in varying tempos.

The child climbs into the mother's lap for a hug and then the mother initiates another game, using different words to the rhyme: "tickle, tickle, tickle" (tickles the child); "tickle, tickle, toe" (move a toe); "tickle, tickle, tickle" (tickles the child); and "around and round we go" (tickle in an unexpected place). The game might also include kissing, hugging, or massaging.

As preparation for nap time, the mother plays some appropriate recorded music and dances with her child. The first selection might involve marching to the beat or twirling and lifting the child in the air. A final selection might be a lullaby where the mother holds the child close, humming to the music and talking in soothing tones. After their dance they sit in the rocking chair and she sings the song "Hush, Little Baby" while he or she drinks a bottle. The mother sings the song first with the words and ends just humming the tune while rocking and rubbing or patting his back.

Strategy #2: Preschool Circle Time (Direct Instruction), Ages Three and Four

Key Concepts: Adult modeling; observation and imitation; action learning through speaking, singing, playing instruments, focused listening, creating and moving

Environment/Materials: A comfortable space for circle time with few distractions; a good quality sound system for recorded examples; age-appropriate percussion instruments; story or poem with a visual and a listening example

Scenario: The teacher rings a bell, indicating that it is time for the children to finish the activity they are involved in and clean up. As children come to join the circle, they see their teacher sitting on the floor, humming a song, and swaying from side to side. The children join in and sway as they sit in the circle. When the group is formed, circle time begins.

Circle time begins with a greeting song that the teacher sings, including each child's name at least once. The song is repeated several times and the children join in singing on the repetitive parts of the song.

continued on following page

The teacher brings out a hand puppet from a "magic" music bag and speaks a new rhyme for the children. He or she uses a variety of facial expressions in reciting the rhyme and speaks with a wide range of vocal inflections. He or she invites the children to speak the new rhyme along with the puppet. The teacher illustrates the motions they will add to the rhyme during the next circle time.

Appropriate sized percussion instruments such as rhythm sticks or jingle bells are distributed, and the rhyme is repeated again with instruments playing. The teacher models playing the instrument on the steady beat, but the children can play as they wish. The teacher observes how the children play their instruments and asks asks one child to show everyone how he or she is playing it. Everyone tries playing that way, and the rhyme is added. Each child is given a turn to be the leader.

As the instruments are collected, the teacher asks the children to look at a picture posted at the front of the room. He or she asks leading questions, and the children discuss what they see. The teacher then tells a story or reads a poem that goes with the picture. They discuss the story or poem. The teacher then directs their attention to a recorded example and asks the children to listen and try to identify what sounds they hear and how the sounds relate to the picture and story/poem. They discuss what they have heard.

The teacher now prepares the children to move as the story or poem is retold, or plays the recorded example again. The movement activity might practice stationary or locomotor movements. The children are given some ideas to help get them started, but they are also encouraged to try their own ideas. (The basic rules for classroom movement have been previously established.) Creative ideas are encouraged with verbal reinforcement from the teacher. Props would be used in some movement activities. At the end of the movement activity, the teacher recites a rhyme that brings the children back to sitting in the circle.

The teacher reviews a known song and invites the children to join him or her. (Note: the songs and rhymes should represent a variety of meters, keys, and tonalities.) The song has phrases that encourage the children to add simple vocal improvisations. The children are invited to share their ideas as they feel comfortable. A small wooden microphone (or stick) is used to encourage solo singing.

The last song is introduced, bringing the music circle time to closure. Everyone participates and waves goodbye to the magic music bag. The teacher congratulates the successes observed and gives directions for what to do as the children leave the circle.

Strategy #3: Multiage Preschool Setting, Free Play Time, Ages Three to Five

Key Concepts: Make-believe play; peer-assisted learning; limited peripheral participation; authentic tasks; scaffolding

Environment/Materials: A center/special interest area. The teacher has created a "concert" center in the classroom. Children are able to participate as performers, audience members, or conductors. Available materials might include kitchen utensils, pots and pans, classroom percussion instruments, one or more conductor batons with rounded tips or rhythm sticks to use as batons, a music stand, printed music, recorded music, and a cassette player

Optional advance preparation: The teacher has shown the students a video of a percussion ensemble, symphony orchestra, concert band, jazz orchestra, or touring musical group such as Stomp.

Scenario: "Children! Do you remember that video of the concert we watched yesterday? Well, today we have a special center where you'll have a chance to pretend you are at a concert. We'll take turns being performers, conductors, and audience members," says Ms. Jones. Some children begin to set up the instruments on the "stage" while others take instruments and begin to play on their own. One or two children select a baton, place a music stand with printed music at the front of the "stage" and begin "conducting" the children who are performing. After all of the instruments are selected, the remaining children sit in front of the instruments in the "audience."

The teacher observes as one or two children may begin to demonstrate how to conduct or perform. One child may say to another, "John, remember on that video they made that cool sound like this?" (The child imitates a sound heard.) John tries to copy the motion on his instrument. As these two children warm up, one of the children who was playing on her own stops and watches these two children. She tries to copy the motion of the other two children. The lead conductor gets the attention of the performers. "Okay, guys, we gotta be quiet to start. When I start moving my hands then you play. Ready? Go!" The children begin to perform their "piece." (The children may prefer to perform to the recorded music or improvise their own.)

The teacher notices that some of the children in the audience are moving or clapping to the music. The teacher also notices that some of the performers insert words and rhythms from the "Eency Weency Spider" song they sang this morning. She approaches these children and comments: "Did you notice how Denis got slower on 'up the spout again'? You might try that too." One of the "conductors" overhears this discussion and decides to try to slow down near the end of the performance. After the performance ends, the teacher notices one of the youngest children in the class who was watching the "concert" from the other side of the room walk toward the center. She picks up an instrument and begins to play the "Eency Weency Spider" rhythm.

Strategy #4: Preschool Free Play/Choice Time, Ages Three and Four

Key Concepts: Make-believe play; free play/centers; physical environment; observation and imitation; holistic experience; flow experience

Environment/Materials: This case highlights the teacher's role as "environment creator." The teacher has set up the classroom with at least four different centers. While these centers might be music-focused (see the previous case), others might include a dress-up corner, a pretend bus, or a finger puppet area (see Andress, 1998 and Alvarez, 1989 for a description of other center ideas). Musical events will emerge during participation in both music-specific and nonmusic-specific centers. The materials should offer a variety of textures and colors and provide a challenge to the students. For example, the dress-up clothes might include zippers and buttons.

Scenario: At the beginning of free play/choice time, the teacher encourages students to select one center area. In the dress-up area, children select various clothes to try on. One girl tries on a long dress and proclaims "I'm the princess, and you can be the prince." Another child in the group puts on the "prince" jacket. As these two children hold hands, two other children pretend to be the court musicians and "play" a fanfare on their trumpets.

In the bus center, the children take turns driving, hopping on and off the bus, giving money to the driver, and turning the wheels of the bus. The driver on the bus makes a "shh" sound when stopping to pick up passengers while two children turning the wheels make the "shew" sound of rotating tires. An improvisation begins between these children as these sounds form a pattern to which other children add other environment sounds. At the same time, the "passengers" begin to act out their roles while singing "The Wheels on the Bus."

In the music center, two children are happily hopping little wooden people along a play mat and singing their version of the accompanying song that was learned in the past several circle times. Their rendition of the song includes parts of the actual song as well as their added improvisations as they play.

Another child is new to this class and she is sitting in a "safe" corner with a doll. She is comfortable observing today, and the teacher brings her a blanket for her doll. She hums a quiet tune to put the doll to sleep. Next week she'll start to venture out and explore the centers.

References

Alvarez, B. (1989). Musical thinking and the young child. In E. Boardman (Ed.), *Dimensions of musical thinking* (pp. 57–64). Reston, VA: MENC.

Alvarez, B. (1981). Preschool music education and research on the musical development of preschool children: 1900–1980. Unpublished doctoral dissertation, University of Michigan.

Andress, B. (1998). *Music for young children.* Fort Worth, TX: Harcourt Brace.

Baker, J. C., & Martin, F. G. (1998). *A neural network guide to teaching.* Bloomington, IN: Phi Delta Kappa Educational Foundation.

Bandura, A. (1970). *Social learning theory.* Englewood Cliffs, NJ: Prentice Hall.

Begley, S. (2000, July 24). Music and the brain. *Newsweek,* 50–52.

Berk, L. (1991). *Child development* (3rd ed.). Boston: Allyn and Bacon.

Brown, J. S., Collins, A., & Duguid, P. (1989). Situated cognition and the culture of learning. *Educational Researcher, 18* (1), 32–42.

Checkley, K. (1997). The first seven ... and the eighth intelligence: A conversation with Howard Gardner. *Educational Leadership, 55* (1), 8–13.

Cohen, V. (1980). *The emergence of musical gestures in kindergarten children.* Unpublished doctoral dissertation, University of Illinois, Urbana.

Collins, A., Brown, J. S., & Newman, S. E. (1989). Cognitive apprenticeship: teaching the crafts of reading, writing, and mathematics. In L. B. Resnick (Ed.), *Knowing, learning, and instruction: Essays in honor of Robert Glaser.* (pp. 453–94). Hillsdale, NJ: Lawrence Erlbaum Associates.

Csikszentmihalyi, M., & Csikszentmihalyi, I. S. (1988). *Optimal experience: Psychological studies of flow in consciousness.* New York: Cambridge University Press.

Deliège, I., & Sloboda, J. (Eds.). (1996). *Musical beginnings: Origins and development of musical competence.* Oxford: Oxford University Press.

Diamond, M., & Hopson, J. L. (1999). *Magic trees of the mind: How to nurture your child's intelligence, creativity, and healthy emotions from birth through adolescence.* New York: Penguin.

Egan, K. (1999). *Children's minds, talking rabbits, and clockwork oranges: Essays on education.* New York: Teachers College Press.

Feierabend, J. M. (2000a). *First steps in music for infants and toddlers.* Chicago, IL: G.I.A. Publications, Inc.

Feierabend, J. M. (2000b). *First steps in music for nursery/preschool.* Chicago, IL: G.I.A. Publications, Inc.

Flohr, J. (1985). Young children's improvisations: Emerging creative thought. *The Creative Child and Adult Quarterly, 10* (2), 79–85.

Gardner, H. (1993). *Multiple intelligences: The theory in practice.* New York: Basic Books.

Gordon, E. E. (1987). *The nature, description, measurement, and evaluation of music aptitudes.* Chicago: G.I.A.

Gordon, E. E. (1997). *A music learning theory for newborn and young children.* Chicago: G.I.A..

Kratus, J. (1985). The use of melodic and rhythmic motives in the original songs of children aged 5 to 13. *Contributions to Music Education, 12,* 1–8.

Kratus, J. (1989). A time analysis of the compositional processes used by children ages 7 to 11. *Journal of Research in Music Education, 37* (1), 5–20.

Lave, J., & Wegner, E. (1991). *Situated learning: Legitimate peripheral participation.* New York: Cambridge University Press.

Marzano, R., Brandt, R., Hughes, C., Jones, B., Presseisen, B., Rankin, S., & Suhor, C. (1988). *Dimensions of thinking: A framework for curriculum and instruction.* Alexandria, VA: Association for Supervision and Curriculum Development.

MENC. (1991). *MENC position statement on early childhood education* (pamphlet). Reston, VA: MENC.

MENC. (1994). *The school music program, a new vision: The K–12 national standards, preK standards, and what they mean to music educators.* Reston, VA: MENC.

Palmer, M., & Sims, W. L. (1993). *Music in prekindergarten: Planning and teaching.* Reston, VA: MENC.

Phillips, D. C., & Soltis, J. F. (1998). *Perspectives on learning.* New York: TC Press.

Piaget, J. (1952). *The psychology of intelligence.* Totowa, NJ: Littlefield, Adams & Co.

Pond, D. (1981). A composer's study of young children's innate musicality. *Bulletin of the Council for Research in Music Education, 68,* 1–12.

Rommetveit, R. (1974). *On message structure: A framework for the study of language and communication.* New York: Wiley.

Scott-Kassner, C. (1992). Research on music in early childhood. In R. Colwell, (Ed.), *Handbook of research on music teaching and learning.* (pp. 633–50). New York: Schirmer.

Sims, W. L. (1990). Characteristics of young children's music concept discrimination. *Psychomusicology, 9* (1), 79–88.

Sims, W. L., (Ed.). (1995). *Strategies for teaching prekindergarten music.* Reston, VA: MENC.

Stauffer, S. L., & Davidson, J., (Eds.). (1996). *Strategies for teaching: K–4 general music.* Reston, VA: MENC.

Valerio, W. H., Reynold, A. M., Bolton, B. M., Taggart, C. C., & Gordon, E. E. (1998). *Music play.* Chicago: G.I.A..

Vygotsky, L. S. (1978). *Mind in society.* Cambridge, MA: Harvard University Press.

Vygotsky, L. S. (1962). *Thought and language.* Cambridge, MA: MIT Press.

Walters, D. L. (1992). Sequencing for efficient learning. In R. Colwell (Ed.), *Handbook of research on music teaching and learning* (pp. 535–45). New York: Schirmer.

Webster, P. R. (1992). Research on creative thinking in music: The assessment literature. In R. Colwell (Ed.), *Handbook of research on music teaching and learning* (pp. 266–80). New York: Schirmer.

Webster, P., and Richardson, C. (1993). Asking children to think about music. *Arts Education Policy Review, 94* (3), 7–11.

Wertsch, J. V. (1985). *Vygotsky and the social formation of mind.* Cambridge, MA: Harvard University Press.

Wilson, B. (1981). Implications of the Pillsbury foundation school of Santa Barbara in perspective. *Bulletin of the Council for Research in Music Education, 68,* 13–25.

Barbara J. Alvarez is adjunct associate professor of music education at Ball State University in Muncie, Indiana, and Margaret H. Berg is assistant professor of music education in the College of Music at the University of Colorado at Boulder.

8

MUSICAL LEARNING AND TEACHING IN THE GENERAL MUSIC CLASSROOM

MARY P. PAUTZ

What an exciting time to be helping elementary school children experience and make sense of music in a general music class. The accessibility of the Internet, the ease of notating musical compositions with MIDI and computer programs, the convenience of CDs, the inclusion of the arts as never before while schools explore integrated learning, the interest in the role of the arts to facilitate *all* learning as promulgated by Howard Gardner, Frances Rauscher, and others, the emphasis on constructivism, design for understanding, brain research, and other key educational topics of discussion—all of these contribute to the excitement.

However, all of this information can also cause overload. While the need to change teaching approaches is readily apparent, initiating the actual process can be threatening. Certainly two attributes that will help teachers through this transition are flexibility and the willingness to try new ideas. Another attribute that may be a key to understanding how to change in a sane manner is the application of appropriate thinking strategies and processes as we consider possibilities for change.

One of the fears of change is the uncertainty that inevitably comes with it. Brooks and Brooks (1999) remind us that "we must rethink the very foundations of schooling if we are to base our practice on our understandings of learners' needs" (p. 18). Even so, we ask, "Is this change better than past practice? Will we be successful as teachers? Will students learn more if the proposed change is instituted?" Sometimes, we simply need to trust—to suspend all desire to hold on to the tried and true and be willing to research the new, ponder it, and then go with abandon to a new way of thinking.

The result of such flexibility and willingness to embrace change may be as surprising and refreshing as the ending of a delightful children's book, *Here Comes the Cat* (Asch & Vagin, 1989). The only text in the book, which is shown both in English and Russian, is "Here comes the cat!" This message is spread by a mouse in page after page of clever illustrations. We see him shouting it from a hot air balloon, riding a bike through the countryside, calling from a street corner, and interrupting a movie. Soon more and more mice join in the message: "Here comes the cat!" Crowds of mice begin to gather. Our logical, predictable, adult minds expect the mice to be afraid, to go into hiding but the wonderful surprise of the story is that the mice are joyously awaiting the cat. He is delivering a huge wheel of cheese for them. The conclusion of the book shows the mice celebrating, eating, playing, and brushing the cat. The cat lies asleep with a contented look on its face.

Just as with the story of the cat and the mouse, this chapter may challenge deeply held but often unexamined beliefs on learning and teaching in the elementary general music classroom. It calls for extensive change regarding the musical goals and means to achieve them. By seriously scrutinizing these beliefs, the result—the decision to change and to act—may be as radical as the ending of *Here Comes the Cat!*

There is another book about cheese that is *not* a children's story. Rather, it is a book that has been read and studied by executives in countless business corporations including Dell, Exxon, the New York Stock Exchange, Time Warner, Xerox, Kodak, General Motors, and many others. It should be on the must-read list of every teacher and administrator as well. The book, *Who Moved My Cheese?* by Spencer Johnson (1998), is a simple parable that reveals powerful truths about change. What does this parable have to do with a book on dimensions of musical thinking? Everything—for the essence of the parable is on ways of responding to change. In his parable, Johnson describes four individuals, each with his or her own reaction to the need for change. In the parable, the cheese is a metaphor for what we want in life or, in the case of the elementary music teacher, what we see as our values and goals for the classroom experience.

A Narrative of Change

As you read the following narrative, ask yourself, "Which of these ways of responding to change is the one I am most likely to use?" The narrative involves four fictional teachers:

Hem is a little person paralyzed by the thought of change; he is angry and refuses to change: "I've always taught these rhythm skills by drill and practice, and I will do it this way until I retire." "It was good enough ten years ago; it is good enough now." "Why should I worry about all this world musics stuff?"

Haw is another little person angry and fearful of change initially but eventually energized as he begins the journey through the maze to find new cheese: "Wow, I hate to admit it, but the kids are really learning more when I take the time to let them create musical compositions. Now that they have a real need to know *how* to record/notate the music so others can play their compositions, teaching music reading makes sense to them and to me."

Sniff's little mouse brain leads him to sniff change early: "I read in the newspaper this morning about a new jazz series that will be shown on PBS this January. It looks as if I should be teaching more jazz. How could I incorporate this into my curriculum?"

Scurry is the mouse counterpart who scurries into action: "The fifth grade teachers agreed that they could integrate the jazz study into their social studies. They will study issues of racial tension and geographic migration of jazz while I help the students listen and become familiar with the music. As Louis says: 'Oh yeah!'"

Our Responses

We might recognize the fact that each of the characters is part of us at some time when change is either thrust upon or initiated by us. At times, being Sniff may be the character to emulate; another time it may be Haw.

As music teachers running through the maze to find the elusive cheese that has been moved (that is, looking for a new set of guidelines for helping children learn), we will have to examine long-held beliefs. When was the last time we questioned what we do in elementary general music? Or have we continued to expect the same old cheese to be there waiting for us no matter what might be happening or what new information is available to us?

Direct instruction with the emphasis on group activity like singing remains the traditional model taught in many college methods classes. Creativity and small-group learning centers are often presented as peripheral activities. Time in college courses is spent learning methodologies that emphasize rhythmic and melodic reading skills. The emphasis on standards and assessment causes teachers to shy away from the important quality of expressiveness because it is difficult to quantify. Classical orchestral music forms the majority of listening lessons. Jazz is usually given lip service despite the fact that it is America's major musical contribution to the world. Neither choral nor band music is commonly used in general music listening lessons. World music is still a sticking point with many music teachers for a variety of reasons: the teacher's comfort level, the unavailability of recordings, difficulty in teaching it, and students' attitudes. New educational theory and practice is often overlooked because it has not been translated into terms directly applicable to the teaching of music.

Perhaps the appropriate starting point would be to look at the first graders sitting in front of us and ask:

- What is it that I want these children to experience in music?
- What are their interests and motivation? What will excite them?
- How can they interact with music?
- What skills and concepts will they really need? (The assumption is that these are not going to be the college music majors of the future but the general public.)
- Will they remember elementary general music time with great delight or will they say, "Why did we ever bother singing those dumb songs and doing all those rhythm and solfège patterns?"
- Are we building memories and a lifetime passion for being involved in music?

Perhaps we need to imagine these first graders twenty years later and ask them:

- Are you passionate about the need for the arts to feed your souls?
- Are you members of churches or community performing groups or subscribers to concert series?
- Do you feel confident singing "Happy Birthday" in a restaurant, singing in your church, and dancing at a family celebration?
- Have you ever created a song to express the joy of newfound love?
- Do you seek solace in music when you experience a loss?

Using every minute to the best advantage, how can we structure general music classes to help students construct their own knowledge? Only to the extent that we make sure that each class experience is valuable and meaningful to our students can we hope for them to turn into the kind of young adults implied by the prior set of questions. We owe it to our students and to ourselves to stay abreast of improvements in teaching and learning because instruction must reflect the best of what we know about how learning occurs. The knowledge explosion with regard to learning is astounding. Every day, new research is released, and new books translating that research into practice are published. Because it is impossible to look at all areas of learning where new information is available as we traverse the maze, let us focus on three: constructivism, learning style, and brain research.

Constructivism

Marge Scherer, editor of *Educational Leadership,* quotes from *The Language of Learning: A Guide to Education Terms* (McBrien & Brandt, 1997), defining constructivism as "an approach to teaching based on research about how people learn." Many researchers say that each individual 'constructs' knowledge instead of receiving it from others (Scherer, 1999, p. 5). Perkins (1999) cites D. C. Phillips as identifying three distinct roles in constructivist-based learning:

The active learner. Students cannot simply sing, listen, read, or practice rhythms; they need to create, to critique, to discuss, to compare, and to contrast. Whole music must be used instead of patterns. Perkins (1999) reminds us that "inert knowledge sits in the mind's attic, unpacked only when specifically called for by a quiz or a direct prompt but otherwise gathering dust" (p. 8).

The social learner. Large ensembles are relevant but not all the time. Equal amounts of small group work, where groups such as quartets, trios, and duos work together to create, to perform, and to listen, must be an integral part of the classroom experience.

The creative learner. It is not enough to re-create others' compositions. To fully understand music and its power, students need to create their own music. This is as true of kindergartners as it is of college majors.

Many researchers say that every individual constructs knowledge instead of receiving it from others, and this is active, hands-on learning during which students are encouraged to think and explain their reasoning. Brooks and Brooks (1999) remind us that there are some simple but profound statements about constructivism that we need to consider as we plan instruction:

- *"Students control their own learning"* (Brooks & Brooks, p. 12). Remember, if you ask a student: "Are you paying attention?" his or her answer may truthfully be, "Yes, but not to you."
- *"Students do not learn on demand"* (Brooks & Brooks, p. 12). This principle challenges the current obsession with standards, assessment, and grading.
- *"The search for understanding motivates students to learn"* (Brooks & Brooks, p. 12). The cheese has been moved. But are we still acting like Hem, refusing to even search for a new route to learning? What does this say about our educational practices?

If we are to find the cheese and help students find theirs, we must build classroom activities around the five principles of constructivist teaching proposed by Brooks and Brooks (1999):

- "Seek and value students' point of view."
- "Structure lessons to challenge students' suppositions."
- "Recognize that students must attach relevance to the curriculum."
- "Structure lessons around big ideas, not small bits of information."
- "Assess students in the contexts of daily classroom investigations, not in separate events." (Brooks & Brooks, p. 21)

Learning Style

For years, there has been an interest in students' learning styles, particularly the perceptual styles: visual, auditory, kinesthetic, and tactile. The result of this interest, when applied in the classroom, has been improved instructional practice. Lessons are designed to involve many perceptual modes in every classroom event. This is essential if we are to reach the maximum number of learners.

Another approach to learning style is Bernice McCarthy's (1996) 4MAT system. The name 4MAT "comes from the fact that we have four major learning styles and that the four quadrants present different formatting possibilities in turn" (McCarthy, 1996, p. 197). It is also an instructional design that "moves from meaning to concepts, to skills, and finally to adaptation and transfer" (McCarthy, 1996, p. 203). McCarthy began her work because of the differences she saw in learners. She also realized that certain kinds of learners were honored in our schools and others, including herself, were not. Her styles are depicted in a circle divided into quadrants: Sensing/Feeling, Reflecting, Thinking, and Doing (McCarthy, 1996).

The beginning point of McCarthy's (1996) work is twofold: perceiving and processing. Perception, she posits, involves sensing and feeling and then thinking about it. It is the tension between these two ways of perceiving that is the central dynamic in learning. "Those of us who favor the sensing/feeling dimension need to understand the beauty and order of thinking. And those of us who move to thinking too quickly need to linger in the sensing and feeling of things percepts and concepts, experiencing and conceptualizing. The most important issue in all this is the issue of growth, of learning itself" (McCarthy, 1996, p. 27).

The second point is processing: "In addition to perceiving, taking things in, we must do something with them if we are to truly learn" (McCarthy, 1996, p. 37). Processing is done by reflecting or acting. We watch and we do. Thus, to combine perceiving with processing creates a natural learning cycle. McCarthy (1996) explains that while sensing/feeling, thinking, reflecting, and acting are all necessary for learning to occur, as individuals we find that different parts of the process more natural. They suit us better, and thus we linger there longer. "Some of us linger in the feeling place where we process through our very skin, filled with the moment, open to sensations—some of us linger in the reflecting place, where we feel how we feel, processing with ponderings and musings, open to our inner quiet—some of us linger in the thinking place where we stand back from and examine and name, converging on the meaning some of us linger in the doing place, where we tinker and explore, and act and accomplish, creating the outcome ... our favorite place or places to hang around in this cycle form our unique learning style" (McCarthy, 1996, pp. 72–73). McCarthy (1996) delineates the characteristics of each quadrant, describing their strengths, as individuals function as learners, teachers, leaders, and parents. Type one is the imaginative learner; type two is the analytic learner; type three is the common-sense learner; and type four is the dynamic learner. While learners have preferences, they must all process through all quadrants in order to learn.

McCarthy (1996) credits her influences as Kolb, Lewin, Piaget, Bruner, Polanyi, Whitehead, Vygotsky, and Dewey. Her intent is to improve the odds for as many students as possible through understanding and honoring how each person learns. "Whether you are a type one, two, three, or four or some combination of the above, your style is how you learn ... it is a comfortable place for you to be and you have every right to learn in that way" (McCarthy, 1996, p. 103). McCarthy's book, *About Learning*, (1996) is a beautiful, unique description of a lifetime of work. One needs to see the book to appreciate its organization and layout. Elliot Eisner's review of *About Learning* said: "Rarely in publications do form and content reinforce each other so well. *About Learning* is the exploration of ideas that afford the reader many opportunities to fashion their own ideational castles. It is intimate, charming, generative; quite an array of achievements." McCarthy's (1996) work is important to know because it not only honors the differences in learning style, but also explains how these differences influence how we deal with each other.

Brain Research

Perhaps the greatest excitement in current learning theory and educational practice circles is occurring in brain research and its implications for learning. Jensen (1998) asserts that we are on the verge of a revolution. He claims that what we are learning about the brain will cause us to "change school start times, discipline policies, assessment methods, teaching strategies, budget priorities, classroom environments, use of technology, and even the way we think about the arts and physical education" (Jensen, 1998, p. 1). One of the reasons is that information about the brain is growing at an unprecedented rate. If this is true, can we afford to be "Hem," resisting change and insisting on doing things the way that they have always been done? Jensen's very practical book *Teaching with the Brain in Mind* (1998) will prove both soothing and invigorating to every arts educator. Rather than fearing change, this book encourages change and propels arts educators to the forefront.

In the first section of their book, Wolfe and Sorgen (1990) provide an overview of the research on how the mind learns, including descriptions of sensory, short term, and long-term memories. The second section of their book explores the general implications of brain research for the classroom, and the third section gives numerous examples of brain-compatible, teacher- tested instructional strategies (Wolfe & Sorgen, 1990). Wolfe (2000) reiterates the brain's need for meaning. Without connections, the information presented will not have meaning and will be lost. As teachers, we must constantly be searching for ways to connect the new with the old, the unfamiliar with the familiar. That is possible by either hooking new material to previous experiences or by creating new experiences with the students. Perhaps the lack of musical retention is due less to the small amount of time given to music learning and more to the use of isolated, random activities.

Brain research is foundational to the understanding of teaching thinking skills. Real life experiences, hands-on activities, and simulations or role playing are important techniques. Rehearsal, chunking, projects, rhyme and rhythm, student journals, mnemonics, graphic organizers, and interactive notebooks are techniques that music teachers need to employ. It behooves us to be Sniff and Scurry as more information becomes available regarding brain development and application to learning.

Implications for Learning and Teaching

In 1989, MENC published *Dimensions of Musical Thinking* (Boardman, 1989) as a companion to *Dimensions of Thinking: A Framework for Curriculum and Instruction* (Marzano, 1989). Association for Supervision and Curriculum Development followed their publication with *A Different Kind of Classroom: Teaching with the Dimensions of Learning* (Marzano) in 1992. That volume translated information and research from *Dimensions of Thinking* into a practical model for teachers to use to improve the quality of teaching and learning, and called for courage on the part of the music teacher in embracing change. (While this chapter stands on its own, the reader might find it beneficial to check out the three books named above for a richer understanding of cognition and learning and implications for teaching.) Emphasis is on the learning process and the learner instead of on the teaching process and the teacher. This chapter on musical thinking in the elementary general music class explores the basic assumptions of *A Different Kind of Classroom*:

- "Instruction must reflect the best of what we know about how learning occurs."
- "Learning involves a complex system of interactive processes that includes five types of thinking—the five dimensions of learning."
- "What we know about learning indicates that instruction focusing on large interdisciplinary themes is the most effective way to promote learning."
- "The K–12 curriculum should include explicit teaching of higher-level attitudes, perceptions, and mental habits that facilitate learning."
- "A comprehensive approach to instruction includes at least two distinct types of instruction: one is more teacher directed, and the other is more student directed."
- "Assessment should focus on students' use of knowledge and complex reasoning rather than on their recall of low-level information." (Boardman, 1989, p. ix)

The principle tenets of *A Different Kind of Classroom* call for courage on the part of the music teacher in embracing change. Learning involves a complex system of interactive processes that includes five types of thinking—the five dimensions of learning:

1. *"Positive attitudes and perceptions about learning"* (Boardman, p. 3). Students will be excited about music class if they are convinced that they can succeed. They will want to be involved in music if the activities are challenging, passionate, and interactive. They must know that they are not playing at music or learning atomistic pieces that do not have meaning. They need to be involved music makers, performers, listeners, and critics. Adults providing thinking strategies for them is vital to their musical growth. Attractive music rooms with engaging, interactive bulletin boards and student displays should not be overlooked. Lastly, a music teacher who is excited about teaching, who is a lifelong learner, who is passionate about the art form, and who clearly likes children will be the most important key in establishing this dimension of learning.

2. *"Thinking involved in acquiring and integrating knowledge"* (Boardman, p. 3). Many school districts have provided in-service programs on processes such as KWL—know (K) want to learn (W) and learned (L); think-pair-share; compare and contrast; Venn diagrams; and advance organizers, graphic organizers, webbing, sequence patterning, and so forth. Unfortunately, many times the examples given are from social studies and language arts teachers or from science and math teachers, and consequently music teachers (as well as art and physical education teachers) mistakenly dismiss the processes because they do not see the connection. An excellent book for arts teachers to examine is *Enhancing Thinking through Cooperative Learning* (Davidson & Worsham, 1992), although once again, the examples are not music examples. Imaginative, insightful teachers will readily see how the examples suggested in the text can be incorporated into music classes. However, careful lesson planning is imperative if a music teacher decides to implement these processes.

3. *"Thinking involved in extending and refining knowledge"* (Boardman, p. 9). Marzano (1992) suggests that a framework for questioning is an important way to cue students' use of specific thinking processes. Comparison, classification, induction, deduction, error analysis, constructing support, abstraction, and perspective analysis are as important tools for a music teacher as they are for a math teacher. Rather than simply listening to jazz recordings of Ella Fitzgerald and Billie Holiday, ask students to compare and contrast. What particular characteristics are similar? Different? Do not be content to classify a piece of music as "jazz." Encourage students to

be able to classify it further as "big band," "swing," "Dixieland," "bebop," or "cool."

Set up multiple lessons so that students do not develop the erroneous opinion that jazz is solely for African-American males. Introduce the music of Ma Rainey, Bessie Smith, and Sarah Vaughn. Introduce Latin jazz musicians and performers, such as Tito Puente, Stan Getz, Mongo Santamaria, and others. Challenge students to see the relationships among jazz, rap, and hip-hop. Investigate why early solos were much shorter than modern day solos. Were they less inventive, less creative? No, 78 rpm records were only three minutes long. Encourage students to research and answer other questions such as "Is ragtime jazz?" "What are acid, free, and avant-garde jazz?" "How is New York and hard bop jazz different from California West Coast cool jazz?"

4. *"Thinking involved in using knowledge meaningfully"* (Boardman, p. 11). The key here is the word "meaningful." If students dismiss the activities in music class as "babyish," "out of touch with reality," or simply unimportant, they will not bother to master the concepts or skills presented through these activities. This does not mean that the teacher should capitulate to the playing of only pop or rap music in the classroom. It does mean that activities must be constantly evaluated for their timeliness and appeal.

Another strand of contemporary research is that of technology. Do students really need to learn how to read music and write music when the MIDI is becoming such a readily accessible tool? Just as classroom teachers agonize over how much drill and practice is necessary in multiplication tables, and the war rages on over the use and misuse of calculators in classrooms, so music teachers must revisit the time spent drilling "tah-tah-titi-tah." What will fifth or sixth graders leaving elementary school do with this skill? Is it a skill more appropriate for instrumental and choral organizations when a need to read is immediately apparent? Is acquisition of this skill developmental, or is it more appropriate for older learners who are more ready to recognize its relevance to the achievement of their music-making goals? Can it perhaps be learned more efficiently when one is older? Would it be reasonable to expect that, given the constraints of time, students in the elementary grades should experience a wide variety of music, learning to respond and create with iconic or graphic representations? Without the reassurance of a firm foundation such as this, it might be relatively easy for students to make the transfer from iconic/graphic representations to symbolic notation when they participate in performing organizations where there the need to acquire such skills is readily apparent.

5. *"Productive habits of mind"* (Boardman, p. 14). Since students will be asked to interact in their adult lives with problems not yet posed, it is impossible to teach the students everything that they need to know. The solution is to help them develop productive habits of mind. Marzano (1992) lists these habits as being: aware of one's thinking, able to plan, knowledgeable about necessary resources, sensitive to feedback, able to evaluate the effectiveness of one's actions; accurate and seeking accuracy, clear and seeking clarity; open-minded, able to resist impulsivity, capable of taking and defending a position, sensitive to others; and willing to push the limits of one's knowledge and ability, able to generate, trust, and maintain one's own evaluation standards, and able to generate new ideas.

One need look no farther than the self-help or how-to-succeed section of any book store to realize that fortunes are being made helping to disseminate the word about the need for these habits of mind. While exhortations such as "Be aware of your thinking," "Plan ahead," and "Evaluate the effectiveness of your actions" might be good for students, they will probably be ignored. What student, however, will not be intrigued by "the handwriting on the wall" (courtesy of Hem):

"Smell the cheese often so you know when it is getting old."

"The quicker you let go of the old cheese, the sooner you find the new cheese."

"They keep moving the cheese!"

Try writing one message a week on the chalkboard and take the time to discuss it in pairs or small groups. It will be time well spent. Throughout class activities, point out concrete examples of such habits of mind.

What we know about learning indicates that instruction focusing on large interdisciplinary themes is the most effective way to promote learning. In the past, a music teacher could close the door and teach. As long as the children were happy, the classroom teachers had a break, and the Christmas and Spring programs were a hit, the music teacher was considered a successful teacher.

In these days of integration, such a situation is not enough. Now the music teacher can move into the mainstream of education. But it comes at a cost. The music teacher will have to change. Planning collaboratively requires time, advance planning, research, problem solving, and thinking strategies. It means addressing fundamental questions such as, "How does one maintain the integrity of the art form?" No music teacher wants to return to the days of teaching inane "tooth-brushing" songs in the name of integration. No music teacher wants to abdicate the responsibility of teaching music by becoming a language arts teacher. It is not enough to simply read the many wonderful books about music. Music teachers want to know how these books become part of a true musical experience for the students. One simple example would be to take the wonderful children's books about music and expand them into learning kits to be checked out of the library. Many books are simply illustrated songs. Rather than students merely reading or looking at a book, include a CD or cassette of the song. If possible, obtain more than one recording. For example, recorded versions of "Froggie Went a Courtin'" by Burl Ives and the Revel Singers can be used for a compare/contrast lesson. Listening to Little Richard sing "Mary Had a Little Lamb" will be a different experience from any child's usual perception of what that little song should sound like. (Note: Purchasing the original, making one copy, and then archiving the original satisfies copyright laws.) Include a brief set of directions for the children and parents. Other interesting books for music students are biographies of composers. Encourage children to read them but then also include a tape of selected portions of their music. There are many child-appropriate books about styles of music, such as jazz. Again, enrich the experience and move it from visual information gathering to actually hearing and experiencing the music while students read.

The second stage of integration would be to hook into established school themes or grade connections. A flexible teacher with the willingness to suspend traditional teaching can teach music in an exciting way while retaining the integrity of the art form and developing necessary musical concepts. This requires time for collaboration and an inventive mind that says "What if ..." instead of "I don't have the time ..." It will mean digging beyond the superficial. We can help children grasp basic musical concepts successfully by using music that relates to animals, families, Native Americans, Olympics, safari, or other themes and units.

An example suitable for the younger grades could be "families." Students could explore who belongs to the family of music. Becoming composers, conductors, performers, and audience will provide insight into the roles of each member of the music family and will provide us with the opportunity to involve students in every possible musical endeavor. Comparing this family to the family of visual artists will cast light on similarities and differences between the two art forms. Working cooperatively to produce a composition about snow or a composition that expresses both delicacy and warmth will lead to unexpected benefits. If students want others to perform their work or to preserve it for posterity, they will have a need for notational skills.

Ultimately, the music teacher will want to be the initiator of themes. One role that can serve the entire school, both in content and in teaching thinking processes, is that of "Detective." It is a perfect tool to latch onto constructivism. What do musical detectives do? They solve problems, think, develop hypotheses, test their ideas, make connections overlooked by "non-detectives," sharpen visual and auditory acuity, and have a zest for tracking down clues.

The K–12 curriculum should include explicit teaching of high-level attitudes and perceptions and mental habits that facilitate learning. This may be the time to pause for some self-examination. Call to mind the saying "What you are doing is speaking so loudly that I can't hear what you are saying." Do we use the higher level attitudes, perceptions, and mental habits that facilitate learning? Which of us as music teachers has not registered for a university summer workshop or summer course in order to obtain recertification credits or credits to help move to the next classification on the pay scale while also secretly hoping that the clinician or professor will provide us with a shopping bag of ideas and materials? Which of us has not been upset to discover instead that the expectation would be that the class would construct the knowledge? Was there perhaps a hint of "I'm paying for this; why doesn't she ... ?" "Why do I have to ... ?" "This is so time consuming." "Wouldn't it be more efficient if she would just hand out a set of materials that give the facts, the resources, and the bibliography and then demonstrate several clever lessons that we can use in the fall to captivate the students?"

We, as teachers, must be examples and models of lifelong learning, possessing a passion and zest for new knowledge. We must be willing and excited about constructing even more knowledge. The material learned in methods class must be constantly updated; the prescriptions handed down from school boards and departments of education must be scrutinized—not blindly accepted. Is the emphasis on assessment causing us to teach to the test? Are important conceptual understandings being ignored because they are not readily written in the language of the standards?

The fifth tenet is indeed comforting in its recognition that a comprehensive approach to instruction includes at least two distinct types of instruction: one is more teacher-directed, and the other is more student-directed. We do not need to throw out all we have been doing. Knowing when to use direct instruction and when it is better to step aside and let students direct the instruction is the challenge.

Finally, we are reminded that assessment should focus on students' use of knowledge and complex reasoning rather than on their recall of low-level information. Brooks and Brooks (1999) call for assessment to be embedded in instruction rather than in separate paper-and-pencil tests. McCarthy (1996) distinguishes between "on the way" assessment and "at the gate" assessment (p. 281). "On the way" refers to progress being made while learning is occurring. "At the gate" is the test at the end, whether it be challenging the first trumpet player for first chair or taking a test to indicate knowledge of styles of music. She calls for a balance of the two but says that elementary schools have far too many "at the gates" tests (McCarthy, 1996). Schank (2000) has damning things to say about schools in his book *Coloring outside the Lines.* He asks parents to separate testing and grading from "smartness." He defines smart as "falling in love with a subject and being intellectually curious about it" (Schank, 2000, p. 40). Schank (2000) states that "while some teachers and a few schools may be following a model that is aligned with how people really learn, most are teaching kids in ways remarkably similar to how they were taught a hundred years ago. It's been said that if you took a doctor from 1900 and put him in a modern operating room, he'd be lost, but if you took a teacher from that year and transported her to a contemporary school, she could go to work right away" (p. xvii). Let's prove him wrong as we search the maze to find better ways of sharing the treasure trove of this wondrous thing called music.

References

Asch, F., & Vagin, B. (1989). *Here comes the cat.* New York: Scholastic.

Boardman, E. (Ed.). (1989). *Dimensions of musical thinking.* Reston, VA: MENC.

Brooks, M., & Brooks, J. G. (1999). The courage to be constructivist. *Educational Leadership, 57* (3), 18–24.

Davidson, N., & Worsham, T. (Eds.). (1992). *Enhancing thinking through cooperative learning.* New York: Teachers College Press.

Eisner, E. (1996). Review of *About learning.* Back cover of B. McCarthy, *About learning.* Wauconda, IL: About Learning, Inc.

Jensen, E. (1998). *Teaching with the brain in mind.* Alexandria, VA: Association for Supervision and Curriculum Development.

Johnson, S. (1998). *Who moved my cheese?* New York: G. P. Putnam's Sons.

Marzano, R. (1989). *Dimensions of thinking.* Alexandria, VA: Association for Supervision and Curriculum Development.

Marzano, R. (1992). *A different kind of classroom: Teaching with the dimensions of learning.* Alexandria, VA: Association for Supervision and Curriculum Development.

McBrien, J. L. and Brandt, R. S. (1997). *The language of learning: A guide to education terms.* Alexandria, VA: Association for Supervision and Curriculum Development.

McCarthy, B. (1996). *About learning.* Wauconda, IL: About Learning, Inc.

Perkins, D. (1999). The many faces of constructivism. *Educational Leadership, 57* (3), 6–11.

Schank, R. (2000). *Coloring outside the lines.* New York: HarperCollins.

Scherer, M. (1999). *Educational Leadership, 57* (3), 5.

Wolfe, P. (2000). Lessons from research about learning within individuals and organizations. Presented at Institute for Leadership, Learning and Service. Milwaukee, WI: Cardinal Stritch University.

Wolfe, P., & Sorgen, M. (1990). *Mind, memory and learning.* Napa, CA: MM&L.

Mary P. Pautz is professor emerita of music education at the University of Wisconsin–Milwaukee.

9

MUSICAL THINKING AMONG DIVERSE STUDENTS

BETTY T. WELSBACHER AND ELAINE D. BERNSTORF

Special children are not just students who have been placed in special education, but students who have a variety of differing needs and are recognized by school districts as needing additional educational services. Walk into the office of the director of special education in an East Coast city, where hundreds of teachers of exceptional children are hired, scheduled, monitored, and inserviced. Find the office of the superintendent of a rural district, whose many duties include the supervision of multicultural classes where migrant students go for a few months of crash courses in English and in American mores. In both of these settings, individuals will be juggling the elements that determine the education of the designated special children under their supervision. For our purposes, such students may be called "children of diversity" or "diverse students."

Professionals have always done their best when threading together the vastly varied pieces required for teaching special education students as they are traditionally identified: curricula, transportation, state and federal guidelines, legal contingencies, workups, testing and placement, hot lunches, certification standards, paraprofessional supply, staffings, validation, IEPs (Individual Education Plans), budgets, and more. Today, with the definition of diversity constantly expanding and the teaching of diverse students in the nation so varied in location and situation, additional variables beyond those that distinguish "regular" education or "special" education are necessary. With so many children who are very different from each other, is there even a chance that teachers can be concerned about the goal of helping these students learn to *think*? Yes, teachers can and should be so concerned.

The hardest part of teaching children of diversity may be acknowledging that it is possible for all children to learn to think. In the past, the learning theory of choice for special education children was basic behaviorism. The whole idea of an instructional process leading toward "thinking" rather than toward "imitating and remembering" may be difficult to envision for special education teachers trained in traditional behaviorist methods. Excellent music teachers have a singular advantage over their teaching colleagues, for they are coming from a different place. The subject area that music teachers share with exceptional students is an art form—not arithmetic, writing, or vocational training, but music. Sharing music with students, as we traditionally do in general music programs, is a far different experience than eliciting predetermined responses in a training program where neither teacher nor students make conscious choices, not to mention artistic choices.

The Reality of Music

A child of diversity is involved in music in exactly the same way, though perhaps at a different level, as anyone else. Music is music, not a model or an approximation of it. The medium is the message, and it requires the same processes and practices for all who engage in it. Further, music is authentically and totally accessible to diverse individuals, even if they lack language. While music may be accompanied by language, it does not depend on language, nor does language depend on music. Both language and music invite their own imagery and share imagery, but they are not dependent on each other's imagery. Thus, music provides a "reality" with opportunities to learn music's content and appropriate behaviors without being penalized for poor language skills.

But is this reality actually possible for special students? After all, aren't some of them special because of a loss of vision, movement, hearing, perceptual clarity, or understanding? As a result of their loss, do these students to some extent possess lesser ability to think?

History presents us with many examples of so-called disabled persons who changed the world through their writing, inventions, art works, compositions, and thinking. Leonardo da Vinci may have been dyslexic (his notes and writings are often in mirror writing). Henri Matisse, the amazing painter, had, of all things, visual impairments. Albert Einstein was considered to be hopelessly slow in scholastic and academic endeavors. Contemporary sports have produced, among many others, Olympic medalists Magic Johnson (basketball) and Greg Louganis (diving), both with learning disabilities, and baseball Hall of Famers Babe Ruth and Nolan Ryan, who were both dyslexic. Musicians? Think about Lincoln Center honoree and enduring performer Ray Charles, who is blind; Itzhak Perlman, who has postpolio syndrome; singer Johnnie Ray, who has a severe hearing impairment; and Mel Tillis, a Country-Western singer known for his speech disabilities, including stuttering. Anyone who has watched Evelyn Glennie, the marvelous percussionist who is deaf, perform her magic has seen and heard thinking in music in living technicolor. So it would seem that thinking can indeed be learned by diverse individuals.

Of course, these extraordinary people could be considered as remarkable exceptions to the rule. But, if we consider the thinking processes used by these artists, we see that they use the same critical and creative thinking skills as all learners. Among these skills are focusing, information-gathering, remembering, organizing, analyzing, generating, integrating, and evaluating. Across the board, in nearly all exceptionality groupings, the majority of students assigned to special categories are capable, to a greater or lesser extent, of utilizing almost all of these stated skills under most circumstances.

So let's look at some children from our own diverse classrooms. Initially, we may notice odd gaps and unexpected holes: a displacement of order, such as erratic performance behaviors, unnerving disparities, and scattering. We also may notice odd strengths. Examples of individual skills exist in abundance, sometimes prodigiously: the girl with autism who can sing every line of every verse of every song she's ever learned; the boy with central language disorders who drowns us with endless facts about his pet subject; the deaf child whose dances are as eloquent as words; the eighth grader who is illiterate due to dyslexia but has taught himself to play the organ by ear; or the immigrant from South America who draws perfect maps having seen the information once. Yet the skills these children demonstrate are often locked in. The girl can't repeat any of the lines of the music she sings; the boy with language disorders absorbs nothing about topics other than his pet topic;

the deaf child does not grasp even signed language; the Hispanic child has no knowledge of the countries drawn so perfectly.

What is missing? Where is the breakdown? What have the world changers mastered that eludes our students, keeping them from using in meaningful ways the thinking skills that they have acquired? Perhaps in the fifth or sixth grade you taught yourself mirror writing, for note passing and to fool your teachers. (It is to many teachers' eternal credit that they never let us know how easily they could decipher our messages.) Such reversed writing looks very similar, sometimes exactly like the typical writing or printing of some children with brain damage. But the appearance of the manuscript has nothing to do with the veracity, correctness, or appropriateness of the words–the content itself. The reason we used the mirror writing was to disguise our messages, but messages were important, and we wanted them to be clear to our intended recipients. These children have no intention of disguising their thinking. While their writing might be undecipherable due to motoric problems caused by brain damage, their core thinking skills may be intact. They simply may not be able to express their thinking skills so that we can relate to them.

Metacognition

No matter how they were placed on the paper, Da Vinci's sketches and words were astounding, illuminating, and world-changing. Matisse's brush recorded breathtaking, highly original scenes and scenarios, magnificent people, and marvelous places. Who of us knows whether his artist's eye or his mind's eye saw and painted them or how much his visual impairment had to do with his genius as an artist? What these two shared and our contemporary world-changers share are their capacity and skill in understanding themselves (self-awareness) and their ability to monitor their own thoughts, ideas, and actions (metacognition).

Among our world-changers, self-awareness and self-monitoring are as fine-tuned as a musical instrument. But for most of the students in our classes, metacognition is the last, the hardest thing to grasp. Perhaps, for some of our students, it is impossible. The inability to monitor one's own thinking very nearly describes the basic problems that occur when teaching diverse children. In *South Pacific,* the song "You've Got to Be Carefully Taught" is about the teaching of prejudice, but its theme can be applied to disabilities as well as social issues. Children dealing with the difficulties of their own diversity, due to either learning or cultural differences, usually cannot monitor their own learning. They cannot learn by osmosis, nor do they have the skills to teach themselves. They are overwhelmed with just living. But they can learn, and they do respond to being carefully taught.

Careful Teaching

As noted at the beginning of this chapter, we are considering all aspects of diversity as it is reflected in our student population. Diversity in school settings includes cultural differences, language differences, and an array of exceptionalities including cognitive differences (both mental retardation and giftedness), sensory disorders (visual, physical, and hearing disorders), neurological disorders (including learning disabilities and autism), physical disabilities (including cerebral palsy, muscular dystrophy, and others), psychological disorders, problems associated with abuse/neglect, and other health impairments (OHI). Students with such diverse needs clearly deserve to have excellent musical experiences, as do their counterparts in regular classes.

Both special education laws and a teacher's common sense require that musical experiences be designed to meet the unique needs of each student. Familiarity with the special education student's IEP may be helpful. To be truly effective, the music teacher—as all teachers do—needs specific information about each student. For the special education student, this may include information from the school's support staff, including social workers, psychologists, counselors, and resource teachers. For the ESOL (English Speakers of Other Languages) student, other information may be necessary. The information that these staff members can provide is essential. Ultimately, how each child can be carefully taught is truly the answer to meeting needs.

While each child is unique and deserves careful consideration, some characteristics may still be generalized for certain groups. In fact, for some children of diversity, difficulties with metacognitive skills may lie at the core of their difference. Among such groups are children with psychological disorders, cognitive differences, and those who have neurological disorders or learning disabilities.

Psychological Disorders. Difficulty with metacognitive skills could actually define the problems of many students who are considered emotionally or behaviorally disturbed. As defined in the new special education laws, a child must have difficulties with internalized emotions to be defined as having psychological disorders. These children are not the typical students with conduct disorders. In fact, many students who qualified for special education services in past years by having behavior disorders are no longer considered special education students. As demonstrated by specialized testing and medical diagnoses, students who qualify for special education services for behavior disorders demonstrate true differences in psychological thinking compared to other students. If a child with psychological or behavioral disorders could monitor his or her central thinking skills, he or she would not be identified as disturbed. To a teacher or a caregiver, work with these students is delicate, full of missteps, and as fragile as a cobweb. But for the students themselves, gaining metacognitive skills is crucial. They cannot function normally without them.

For teachers, approaching the skills as thinking strategies is a different and potentially more productive way of engaging these children in their own learning than is the usual method. The traditional management model for children with psychological disorders is behavioral modification. For success, behavior modification techniques like imitation, repetition, and drill must permeate every aspect of the school day and perhaps beyond. However, using these techniques cannot help the child monitor his or her own faulty thinking or help him or her to learn to think in better ways. Metacognitive skills, which can be learned, offer the option of questioning. This technique, too, can be learned, first, through a teacher's gentle asking of the questions and then by helping the student formulate his or her own questions ("What happened?" "How did it happen?" "When, where did it happen?" "What if this had happened differently?"). As the student explores and practices asking and answering the questions independently, the answers that come may be the student's own. If the questions are self-generated, there may be self-monitoring, and the beginnings of self-control may then enter the process.

While the goals of behavioral modification and metacognitive techniques may be the same (they are not always), there are more likely to be statements than questions in behavioral modification or similar management approaches: "Control yourself"; "Remember the consequences if you ..." In such situations, the payoff for the student tends to be negative: "Control yourself and your privileges won't be removed"; "Remember the consequences and you won't have to go to time-out." When the learning situation is pointed toward the acquisition of thinking skills, however, the tone is more positive, and the student becomes an active participant. When teacher's statements are replaced by gently probing questions with many correct answers possible, the learning situation does not carry the implied anxiety load of expected failure. The payoff is positive. The elusive feeling of doing something well—the "prize" of education—may occur often if thinking skills can be attained.

Cognitive Differences. Students with mental retardation also may demonstrate metacognitive difficulties, including difficulties with abstract thinking and with language learning, especially in the areas of vocabulary and grammar. Language is itself abstract, in that words stand for or represent things or ideas. These children do not understand "standing for"; they understand things only that are real or concrete. They are, literally, at a concrete level of learning. For example, many methods of teaching reading use pictures of objects to teach the words, for example, a picture of a ball to teach the word "ball." Children who lack abstract thinking—whose thinking is entirely at the concrete level—will not comprehend the picture of the ball. The picture will be an object in itself, and thus it will have no connection with the ball. To these children, a ball is a sphere, and the picture is flat and square; a ball bounces when dropped, the picture doesn't. A ball is somewhat heavy, and the picture is light; a ball makes no sound when shaken, and the picture rustles. At the concrete level, only actual objects can serve as learning aids. This does not demonstrate lack of intelligence, only a lack of the ability to abstract. Thus, for a concrete learner, a picture of a ball is a big jump from the ball itself. The learner needs a transition in order to learn to abstract.

We must be careful, however, that we do not equate concrete thinking with concrete experiences. What we think are concrete ideas may still be very abstract to children with cognitive differences. In other words, some children need "thing-things," not "thing-thoughts." When we consider most teaching, the transmission of information through language is the primary technique. Since language itself is abstract, words stand for things as well as ideas. Our assumption is that we, as teachers, can describe things or ideas using language and make the experience real—concrete. But describing is not the same as experiencing. In the arts, we are very clear about the fact that talking about a piece of music bears no relation to experiencing the music. For children at a concrete level of learning, music may provide evocative sensory experiences that can be authentic expressions of ideas without the meaning load of language.

On the opposite end of the spectrum are those students with cognitive differences whom we term gifted. Some of these students may have vast vocabularies and perfect grammar. However, many such students experience their own difficulties in expressing themselves to others because they cannot verbalize their insights in ways that others can understand. For them, the words may literally get in the way or they may not have sufficient vocabulary for their advanced insights. Is this why geniuses like Albert Einstein and Thomas Edison were described as slow? For gifted students, the arts provide avenues of expression that allow these diverse thinkers to manage ideas in nonlinguistic ways. For many of these students, an internal version of life occurs in pictures or schemas, internal actions and reactions, and imagined manipulations of sounds, sights, and events that are beyond what they can express outwardly. This type of metacognition may eventually develop into a new invention, philosophy, or system of management that becomes useful to others. During the school years, however, these children may be such diverse thinkers that they are outcasts among their peers or frustrations to the school system. Music, as well as the other arts, may provide the only outlet for some of these students where they are able to be themselves. When we encounter students for whom music is the dimension of thinking with which they can relate to others, it behooves us to support and advocate for such students even when the general system cannot.

Neurological Disorders/Learning Disabilities. Students with neurological and learning disabilities often cannot interpret sensory input accurately. They actually receive faulty information; thus, they have difficulty in focusing and attending. For quite different reasons than students with psychological/behavioral disorders or mental retardation, a lack of metacognitive understanding may also be at the core of these children's disabilities. With these children, the problem is not so volatile or erratic as with students who have behavior disorders, but is the result of mixed signals, improperly transmitted neural patterns, and incomplete or distorted sensory reception. For learners with neurological disorders or learning disabilities, metacognition becomes a matter of self-recognition of problem areas; trial-and-error attempts to trick or circumvent faulty perceptual tracks are undertaken knowingly and deliberately by the student. We, as professionals, must learn not only to recognize these compensations when we work with students. We also must look beyond what may be termed wrong answers or incorrect approaches by allowing students some latitude during the learning process.

The fifth-grade child with a learning disability who has trouble with midline crossing because of motoric perception and laterality problems falls apart when presented with a crossed-arms finger-snapping pattern in a hand-jive activity. At first, he denies it happened and refuses to try again. But asked to become aware of how it really feels to do the exercise—and to try to figure out a way to fool his arms and hands into doing it—he tries again. First, he may respond without crossing the midline at all, and then a little at a time, crossing and moving tentatively as he monitors his own movement. In time, he may be successful to some degree; he'll not be perfect, and the movement won't always be comfortable. But he'll have done it. And the next time, he'll remember his self-learning and find the activity less difficult. The whole effort has been much easier because of the security provided by the music itself and the carefully monitored practice of the skill. For children with neurological and perceptual disabilities, such self-awareness, attention, and self-control are the only known ways for them to alleviate the effects of their disability.

Sensory Disorders. For some children with exceptionalities, serious problems with metacognition may exist, but metacognitive difficulties are not the very heart of their problems as with previously described groups. Students with developmental disabilities and those with visual, hearing, and physical disabilities tend to live in an educational world that seldom reaches beyond imitation and a rote accumulation of certain facts. These children seldom have opportunities to exercise judgment or to make personal choices. This is understandable, given the necessity for learning academic material correctly. Traditionally, arithmetic, grammar, and spelling are not subjects with which one can take liberties. When a sensory disorder is present, students may have more restricted learning modalities in all of their core subjects. In addition, they may attend highly structured, prescriptive therapy sessions in speech, occupational, or physical therapy. But music classes are ripe with circumstances allowing these children to engage in thinking opportunities unavailable to them elsewhere. When these children are first offered chances to exercise personal judgment in music situations, they may not really comprehend them. If they are asked, "Which way sounds better to you?" they may think, "Sounds better? There is a 'better?' And I can choose it?"

Personal choice is a new idea for most children with sensory disabilities. While personal choice does not deal directly with creative or critical thinking skills, though those are clearly involved, it does deal initially with developing the skills of metacognition. "What if I …" and "Maybe I'd better …"—such questions predicate the existence of control and choice. Choices require options. Options mean choosing, knowing why, judging, and recognizing the reasons. Dealing with choices and judgments in music is a beginning of metacognitive thought, both simple and sophisticated. Choice will be effective at all levels of a child's abilities and skills. It can take place in a music setting easily and naturally. When listening, children may choose to focus on any of many facets of the music. On the first listening of a new recording, the child may choose to focus on the melody or the percussion accompaniment, or the child may choose to listen for dynamic or tempo changes. All are appropriate metacognitive choices. Music class may well be the only setting in the education program where making choices occurs naturally.

Other Health Impairments. This category of disability frequently confuses professionals. There are so many factors that may contribute to a child's being labeled as other health impaired. Some health impairments may cause changes in attention, either due to fatigue or due to chemical reactions from medications. Changes in body chemistry due to diabetes or chemotherapy may affect a child's level of alertness, concentration, and even mental associations. Students may be taking medications that affect their ability to concentrate in school settings. When students experience fluctuations in attending ability, pain levels, physical flexibility, and general mental alertness, learning and the development of metacognitive skills may be affected. In addition, students with health impairments frequently may be absent from the classroom. Such interruptions in learning opportunities may cause gaps in knowledge and experience. Music, with its recurring elements of timbre, pitch, intensity, and duration, provides a medium with consistencies. Structures in music may be experienced over and over again in different settings, on different days, with different materials. The spiral nature of most music curricula offers students multiple opportunities to learn concepts. As students experience the same elements during their different states of health, they are afforded opportunities to develop schemas that they can retain over time. Drill and repetition are not always necessary for understanding musical concepts. One evocative encounter with the Surprise Symphony is enough for a student to understand what sforzando means. Children with health impairments may have problems with metacognition, not because they cannot self-analyze, but because their states of physical and mental concentration may influence their metacognitive ideas. On days when it is difficult to think because of pain or medication side effects, students may still gain from the music experience as passive listeners. On days when they are alert and feel well enough to participate, they may gain skills and be able to analyze the music in more traditional ways.

Situations of Abuse and Neglect. In much the same way, students who experience abuse or neglect may find difficulty with metacognive processes. For these children, it is safer not to have ideas or opinions. Merely existing is difficult. Preoccupation with physical survival and mental self-preservation takes most of their energy. Music class may provide a nonverbal world where they can experience emotions without feeling threatened or abandoned. The group ensemble, handled correctly by a supportive teacher, can provide a feeling of belonging for these children. They may blend into the group in large ensemble experiences. But they may also have the opportunity to be special through small ensemble and solo experiences. Children who never have a kind word spoken to them may feel more human through the interaction with peers in a music setting. When applause comes, they may feel truly appreciated, a rare feeling for many children of abuse or neglect. Such experiences bolster the child in ways not easily found in other academic activities. Some may have opportunities in sports, but most sports events have winners and losers. For these fragile children, music activities offer win-win opportunities. It is very important that teachers provide these children with many opportunities for self-expression without risk of failure. No matter how talented, an abused child may decline auditions due to fear of rejection. It is important that teachers be aware of such students and look for opportunities to reach out and respond to their need for inclusion.

In addition, students who have been abused or neglected may have odd ideas about musical selections. Depending on their background, they may demonstrate inappropriate gestures or make unusual associations when discussing what a particular piece of music means to them. If these children were asked to draw a picture to represent the animals while listening to "Carnival of the Animals," all of the animals may be angry or violent. Teachers should know not to automatically think of odd behaviors or comments as intentionally disruptive, but rather as small revelations of metacognitive associations based on a cruel or limited world. Consultations with the school social worker may be helpful when teaching these children. In any case, it is important not to reject the children's ideas, but rather to enlarge the spectrum and show them that the world is larger than their world of fear or depravity.

Cultural/Language Differences. Differences in cultural background may also affect a child's metacognitive choices. Each culture has special characteristics. When working with children from a different culture, it is important to realize that there are factors that influence learning and thinking in different cultures. Such factors may include:

- the time spent in their original cultural setting
- the age of the child when he or she came to the United States (how much other language experience the child had before beginning to learn English)
- the influence of extended family
- the size of the cultural or language group living in the area
- the attitude of the family toward assimilation
- the occupations of family members (the extent of contact with the general public, professional contacts, or educational level)
- the presence of any disabilities or learning problems.

In a music setting, these children may provide a richness of ideas as they assimilate their prior metacognitive awareness with the new ideas that they learn in their new world. Many of us have experienced the feeling of being foreign. We do not understand the mores, the language, and even the sights, smells, and sounds of the new land. Most often, we enjoy the stimulation of the new experiences. But who among us has not experienced the fatigue of trying to cope with new customs, new sounds, and new foods during a vacation to a foreign country? Children who are asked not only to live, but to think and learn in a new culture may find that they do not perform as well as they did in their former culture. They may be frustrated or depressed. They may feel a sense of grief or loss as their identity is forced to change. By allowing opportunities for these students to bring in examples of their music, musical learning can occur with materials familiar to them. Additionally, the nonverbal nature of music may allow these students to experience music in the new culture through movement and playing activities in which they can perform well, thereby increasing their desire to assimilate new ideas into their learning schemas more readily than in language-based activities.

Strategies for Developing Metacognition

How can we help our diverse students acquire appropriate metacognitive processes? In the first edition of this book, Pogonowski (1989) speaks of students who see themselves as "designers of their own learning" (p. 9). In so many ways, society and the schools that mirror it seem to believe that if that descriptor is true at all, it certainly does not apply to these children, who in common parlance don't learn. We know that they do learn, and we can teach them the processes of metacognition by relinquishing a bit of our ownership of the music. We can stop spooning it out, one measured dose at a time, and give music back to these children, providing the materials they need, carefully constructing schemas to move down roads of discovery, and stepping back when they arrive to let the learning be theirs. We can place them in new roles:

- As translators of sounds into meaningful patterns (For example, "Show me with your fingers how rain sounds ... more rain ... less ... make a rain shower, now a hard storm. What made it sound like rain? How did you change it? What if you had used something else for the rain?").
- As discoverers and makers of instruments and sounds (For example, "Search for and find, just in this room, things that can be instruments. Find many ways to make different sounds with them. When, in this song, would be a good place to play the instruments? When would be a poor place? Why? Which of your new instruments would be better? Why?").
- As makers and arrangers of music (For example, "There's new snow today on the playground. Let's say snow words, sing snow words, and put snow words together to show how the snow felt. Let's use your new instruments to play snow words. Will they sound right? Which are

the best? Why? Can you find some new ones that sound right? Let's make a music piece from our words and sounds. How? What shall we do? Where shall we do it? What shall be first?").

- As performers (For example, "Let's tape the two ways you decided to arrange your song: once with instruments and once with soft clapping. Are they just the way you want them? Fast enough or too fast? How about loudness: all the way through, or not? Who can think of a way to clap and still hear the words of your song?").
- As critics (For example, "Which of the two performances that you taped do you think sounds best? Why? Would it be better if you tried another way? What way? Here are two different ways that an orchestra played a piece of music: Which way do you prefer?").

There is nothing new here. These are basic self-generative approaches used often in regular classes. We use them less often with children of diversity, perhaps because their lack of traditional academic skills or their language limitations have convinced us that music is unavailable to them, too. But it takes only a little experimenting to discover the satisfaction, for both student and teacher, of an approach based in metacognitive process development.

For not-very-big adjustments in the usual strategies for working with children who have disabilities or language differences, the outcomes can be disproportionately large and thereby immensely satisfying for both teacher and student. With regular children, developing thinking skills at all levels can improve their school progress and can carry over into their futures. For children with diverse needs, possession of these thinking skills is often the difference between succeeding in anything and failing. In terms of individual children's lives, the stakes are high, and the rewards can be sizeable. In this world, no one wins them all, but control over even some of the rules of thinking can make it possible for every child to be the designer of his or her own learning.

References

Pogonowski, L. (1989). Metacognition: A dimension of musical thinking. In E. Boardman (Ed.), *Dimensions of musical thinking*. Reston, VA: MENC.

Betty T. Welsbacher is professor emerita of music education in the College of Fine Arts, School of Music, at Wichita State University in Kansas. Elaine D. Bernstorf is associate professor of music education in the College of Fine Arts, School of Music, at Wichita State University in Kansas.

10

MUSICAL THINKING AND LEARNING IN THE BEGINNING INSTRUMENTAL MUSIC CLASSROOM

JOSEPH L. SHIVELY

The day a child enters a band or orchestra classroom for the first time can be the beginning of a marvelous journey of musical and personal growth. On this same day, the teacher sets the tone for the nature of this journey. Will this teacher function as band director or orchestra conductor leading children through the rehearsal and performance of music, through scales and exercises, telling the learners how to play each step of the way? Or will the teacher guide a journey where each child not only learns to play an instrument, but more importantly develops the ability to know about and think about music, thereby developing a much greater musical knowledge that can be demonstrated on the instrument? Is it a classroom where the varied and complex experiences of instrumental musicians are the focus? It is the premise of this chapter that music education is a matter of leading the learner to musical autonomy and of placing learners in the position of being able to think like expert musicians and apply what they know to new musical experiences.[1] Creating this sort of classroom presents unique challenges for the instrumental music teacher.

Participants in any discussion of curricular matters in instrumental music usually agree that the development of independent musicians is a major goal. Often, however, little thought is given beyond developing lists of skills as to how this might come about. Whether individuals design curriculum or author method books, the focus has typically been on sequencing those activities that have always comprised beginning band and orchestra instruction—the process of learning the skills and techniques necessary to play an instrument. Furthermore, little emphasis has been given to basing the activities of the classroom on how children learn; rather, the emphasis has focused on discussion about how to teach band or orchestra. The main focus, however, should be on how children learn with the implications for teaching emerging from this discussion.

The purpose of this chapter is to examine the nature of learning in the beginning instrumental classroom and the implications for developing musical thinkers. This discussion is grounded in a constructivist approach to learning. In other subjects, constructivism has greatly informed teachers about how they might provide learning environments for children. In music, little attention has been given to this approach. However, the music classroom has great potential for successfully using this approach to learning.

The Constructivist Classroom

Learning requires an environment in which learners are immersed in experiences that reflect the activities of those who function in a knowledge domain. In a music classroom, the activities of instrumental musicians are the focus. It is through these experiences that learners make sense of the world and construct or build knowledge that reflects their understanding of the experience. Learners will apply what they already know to strengthen their knowledge bases. Classrooms based on constructivist approaches to learning are classrooms where the responsibility for learning has been shifted from the teacher to the learner. It is not the role of the teacher to tell learners what they need to know about music. In a constructivist classroom, teachers provide learners with an array of experiences that afford them the opportunity to build a greater understanding of music and to demonstrate this understanding in much the same way as expert musicians do.

The basic premise of constructivism is that knowledge is something that the individual constructs based upon experience, not that knowledge is something that exists independent of experience that is packaged for delivery from teacher to learner.

There are several underlying principles of knowledge construction in a classroom setting. These principles will serve as a framework for discussing the critical attributes of a beginning instrumental music classroom employing a constructivist approach. Knowledge construction is dependent on experiences where:

- Learning is the active process of making meaning out of one's experiences
- Learning is enhanced by exposing learners to experiences reflecting practitioner culture
- Learning is enhanced by involving learners in experiences that involve individual and group knowledge construction
- Learning is enhanced by engaging learners in experiences reflecting multiple perspectives
- Learning is enhanced by offering students multiple means of representing knowledge
- Learning is enhanced by individuals who distribute the process of knowledge construction among other individuals and artifacts
- Learning is enhanced by experiences encouraging the reflective use of a learner's knowledge base.

A constructivist classroom offers new ways to think about the process of learning and the subsequent implications for teaching. With this in mind, it is worth noting that several points should be addressed:

- There is much to be gained from examining a constructivist approach to learning, whether one agrees with the overall premise or not, because the focus is on learners having greater facility with knowledge.
- Shifting the responsibility for learning from the teacher to the learner can be problematic for the learner in many ways. Rather than being told what they need to know, learners will need to be able to respond to a teacher who models and coaches, reconciling what they already know with the experience at hand. This is the process that leads to new knowledge.

While a constructivist approach to learning may seem at times to be one where there is little for the teacher to do in planning for learning, this is hardly the case. The development of learning environments for beginning instrumental classrooms requires that teachers consider the experiences they will provide learners as context for knowledge construction. This framework (Figure 1) for developing learning environments is based on the principles of constructivist learning presented in this chapter. The major components of this framework are (1) Background, (2) Development, and (3) Process.

Background

Developing musical thinkers in the beginning instrumental music classroom requires learners to become immersed in activities authentic to instrumental musicians. Musical thinking requires that learners bring their previously acquired knowledge to bear on their new experiences. Knowledge is what the learner understands as the meaning of an event or concept based on an experience. Learners construct deep knowledge bases and use those knowledge bases to interpret musical experiences. Knowledge bases reflect the knowledge that learners have in order to be able to think in different knowledge domains. A knowledge domain is the knowledge that a particular group of practitioners uses. It also reflects how they use this knowledge. In this chapter, the focus is on the knowledge domain of instrumental musicians, with additional attention being given to other music knowledge domains, such as conducting and composing. So in a music education class, learners engage in activities in which they experience what instrumental musicians and other musicians experience. The learners then make their own meaning of these experiences with the aid of other learners and the teacher. The knowledge they construct allows them to better interpret new experiences.

The teacher's first activity is to consider the knowledge that domain practitioners use, as well as how they use it, and to consider the knowledge bases of the learners. Analyzing the knowledge domains, especially that of the instrumental musician and the knowledge bases of the learners, provides teachers with the necessary background to make decisions that will support the development of learning environments. The ability of the teacher to do this analysis is largely dependent on the teacher's domain knowledge. Being a constructivist teacher requires deep and broad music and teaching knowledge.

Knowledge Domain. A knowledge domain consists of the knowledge a group of practitioners uses and how they use this knowledge. The simplest way to identify the components of the domain is to examine the activities of the domain practitioners. What instrumental musicians need to know to perform and how they use that knowledge in their performances is an example of a knowledge domain.

(1) BACKGROUND
- **Knowledge Domain**
- **Knowledge Base**

(2) DEVELOPMENT
- **Context**
  - *Authenticity*
  - *Multiplicity*
  - *Collaborative potential*
- **Classroom Roles**
  - *Learner autonomy*
  - *Teacher involvement*
- **Constructive Supports**
  - *Learner interaction*
  - *Support artifacts*
  - *Practitioner models*
  - *Process strategies*

(3) PROCESS
- **Process Events**
  - *Introduction*
  - *Experience*
  - *Interaction*
  - *Evaluation*
- **Process Extension**

Figure 1. Framework for developing learning environments

Although certain aspects of this approach to teaching music may seem to shift away from instrumental techniques and skills, this is not at all the case. The development of techniques and skills should rise out of a need to use the instrument to represent what a leaner knows about music. Nonetheless, knowledge domain analysis should not lead to the teacher making a list of skills and tasks. The focus should be on the activities and experiences of domain practitioners.

Knowledge Base. Knowledge bases consist of the knowledge learners have built, and the application of knowledge to new experiences is critical to this process. It is not at all valuable to learn facts for the sake of learning them. Information about musical terminology or composers should be learned in a musical context. The application and building of a knowledge base are not necessarily distinctive, nor should they be. The first year of band or orchestra should be one in which knowledge bases expand rapidly, and learners have an opportunity to experience music using instruments as the medium. The teacher will need to provide experiences that allow learners to apply the knowledge they have constructed and to create new connections. For example, students should have opportunities to play new music in a particular key and to play something they already know in a new key.

One critical item is the knowledge base that learners bring into the classroom on the first day. Consider the knowledge base that beginners bring to band or orchestra. Even without music classes in the schools, they have certainly had music experience in the home, and through radio, television, and recordings. Their learning environment should reflect this variety of musical sources, giving the learners opportunities to make meaningful connections. In addition, teachers should value students' previous musical experiences. Learners should have the opportunity to use music they know from outside of the school setting, instead of the teacher being the sole provider of music. The learners may know a great deal about music, but they likely won't use the vocabulary of practitioners. At this point, it is critical that teachers build on the understanding and knowledge that learners bring to the classroom. It would be all too easy to dismiss the knowledge that learners possess at this point, especially knowledge that came from musical experiences outside of formal schooling. Learning to play familiar songs on their instruments is a very useful approach to learning the instrument, because it aids learners in making connections between what they know and what they do not yet know. It also provides a variety of music-learning experiences.

Design and Development

Designing and developing learning environments is the teacher's role. The term "design" most often refers to traditional instructional design where a task analysis is performed, and a sequenced list of skills results. In the case of the constructivist music classroom, however, the teacher focuses on selecting experiences for learners: choosing to teach ensembles, compositions to conduct, and solo performances to coach. The role of the teacher is to provide rich musical experiences for the learners and to consider how the learners will be involved with these experiences. The many critical components that the teacher should consider in developing learning environments are discussed below.

Context. The teacher must first consider the context of the musical experience because it generally serves as an index for the knowledge that the student is building. The index establishes for the learner how knowledge relates and when and how to apply it. If the learner is given a music vocabulary list, for example, the knowledge that results will be simplistic, temporary, and, most disconcerting of all, inert. However, if musical terms are learned and used in the context of musical experiences, the result should be knowledge that will be constantly reapplied and will become a part of the learner's knowledge base. After all, it won't take long for a learner to realize that *piano* and *forte* mean much more than soft and loud: how these terms are applied is dependent on the style of music, the instruments in the ensemble, and the nature of the orchestration. Of course, we need to provide learners with experiences that reflect the nature of dynamics and allow learners to make sense out of these experiences. It is also important that learners have an opportunity to manipulate dynamics in a variety of ways. In other words, learners must be provided with opportunities to think and listen for themselves in learning environments that reflect three important aspects of the experiences that the teacher should consider: authenticity, multiplicity, and collaborative potential.

Authenticity. Authenticity is determined by the extent to which the learning environment reflects real-world experiences. The teacher should consider what instrumental musicians, as well as other musicians, do and how they think about what they do. This is a potentially powerful aspect of the music classroom, as music educators often provide learners with authentic experiences. However, it is important that teachers don't instruct learners about every aspect of playing the music, but rather allow learners to work on their own, guiding them when necessary.

With the emphasis on authenticity comes the question of complexity. It is most doubtful that the beginning band will tackle "Lincolnshire Posy" or that a sixth-grade orchestra will master a Mozart overture. Nonetheless, it is imperative that students focus on real music rather than contrived exercises. In all music there will be naturally occurring complexities, and teachers should not be in a rush to oversimplify or break down learning. When teaching the learners a song by means of a model, play the whole song first, let them get it in their ears—let them find the starting pitch, and let them try to play the song. If they can sing it and they have the fingerings, they can often learn to play the song on their own. It is also important to model using fingering charts, demonstrating to learners how to teach themselves to play new pitches. Teachers must fight the urge to immediately explain everything. Of course, subsequent learning environments should be developed that provide an opportunity to apply the knowledge in a related context. Once the learners have experienced 6/8 time, for example, they need to have more opportunities to work in that meter.

The question arises about whether scales and exercises will be a part of the constructivist music classroom. Granted, instrumental musicians play exercises and scales for the purpose of improving technique, and this desire to improve is based on the needs of the performer. Largely, learners will identify the need to play certain scales or exercises because the teacher will model how practitioners use them to play the music they want to play and to play the instrument well. The beginning levels for most of school instrumental music experiences are restricted to band keys and orchestra keys. What prevents learners from exploring a variety of keys? While scales are important, learners are all too often asked to learn scales, then rarely if ever play any music in those keys. The teacher will want to have a wide-ranging repertoire of songs to teach both by model and by notation. There are many good sources for this material, but the teacher should transpose songs to explore other keys.

The context in which learning to read and play from music notation occurs is important. This skill is critical for instrumental musicians, although it should be recognized that not all instrumentalists read music. However, nowhere is the need for multiple experiences as great as in learning to manipulate notation. The activities should be varied—playing from notation, composing with notation, and conducting from notation.

Notation represents sound, and it should be learned from an experiential base. Teaching a beginner trombonist that "F" is first position, that it is on the fourth line, and that a whole note receives four beats creates learning void of context. Learning occurs better when music serves as the context, whether it is via aural model or written notation.

How and when children should learn to read notation has always been a subject of disagreement among band and orchestra teachers. Some believe in an aural modeling approach, and others believe students should learn to read notation as they learn to play the instrument. Of course, there is every variation on these positions. An aural modeling approach is preferred in the constructive classroom, because experience plays such a role in the development of the knowledge base. A rich environment for learning and evaluating is created when the teacher plays a song such as "Twinkle, Twinkle, Little Star" and has the learners model it. (Different approaches to modeling are discussed later in this chapter.)

Multiplicity. Multiplicity means offering many ways to represent knowledge and sources of knowledge. Involving learners in activities such as performing, composing, conducting, improvising, coaching, and discussing music provide not only multiple ways for them to demonstrate music knowledge, but also multiple ways for building the knowledge base. Multiplicity contributes to a much richer knowledge base, making it easier for the learners to apply what they know in new learning environments.

The music used in class should be as varied as possible in almost every way imaginable—for example, in styles, meters, and modes. Certainly, music that learners know when they come into the classroom from their experiences both in and outside of school should be used. As with authenticity, complexity should be considered with regard to multiplicity. In developing learning environments, consideration needs to be given to finding a balance in technical difficulty. Many method books offer a very limited exploration of keys, and they are usually based sequentially on rhythm and meter. Music educators need to provide opportunities for learners to explore music with variety in areas such as key, meter, and duration, as well as in dynamics, articulation, and other expressive attributes.

Learners need a variety of ways to represent what they know about music, which can then be used to create a variety of experiences within the beginning instrumental music classroom. The experiences that learners have in the beginning instrumental music classroom should reflect a wide array of sources of music.

Learners need multiple ways to represent what they know. The experiences in the beginning instrumental classroom should afford learners the opportunity to:

- Perform—While performance is an obvious feature of the instrumental music classroom; it is critical that the experiences extend beyond what has traditionally occurred in most band and orchestra classes. There should be a variety of ensembles with an emphasis on small ensemble and solo performing. As with much of what is discussed in this chapter, focusing on solo and small ensemble experience requires restructuring the classroom and the approach within that classroom. Granted, this restructuring may sometimes present a logistical challenge, but it should be noted that its purpose is to address how best that learning might occur and to try to incorporate as many of these ideas as is feasible. The result should be worth the effort.

- Compose—As soon as notation is introduced, the learner is ready to compose. His or her music reading skills will also improve as a result of manipulating notation and organizing sounds. Most important, however, learners will develop a much keener understanding about the relationship of sound and notation.
- Improvise—Send learners home the first day inventing songs using the pitches they have learned. They will probably explore their instruments' pitches, which can help them to understand more about how their instrument works. It will also stretch their desire to learn notation—they'll certainly want to hear their improvisations again.
- Write about and discuss music—Verbal knowledge representation is important in the music classroom because it provides beginners an opportunity to share knowledge in ways more familiar to all.
- Conduct—Learners need an opportunity to look at scores and to hear what an ensemble sounds like from the front of the room. Even more basic than this is learning that basic conducting patterns provide greater insight into what they see the conductor doing as they play.
- Coach—The opportunity to coach a small ensemble provides another means for learners to represent their knowledge. Further, the discussion that results not only with the coach but also among members of the ensemble provides opportunities for learners to share what they know and learn from each other to further solidify knowledge. In this case, they are discussing music with one another in a rich, authentic context.

Each of these suggested strategies is not just a way that learners can represent their music knowledge, but is a guide for the type of experiences that should occur in the instrumental music classroom. For example, students learning notation can also learn to play, compose, conduct, and coach from it. The more ways they manipulate it, the greater a part of the knowledge base it becomes. Learners who are able to use the same knowledge in different ways and in different settings can learn to work more confidently in a new context.

Collaborative potential. The learning environments developed should encourage different modes of collaboration. Having different ensemble groupings can help. While the need for small ensemble and solo experiences is highly valued in the constructivist classroom, large ensembles are still very important, for they provide learners with a large body of literature and require them to listen differently and interact with a conductor, all of which are authentic activities. Placing learners in roles such as conductor, coach, or teacher builds on the notion that one of the best ways to learn something is to teach it. Focusing on authenticity, especially in terms of multiplicity, will aid the teacher greatly in cultivating collaboration.

Classroom roles. The implementation of a constructivist approach in the beginning instrumental music classroom requires that the teacher lead the way in rethinking roles. The teacher must be an advocate of this approach to learning.

Learner autonomy. Above all else, the development of learning environments that encourage learner autonomy goes far in assuring that all learners are actively engaged in the learning process and that each learner and what that learner brings to the classroom experience are valued. In shifting roles, however, learners should be reminded that the teacher is there as an important resource—the teacher is an instrumental music practitioner who will coach, model, conduct, and advise.

Perhaps the greatest difference in a classroom in which the teacher incorporates a constructivist approach is that learners are given the opportunity to make sense out of their experiences. Rather than being shown a rhythm chart with the teacher explaining that a whole note receives four beats, a half note receives two, and so forth, the teacher might perform a piece of music, have the learners model it, and ask them to compare the rhythms or to think of ways they might write or draw the rhythms. It is critical that learners be actively involved in the process of learning. The question may arise: if learners are playing instruments in band and orchestra classes, aren't they already actively involved in learning? The answer to this question is both yes and no. Yes, they are actively involved, but mostly to the extent that playing an instrument is an activity. In most cases, they are playing the instrument under the direction of the teacher. In the constructivist classroom, learners are free to explore music and to make decisions for themselves.

Allowing learners to interpret experiences may appear to be a relativistic approach where anything goes. While there are constructivist approaches that reflect this view, this is not being advocated. Rather, it is the recognition that all of the learners in the classroom and the teacher, as practitioners, will serve to monitor the process of knowledge construction. For example, a learner would not be able to perform a composition while totally ignoring its notation. The teacher and the other learners would comment on how they didn't agree with the performer's reading of that notation. In addition, notation itself is a socially negotiated symbol system. A whole note in 4/4 time represents a duration of four beats only because musicians have agreed that is how this particular symbol will be interpreted.

Teacher involvement. The teacher sets the tone for this approach and must communicate a productive attitude by functioning as someone who is guiding learning rather than delivering information. Determining when to intervene and to what extent is a decision that each individual teacher will need to make, and it will largely be dependent on the specific group of learners and the overall classroom environment.

While this discussion has focused on learning, what is expected from a teacher in such a classroom is challenging. The most significant requirement of the teacher is domain expertise. To be able to model both product and process requires someone with a significant understanding of music. Flying in the face of the old adage (if you can't do it, teach it), teachers must be able to "do" to be successful in the constructive classroom. For example, significant knowledge of many instruments is critical to the instrumental music teacher's domain. Conducting, improvising, and composing knowledge is also very important. This unique combination of skills leads to the observation that being a music teacher is yet another knowledge domain in music, because the knowledge base required of a music teacher is so varied, and the teacher uses the knowledge in a specific manner.

Constructive Supports. Knowledge construction is greatly enhanced when learners recognize the need to depend on other learners, the teacher, and support artifacts. It is neither necessary nor desirable that learners depend solely on themselves for the constructive process and for holding their knowledge bases. In addition, the teacher should serve as an active participant in the learning process, functioning as a learner.

Learner interaction. In the constructivist classroom, learners are immersed in the experiences of instrumental musicians and encouraged to interpret these experiences and to construct knowledge from them. These experiences are both individual and social. The interaction that occurs while individual learners are constructing knowledge bases can lead to rich, deep knowledge. The nature of this interaction is a natural fit for the beginning instrumental music classroom—if the teacher is prepared to abandon the notion of standing at a podium and providing learners with all of the information.

The potential created as a result of authentic collaborative experiences in the classroom is quite powerful. Fortunately, the instrumental music classroom can provide numerous and varied opportunities for these experiences.

Support artifacts. Learners should be made aware of artifacts important to knowledge construction. For the instrumental musician, these might include a tuner, metronome, audio or video taping, fingering charts, and part-marking. From the beginning, the teacher should model how to practice and use these important artifacts. This will go a long way toward empowering learners to construct deep knowledge. For example, expert musicians do a great deal of part-marking. After all, the goal is a high quality performance, not a performance with a clean copy of the music.

Practitioner models. The teacher should constantly model strategies and sounds and provide aural models of expert practitioners on all of the instruments. These models could come from other learners in the classroom, practitioners visiting the classroom, or older learners in the music program. The key for the teacher is to allow the learner to work with these models and not to immediately tell the learners what they are to take from the experience.

Learning environments should include models of both process and product. An example of a "process model" is demonstrating how to practice, whereas an example of a "product model" is a performance—both are essential. In both cases, learners should be provided opportunities to discuss or demonstrate what they gleaned from the model. Other process models might include marking music or using a fingering chart. The teacher should not only model each process, but also discuss the strategies that comprise the skill or activity being modeled.

The product model allows the learner a great deal of freedom to interpret what is going on, for example, when the teacher or another learner performs a piece of music. A performance provides an experience that is entirely implicit and a model that is entirely open to interpretation by other learners. A product model lacks the commentary of the person providing the model. The process model is based on the notion that modeling the process requires the person who is providing the model to "think aloud." In both cases, the learners must have every opportunity to make sense of these models on their own. The process of performance provides an experience. Above all else, the learners must have every opportunity to make sense of these models on their own. For learners to have ownership of this knowledge, it is critical that the teacher not break it down for them.

Process strategies. Process strategies are critical components of every learner's knowledge base, and the ability of the learner to develop these process strategies results from experiences that reflect knowledge domains. The three types of strategies most useful to the music student are music strategies, distribution strategies, and interaction strategies. Music strategies are those that the learner can call upon when making musical decisions or reading notation. The teacher should model how counting systems are used, but this should be based on rhythms that have already been experienced. Distribution strategies involve support artifacts, such as using a metronome or marking music. Interaction strategies contribute to the learner's ability to interact with other learners and the teacher as a member of an ensemble or as a conductor. The teacher will want to model many of these strategies and make them as explicit as is natural in learning environments. A teacher might model how to practice, and the learner might be asked to adapt what the teacher does and even to develop a written list of strategies for practice.

Process

Process lies at the heart of a constructivist classroom. During process, learners are immersed in learning experiences that provide them opportunities to apply their knowledge. It should be recognized, however, that no matter how much a teacher plans, being prepared for a variety of perspectives is crucial. There is no guarantee that the learner will be interested in focusing on the particular knowledge that the teacher focuses upon in developing this experience. In some ways, this is no difference from the traditional classroom. However, in the traditional classroom, the instructions a teacher gives and the types of materials presented can limit the directions in which the learners might go.

Process Events. These are the activities that occur in the constructivist classroom. While process events share similar structures, they don't always have to occur in a specific order, and they may be adapted to what the teacher has in mind to support the needs of the learners.

Introduction to learning experiences. At the beginning of this chapter, it was recognized that the teacher sets the tone for learning from the first day of class. It is the same with the introduction of each learning experience. The teacher should not specify to the learners how they will apply their knowledge bases. However, it may be necessary to provide some instructions to the learners. For example, the teacher may pass out a piece of music to a small ensemble informing them that they are to learn it for performance. From there, the ensemble may make decisions about who is going to play which part, how it will be played, what rhythm will be used, the quality of the playing, and how the piece will be interpreted.

Experience. This is the point in the process where the teacher allows students to begin to interpret the experience and to apply their knowledge bases. It is also the point in knowledge construction about which the least can be anticipated. Learners will go in a variety of directions within any single experience. Some learners will want to play a piece they hear, whereas others may want to conduct it. The purpose of the experience may be to work in a new key, but some of the learners may want to talk about the style of the piece or improvise in that style. The teacher has the tremendous challenge of guiding all of these activities. Sometimes the guiding will require active involvement, and other times it will require that the teacher be a tacit observer.

Interaction. While interaction works on many levels during an experience, the most common interaction is a group of learners playing together, which may lead to an overlapping of individual knowledge bases. Along with playing together, discussion about what they are playing and how they are playing it will no doubt ensue. At some early point, the teacher will likely participate in the ensemble or coach it to model the sort of discussion that instrumental musicians might have in such a setting. Of course, as learners take on the role of conductor or coach, the nature of the interaction will change. By placing the responsibility on the learners, the teacher creates musical problems for them to solve and structures practical reasons for solving them.

Evaluation. The process of knowledge construction includes the process of evaluation. Learners must continue to reevaluate how well their knowledge bases serve them as they interpret new experiences. When the learner does not have sufficient knowledge, there is a problem. The teacher should use this lack as a possible context for a future learning environment.

While much of the evaluation in a constructivist classroom resulting from the process itself will be informal, there is a place in the constructivist classroom for formal evaluation. One of the challenges in all instrumental music classes is how to evaluate learners. Often they are given pencil-and-paper tests on material best demonstrated in context. A learner writing a definition for each of the dynamic markings is well and good. However, much more can be gleaned from how a learner applies dynamics in a performance or composition. Most importantly, the knowledge will be applied in context.

Instrumental musicians do not typically listen to a performance with a checklist. Rather, they identify what they like and dislike as they respond to the emerging qualities of performance. As much as possible, formal evaluation of performance in the classroom should be as authentic as possible. Why ask a learner to define legato and staccato when he or she can demonstrate knowledge through performance or composition?

Process Extension

The application of knowledge in new contexts is critical to the process of knowledge construction. The teacher should consider how new learning environments might be developed to encourage the reapplication of knowledge already constructed. As with any constructivist learning environment, there are no guarantees that learners will focus on what the teacher expects.

The notion of transfer has always presented a special challenge for teachers. In the case of the constructivist classroom, it should be thought of as the students' reflective use of the knowledge base. Because learners have constructed knowledge though experiences that reflect the rich and complex nature of music, they will be able to apply the knowledge to new experiences. It is from this viewpoint that the role of knowledge as a tool is most clearly understood.

Conclusion

There is still a place for direct instruction in the beginning instrumental music classroom. There is little need for having the learners "discover" how to put an instrument together, and we should not allow them to develop poor physical habits. However, these matters relate to using tools. Exploration of and knowledge of music should be the primary goal of beginning instrumental music classes. Of course, setting this foundation in the first year will likely alter experiences in subsequent years. Regardless of whether a teacher has an interest in shifting the focus to the learners or whether or not he or she sees any validity in a constructivist approach, there is much to gain from the underlying principles and specific ideas presented in this chapter.

Beginning instrumental classes provide important experiences in the development of musical understanding. There is a strong tradition of very successful band and orchestra programs in the schools; however, it is worth examining approaches that reflect contemporary thinking about the process of learning and how that process might contribute to the development of musical thinkers.

Beginning instrumental music classes should be environments in which learners are encouraged to explore and learn about music using an instrument as the most important tool. Many students sign up for band or orchestra to learn to play an instrument. In no way is the suggestion being made in this chapter that this should not be a significant focus. Rather, the suggestion is made that there is a way to approach learning in the classroom that will allow learners to be not only better performers on their musical instruments, but also more knowledgeable, independent musicians. For learners to be able to think musically, they must have ownership of knowledge, and to gain ownership they must be encouraged to use this knowledge repeatedly to build new knowledge.

Note

1. This chapter is based on a dissertation by J. L. Shively (1995), A framework for the development and implementation of constructivist learning environments for beginning band classes. *Dissertation Abstracts International,* 57, 1535A (University Microfilms No. 9624497). For further discussion, and to become familiar with the research that formed the basis for this chapter, the reader is urged to refer to this dissertation.

11

MUSICAL THINKING IN THE INSTRUMENTAL REHEARSAL

RICHARD KENNELL

Several years ago, I observed a student teacher at a nearby high school. This student was already a reasonably experienced teacher, and she was introducing a new piece to her band. The initial results from the students were imprecise and unrefined. The student teacher went to work. As she worked on a crescendo here and a phrasing detail there, the ensemble's precision improved. Individual students improved their scale passages, and the accompaniment jelled. I noticed that the ensemble was improving on each reading. Their progress even exceeded the directions of the novice teacher. While the student teacher was working at a micro level to improve a few specific trouble spots, the students were independently improving at the macro level of performance. I later commented to the cooperating teacher, "You certainly have a very intelligent band."

What later struck me about this encounter was my selection of the word "intelligent" where I might have been expected to use "well-trained." These students were not trained in the sense that their director had placed all the notes and nuances for them. No, these students were displaying definite musical independence, going far beyond what their student teacher/conductor was asking of them. They were solving problems and making musical decisions on their own. Their steady improvement demonstrated working musical intelligence rather than conformance to the student teacher's directions.

Ten years ago, I commented on how strange and unique it was to use an academic term like "intelligence" in a musical context. Since the original publication of *Dimensions of Thinking* by Marzano et al. (1988), however, there has been a veritable revolution in instrumental music education. Ten years ago, we were different. Music teaching seemed separate from the basic classroom education that was taking place around us in the schools. Our colleagues used textbooks; we prepared individual musical compositions for concerts. They held discussions; we conducted rehearsals. They gave paper and pencil tests; we went to contests. They assigned homework; our students practiced. Their students studied; our students played. Within the semantics of these contrasts lay a sense of the way we viewed our profession and were in turn viewed by others. Ten years ago, the presentation of music instruction in the schools remained outside the public's expectations for an academic discipline.

Much has happened in the intervening years to cause us to rethink what we do and to better understand the unique benefits that students enjoy from engaging in music experiences. Howard Gardner (1983) has challenged us to consider the implications of multiple intelligences. Frances Rauscher (1997) has suggested that listening to music fosters improved student performance on some kinds of tests. As a result of such research, academicians are at least curious about what music experience might contribute to the education of the whole child, and musicians have appropriated a new professional vocabulary. We have fundamentally changed the way we view our subject matter and the importance of our contributions as music teachers.

Over the past ten years, many prominent educational researchers—perhaps best represented by the writings of Jerome Bruner (1996)—have shifted their attention to the influence of culture on learning. As a socially constructed cultural system (Bruner, 1996), the teaching of music offers the education researcher new opportunities to study how experts in a culture assist novices in acquiring the necessary cognitive strategies and competencies to function independently. What music teachers do, how we do it, and why we do it are now of central interest to a larger research community that heretofore has considered us a deviant tradition in the family of education. This shift in professional attention signals the start of a realignment of the relationship of music education to our larger parent endeavor, human education.

As music teachers, we have always been involved with the teaching of thinking skills. We just call it by a different name—"musicianship." While our classroom colleagues deal primarily with the world of verbal discourse, we seek to develop a similar set of intellectual skills through the nonverbal medium of music. Our problem-solving activities involve decoding complex musical symbol systems into live musical performances. These problem-solving exercises are guided by traditional rules and conventions that have been passed down from generation to generation. In order to function independently, our students must learn to apply these rules to new musical situations. The more musical independence our students achieve, the more musical intelligence or musicianship they exhibit. Music teachers promote the development of musical intelligence to achieve musical independence.

Almost ten years ago, renowned pianist John Perry (1992) remarked, "Not only is it often difficult to verbalize what we do in teaching music, our subject matter—what we teach—is also often impossible to verbalize." Today, as we search for a greater understanding of human cognition, music teaching offers the education researcher a convenient laboratory in which we can study the processes of teaching and learning. The paradigm shift of the cognitive revolution has moved music teaching from the periphery of education research to center stage.

Metacognition and Executive Control

When music teachers teach, they simultaneously perform. We make music with our students. I cannot think of another subject area in which the roles of teacher and student are so intertwined. Our music making is a joint activity that combines the responsibilities and actions of the teacher with the responsibilities and actions of our students. This tradition presents a unique problem for the development of the executive control processes of planning, evaluation, and regulation in our students because much of our executive decision making as teachers takes place out of view of the student.

Traditionally, the teacher selects the music to be performed, plans a set of rehearsals, and monitors student progress toward performance standards. These are examples of executive control processes that we rarely reveal to our students. Either our planning takes places out of sight from our students, or our actions and decisions are so automated that they seem invisible to them. In addition, we rarely put our students into situations that require them to use their executive control functions in meaningful ways.

How might instrumental music teachers transfer executive control process experience to their students? Initially, we can briefly discuss the criteria for selecting music with our students. We can reveal our choices by explaining the process undertaken to clarify why we picked one piece over another.

As students become aware of the process involved in this choice, we can assign small groups of students to participate in the music selection process for the ensembles in which they perform. We can make these students responsible for identifying specific goals for the next rehearsal, as well as for determining the performance standards to be achieved. In this interaction between teacher and students during such planning activities, the teacher's executive control processes become accessible to the student.

Another possibility is to assign students to chamber music groups that complement the large-ensemble experience. In chamber-music ensembles, our students could gradually become totally responsible for selecting the literature, planning and conducting the rehearsals, and presenting their work publicly. This independent activity forces the student to exercise executive control processes in a meaningful way.

Problem Solving

Fluid performance requires the automatic execution of complex skills. An important principle of music performance is that numerous smaller units combine to form larger units. In the same way, music teaching is a higher level cognitive process that draws upon highly automated decision making and problem-solving subroutines. These basic functions must be secure and be immediately accessible to the teacher. But these automated teaching skills may not be visible to the casual observer; the complexity of the teaching strategy may simply not be apparent in the classroom.

I can best illustrate this by considering sight-reading at a contest. When the teacher opens a score for the first time, he or she employs a personal routine to retrieve significant information from the printed page. Try making a list of all the questions you ask yourself upon first exposure to a score. Your list will no doubt include many of these questions:

1. How is this score similar to or different from others that I have seen?
2. What is the key signature? Are there any changes of key?
3. Is the work melodic, rhythmic, or textural? Where is the melody and accompaniment, and how does this change?

4. What is the time signature? Does the time signature remain the same, or does it change?
5. What is the tempo marking? Are there any changes in tempo?
6. Are there clearly defined sections? What is the character of each section?
7. What are the stylistic features? What changes in texture occur?

In the brief time it takes to open the score until giving the first downbeat, the conductor must craft answers to all of these questions. He or she must form a specific schema or mental blueprint of this work to use in conducting the new score.

Back in the rehearsal hall, however, how many of us take the time to share these specific musical problem-solving strategies with our students? Our cognitive strategies are often invisible as we work with our students. In fact, they may be so automatic that we may not even be aware of them ourselves.

In rehearsals, we have an opportunity to reveal our personal strategies for solving musical problems. Demonstrating highly automated instructional strategies to our students takes concentrated effort and attention. In approaching any musical problem—sight reading, ensemble balance, precision, rhythm problems, and the like—we need to first be aware that higher level strategies consist of tightly connected smaller units of attention, thought, and action. We must break the larger strategy down into its complex components to show our students how the parts fit together.

In teaching instrumental music, our interactions with our students—our verbal and gestural instructions—support our students' performance like a scaffold. Our instructions help the students to reach beyond their current capabilities. Our assistance is temporary and is removed when no longer needed. In musical scaffolding, there are three basic ways that music teachers offer support: marking a critical feature, offering a demonstration, and manipulating the task.

The most frequently used teacher intervention is marking a critical feature. This involves a teacher statement, question, command, or gesture that functions to highlight a specific feature of the task, such as "Forte!" or "What's the dynamic marking at rehearsal number six?" This class of teacher intervention draws attention to a feature of the task or the students' performance. It reminds the students of specific details they have already learned but not yet mastered.

Less frequently employed interventions are offering a demonstration and manipulating the task. We easily recognize teacher demonstration in the rehearsal. From time to time, teachers provide direct models for their students to emulate or avoid. Communicating such models might include singing, playing on the piano, or clapping. These actions typically function to introduce new concepts or new nuances in existing concepts. Thus, the teacher selects and employs the demonstration strategy to build a new concept or a common understanding within the student ensemble.

Conductors use the manipulating-the-task strategy to move the students from one skill level to the next. They do this by first simplifying the demands of the task, saying, for example: "Let's slow down the tempo" or "Put your instruments down and let's clap the rhythm." Then they make the task increasingly more challenging until the desired level of skill is achieved. The manipulating-the-task strategy is used to help automate musical skills.

Music teachers employ different strategies to accomplish different instructional goals. By creating functional labels for these basic genres of interaction, the notion of scaffolding allows teachers to identify strategies and combinations of strategies that otherwise might be invisible to the student.

The next time you record a rehearsal on videotape, review the results of your taped recording carefully. This is what your students see when you rehearse them. They see only the largest outcomes of your cognitive involvement in the rehearsal. Next, review your tape and look for instances of scaffolding. You'll be surprised at how easy these interventions are to spot once you know what to look for. You will no doubt remember the reason you selected each strategy. Students rarely are privileged to understand the private reasons that lead up to public instructions. It may be useful from time to time to slow down your rehearsal interventions and to share your inner strategies with your students. The scaffolding labels (marking a critical feature, offering a demonstration, and manipulating the task) offer a potentially useful vocabulary with which to explain your instructional choices and the interventions that you initiate during a rehearsal.

And there's the other problem: the actual steps you go through to construct a pedagogical intervention are so automatic that you may not even be aware of the details that underlie your own instructional choices. You might employ the basic notions of scaffolding listed above to deconstruct the reasoning that supports your pedagogical decisions. The more we can reveal about our moment-to-moment musical problem-solving strategies to our students, the more we promote musical independence in their performance.

Have you ever noticed how truly outstanding studio teachers of music performance will offer their students several possible strategies for solving musical problems? How many times have we heard studio teachers say, "This works best for me but you may also want to try … "? As teachers of ensemble performance, we also need to be collectors of musical problem-solving strategies. We collect these strategies from numerous sources: other conductors, colleagues, mentors, and, of course, our own students. Sometimes, strategies appear spontaneously in a rehearsal that work exceptionally well for the moment. We can evaluate that strategy in other contexts and add new techniques to our collection of rehearsal strategies.

As we employ these successful strategies in rehearsal and make our students aware of them, we encourage each student to build a repertoire of personal problem-solving strategies. The more they automate the strategies, the more "intelligent" they become as musicians and the more independent they become. It is musical independence that is, after all, a significant lifelong benefit of music participation.

Creativity

Musical performance is a "re-creative" experience. Performers transform the limited instructions provided by the composer's notation into a live expression of the composer's creation. This transformation involves interpreting written symbols to which we also bring a wealth of common-practice knowledge and understanding. But many of the creative decisions involved in this re-creation process are either assigned to the exclusive role of the teacher or are internal and invisible to the student.

Our rich ensemble tradition has produced a rather restricted view of music making. The music experience for most instrumental music students consists only of the performance of other people's ideas. They seldom solve musical problems as composers or even make musical decisions as listeners. Yet, we know that, for most of our students, listening will be their primary mode of musical involvement in adulthood. Our school music-making experiences, therefore, must somehow include creating, listening, and evaluating, as well as performing.

There are a number of creative possibilities for instrumental music students short of the "write your own overture" assignment. One of my personal favorites continues to be *A Contemporary Primer for Band* by Sydney Hodkinson (1973). This series introduces the basics of interpreting graphic music composition. The primer can be introduced as early as junior high school, and it encourages students to write their own graphically represented compositions. Student compositions can be easily duplicated and performed, which provides an excellent opportunity for the student composer to teach the new work to the student ensemble.

Another exercise I have found to be very successful is the "reconstruct the melody" activity. I was first introduced to this activity by a high school

English teacher who was using a "reconstruct the poem" exercise. The principle is the same in either medium. An unfamiliar poem or melody is cut up into brief phrases. These phrases are randomized and numbered. The student's task is then to examine each phrase and to attempt to reconstruct the original order. By considering sequences, line direction, cadence points, and other contextual details, students are quite capable of reconstructing unfamiliar melodies. From this exercise, it is but a short step to applying these same principles to original student compositions.

It is ironic that there are so few opportunities to listen to music within our traditional instrumental music ensemble rehearsals. We are so busy making music that there is little time to listen to it. Listening to music, however, provides an ideal experience for exercising thinking skills like focusing, information gathering, remembering, organizing, analyzing, generating, integrating, and evaluating, which are the basic components of other high level mental processes (Marzano, 1988).

Music listening allows us to use all of these core skills. For example, as the rehearsal proceeds, students can be asked to determine through listening "Which instruments have the melody?" "Have you heard this line before?" "Can you think of another accompaniment figure that would compliment this melodic line?" "How far apart are the highest and lowest pitches in this melody?" "From where in the melody line does the accompaniment figure come?" and "Which note in this cadence sounds as if it doesn't belong?" In comparing an early rehearsal tape with the final recording of a performance, students can participate in the assessment of their own musical growth. Additionally, listening to a recording of music from a different world culture can challenge students to develop a deeper understanding of their own cultural assumptions and expectations.

The Teacher's Role

The music teacher should always be a model for successful music thinking skills. As we display personal commitment, positive attitudes, and intense attention, we communicate successful thinking strategies to our students. We need to bring these control processes to the attention of our students. As individual students exercise these qualities and achieve success, we have the opportunity to point these out to the other students. Then we need to create opportunities for students to apply these successful strategies to appropriate musical contexts.

The music teacher should also model diverse musical roles. Our students should have opportunities to see us engage in different musical experiences: conducting, performing, listening, and composing or arranging. Students should see examples of how adults experience music in their lives. And students should see how adults create links between music and other subject areas: how historical and political forces affect the musical culture of a time, and how the music and arts contribute to the politics and events that comprise our understanding of history.

Reflect for a moment on the truly gifted teachers who have influenced your life. Chances are they taught you more than their professional subject matter. They taught you about the meaning and value of that subject in the larger community of ideas. Much of this connecting was taught through storytelling. In between musical selections, at breaks and between rehearsals, teachers are able to share small pieces of themselves through their personal stories. It is through such personal exchanges that students begin to learn about the larger world around them.

The narrative is tremendously powerful for transporting students beyond the classroom and into the adult world. Through sharing your personal story, your professional experience becomes accessible to your students. They connect what they do in the rehearsal with the concert hall. They situate their new knowledge in a community that gradually becomes more familiar. As we reveal links between the experience of music and other human experiences, we provide a model for our students' future lives.

The instrumental music program that draws on musicianship-fostering strategies will be very different from the traditional instrumental music program of the past. It will include a greater variety of learning contexts, place the teacher in new and demanding roles, and offer students a broader range of musical experiences. In short, instrumental music education will continue to evolve to make ever greater contributions to the intellectual and aesthetic development of young people.

The historical traditions of the school music program emulating the college and military band have served us well over the past sixty years. There are indications, however, that music teachers across this nation are seeking new answers to our professional dilemmas: What shall we teach? Whom shall we teach? How shall we teach?

To illustrate some of these changes in the focus and structure of instrumental music programs, let me briefly describe one of the high schools that I visit to supervise student teachers. It is a typical instrumental music program in a typical town. What is atypical, however, is the consistently high level of musicianship its students display. At this school, the teaching staff has established a set of after-school musicianship requirements. These requirements include some music theory, as well as creative and performance-skill enhancing activities. Each student's class grade is tied to this out-of-class work. And the students bring what they've learned to each rehearsal.

Whether the superior performing skills of this band can be attributed to this musicianship-fostering program is subject to debate. I point to this program only because it is representative of a growing number of instrumental music programs around the country that are redefining the expectations of instrumental music education. They provide students with music learning experiences to improve basic musicianship skills as a step toward improving their performance skills.

Some instrumental music teachers will view fostering personal musicianship skills within the daily rehearsal as a choice: "Do I sustain high performance standards, or do I develop student musicianship skills?" The development of personal musicianship skills is a means of attaining and sustaining excellence in performance. The instrumental music program of the future can connect the worlds of musical knowledge and musical skills as it makes a truly special contribution to the total development of the child.

References

Gardner, H. (1983.) *Frames of mind: The theory of multiple intelligences.* New York: Basic Books.

Rauscher, F. H. et al. (1997.) Music training causes long-term enhancement of preschool children's spatial-temporal reasoning. *Neurological Research, 19* (1), 2–7.

Bruner, J. (1996.) *The culture of education.* Cambridge, MA: Harvard University Press.

Sheehan-Campbell, P. (1991.) *Lessons from the world.* New York: Schirmer Books.

Perry, J. (1992.) *Qualities of successful teachers.* Paper presented at the meeting of the National Conference on Piano Pedagogy in Schaumburg, IL.

Hodkinson, S. (1973.) *A contemporary primer for band.* Bryn Mawr, PA: Merion Music.

Marzano, R., et al. (1988.) *Dimensions of thinking: A framework for curriculum and instruction.* Alexandria, VA: Association for Supervision and Curriculum Development.

Richard Kennell is interim dean and professor of performance studies at the College of Musical Arts at Bowling Green State University in Bowling Green, Ohio.

12

MUSICAL THINKING AND LEARNING IN THE CHORAL CONTEXT

SANDRA SNOW AND HILARY APFELSTADT

How will the choral classroom of the twenty-first century interface with wider educational reform efforts in the schools? Has the nature of the choral classroom changed or expanded in the past hundred years? Does the choral profession critically examine issues of pedagogy, curriculum, teaching practice, and assessment? What does it mean to demonstrate musical thinking and learning in the choral domain?

For those choral educators who emphatically believe in the intrinsic value of music making and learning, these questions need probing and clarification. The purpose of this chapter is to examine musical thinking and learning in relationship to the student and the conductor/teacher as it is manifested in the choral classroom.

The Student

Ever-increasing advances are being made in the understanding of how humans learn and use knowledge. In education, a continuing challenge is the practical application of research results to teaching practice. Research in music education, in the wider educational research body and in the cognitive sciences and psychological domains, provides important information about how students learn in the school environment. The foundations section of this book renders an excellent overview of these strides. This section will bridge aspects of recent theory to particularized learning in the choral setting. In the choral classroom, educational theory has been translated into various educational practices in recent years. These include a focus on comprehensive musicianship, portfolio assessment of learning, development of critical thinking skills, and emphasis on active listening, performing, and creating. Improvisation and composition have become increasingly important in both performing and general music classrooms. A commonality among these trends is a focus on development of musical independence by learners.

Current brain research indicates that the arts do more than develop a cultured child. "A strong arts foundation builds creativity, concentration, problem solving, self-efficacy, coordination, and values of attention and self-discipline" (Jensen, 1998, p. 36). Researchers cite three effects of music in relation to brain development:

1. "Reading music engages both sides of the brain."
2. Music serves as a carrier of various concepts (i.e., children may remember words better if set to music that reinforces their rhythm).
3. Music "can actually prime the brain's neural pathways." Because of that, music may be "critical for later cognitive processes" (Jensen, 1998, p. 37).

In light of these statements, one can agree that not only is choral subject-matter content important for aesthetic and artistic reasons, but it also relates to brain development and the general capacity to learn. The so-called "Mozart-effect," while controversial, is spurring interest in the value of music in cognitive processes (Jensen, 1998, p. 38).

The rehearsal setting offers a rich context for achieving the goals of musical independence, the development of thinking skills via problem solving by ensemble members, the development of questioning techniques to elicit reflective thought by students, and the empowerment of students in a classroom where critical thinking takes precedence over noncurricular pressures such as performance (Apfelstadt, 1989). Three areas of contemporary research interest include the development of expertise as a primary goal of instruction, the cultivation of a subcommunity of practitioners (in this case, choral singers), and scrutiny of verbal and nonverbal ways of knowing in relationship to developing musicianship.

The Expertlike Mind Set

Considerable research exists about expertise as it relates to cognition, behavioral and social manifestations, and examination of domain-specific experts in widely diverse fields (Bereiter & Scardamalia, 1993). One might wonder why it is important to study an expert like a professional conductor or singer when the choral classroom is probably not geared for creating professionals as its primary mission. Expertise is a rich form of situated knowledge embedded in a particular domain. In choral music, an expert might demonstrate a masterful understanding of vocal production and tone, style in relationship to standards of musical practice, or knowledge of formal elements such as form and structure of music. An expert or professional choral musician may not be an expert choral conductor because the situated understanding of gesture and communication is an additional skill requiring other forms of knowing.

Bereiter and Scardamalia (1993) make useful distinctions between an expert and an experienced nonexpert in a given field. These professionals might have had the same background, training, professional development opportunities, and career paths. One is regarded by colleagues as a master teacher, the other as a competent teacher. If each professional has had benefit of similar training, how is it that one becomes a master teacher? Bereiter and Scardamalia (1993) posit that expert teachers approach their craft constantly searching for new ways to increase their knowledge. The expert maintains a curiosity and openness to new ideas and is in a continual cycle of self-reflection and renewal. The expert is willing to experiment and improvise, even risking failure of a given action in order to further knowledge and understanding.

The experienced nonexpert, on the other hand, takes knowledge or skill acquired and attempts to reduce a set of possible actions to replicable and familiar responses in new situations. The experienced nonexpert choral teacher might respond to a musical challenge presented by a choir in the same manner each time it is presented. For example, if the sopranos sing sharp, this teacher might have mapped out one or two possibilities to diagnose an intonation fault such as lack of breath support. This musical challenge would be evaluated and rehearsed in a similar fashion whenever it occurs. The teacher might not consider other possibilities germane to a specific instance, because his or her intellectual energy is used to call on familiar responses rather than searching for new solutions.

Expertise, according to Bereiter and Scardamalia (1993), is a never-ending process of growth and renewal. Humans can take on the orientation of experts by adopting an expertlike mind set. Learners in the choral classroom, reflecting expertlike actions, would be encouraged to work at the upper level of complexity for their individual knowledge base. These students would necessarily be involved in many layers of musical decision making as they try out new ideas in order to expand their thinking and learning. The term "expertlike mind-set" is deliberately chosen over more commonly encountered phrases such as "choral artistry" to provide connection between recent research on thinking and learning and how choral musicians learn their craft. Artistry may well be an exquisite outcome of expertise and expression.

Choirs: A Mini-Community of Practitioners

If situated knowledge defines understanding in a given domain, the choral musician necessarily depends on others to further his or her growth and comprehension. One of the joys of choral singing, in fact, is the opportunity to make music in a group setting. It may be true that the corporate unit, the choir, can achieve levels of expertise beyond the capacity of a single member. The knowledge demonstrated by a particular choir includes the musical and nonmusical contextual experiences formed by long-term association. In order to optimize the development of corporate expertise, several features might be noted. First, the role of the learner takes on increased importance as the role of the conductor/teacher shifts toward that of facilitator. The students as a whole need multiple opportunities for musical decision making.

Second, the choir might function as a reflective practicum, one in which the expertlike mind-set is explored. The notion of reflection, or reflection-in-action, has become central to discussions of expertise. As Donald Schön (1983) notes, it is possible to evaluate what we are doing as we are "in-the-action." This occurs in real time and differs from reflecting on one's actions either prior to or following an experience. In the choral setting, reflecting in action might be framed by a teacher's guidance of the rehearsal moment. For example:

> *Teacher:* "Begin at measure five. As you sing through the A section, become aware of the vowels that affect pitch. Are there any places where an improved vowel would result in improved intonation? Please sing your answer."
> *Choir:* (On teacher cue, sings A section)
> *Teacher:* "Excellent. Your decision to brighten the "ee" vowel indeed improved pitch."

This teacher-guided reflection might be verbalized prior to the experience, but the teacher is asking the learners to attend to a particular musical challenge within the actual singing experience. The musical decision making by ensemble members is nonverbal and demonstrated in the singing action. This differs from a nonguided sing-through in which the learners are questioned following the experience but without prior guidance for active listening in singing. A reflective practicum in the school setting, as defined by Elliott (1995), emphasizes the induction of students into authentic musical practices by placing productive musical action at the center of the curriculum. The choral classroom, with its focus on production, is a natural vehicle for development of musicianship. Production in the choral setting includes active listening and creating, as well as singing.

Finally, corporate expertise develops when musicianship is a prominent goal of instruction. The term "musicianship" is complex and has been defined in various ways through time. It, along with "choral artistry," is a catch-all term often used to describe the elusive qualities associated with a masterful or moving performance. Elliott (1992) views the development of musicianship as constituent of various kinds of knowing that include at least the following categories: formal knowledge, informal knowledge, impressionistic knowledge, and supervisory knowledge.

Formal knowledge can be thought of as verbal facts and principles within a domain. In choral music, this knowledge might include performance practice and historical and theoretical knowledge about a choral work. Formal knowledge often serves to contextualize learning.

Informal knowledge is gained through experience. It represents those tacit learnings that a musician collects over time in relationship to specific standards and traditions of musical practice. For example, the ability to sing Baroque choral repertoire is likely the result of both formal knowledge (historical precedent) and informal knowledge gained through sustained exposure. Informal knowledge informs in-action musical judgments. Using Bach as an example, the musician might treat two-note phrases with similar articulation due to past experience with like musical instances. When the musician encounters two-note phrases in Stravinsky's music, however, the rules have changed, and one cannot assume that the first of the two notes will receive the emphasis. Choral musicians must make in-action judgments as the singing progresses.

Impressionistic musical knowledge, according to Elliott (1992), is a felt sense of directionality in musical decision making. He argues that cognitive scientists now acknowledge the relationship between thinking and feeling. The filtering of experience in relationship to personal understandings, emotions, and feelings gives meaning to the music-making process. In the choral classroom, impressionistic knowledge is inextricably tied to the corporate experience of these members of the ensemble. This form of knowledge might be facilitated when students have sustained opportunities to encounter both breadth and depth of choral literature, as well as the contextual understanding gained through a variety of performing experiences.

Supervisory knowledge, or metacognition, relates to the ability to monitor one's actions in a given set of circumstances. Becoming aware of one's learning and the ways in which one learns sensitizes humans to their strengths and weaknesses. In terms of musical knowing, supervisory knowledge is responsible for large-scale abilities to monitor, adjust, and oversee musical thinking. The development of supervisory knowledge is likely heightened in a classroom where reflection and self-evaluation are preeminent. Student leadership roles, including peer teaching assignments or student conducting opportunities, are an excellent way to encourage students to monitor and sort through their own thinking and learning.

Role of Verbal and Nonverbal Knowledge in Musical Decision Making

When musicianship is viewed through the complex lens suggested by Elliott (1992), the development of such knowledge requires a reevaluation of ways in which choral classrooms function. Recent underscoring of the need for reflective practice, as well as the challenges inherent in the influential voluntary *National Standards for Arts Education* (MENC, 1994) has resulted in suggested educational techniques and practices to address these concerns.

A primary misconception about reflective practice, particularly in the classroom setting, is that musical understanding is largely verbal in nature. This is embedded in teacher practice, as well as in assessment tools. For example, a teacher might equate reflection with lengthy verbalization following a rehearsed section of a choral work. The sing-through may have taken three minutes, while the ensuing talk from the teacher comprised another ten minutes.

Rather than being primarily verbal, music is foremost a nonverbal form of procedural knowing. This knowledge, according to Schön (1987), may involve thinking that does not result in verbal concepts or need not be mediated by language. Thinking in singing does not equate with talking about singing. A rehearsal, therefore, that is characterized by an emphasis on talking about the music under study rather than in the singing action may reorient the experience away from developing musical thinking.

It may be that the teacher's role in this situation is to guide or facilitate the musical activity, in this case singing, so that production is central to learning. Verbalization might be restricted to small chunks of a rehearsal and carried out in direct relationship to the musical sound, either beforehand to target attention or afterward to deconstruct the learning. Verbalization, then, is a specialized teaching strategy used to target learner attention rather than a prescriptive set of teacher-generated instructions that require little student thinking.

It is considerably easier for teachers to identify verbal thinking and knowing than it is for them to understand nonverbal thinking. In the choral classroom, students can participate in a variety of nonverbal learning strategies coached by the teacher. For example, they can conduct the phrase, draw phrase shapes through the air, chant text in rhythm, solfège problematic passages, or move around the room in relationship to the style of the music. In a rehearsal where nonverbal thinking is prized, musical decision making by ensemble members is ongoing, corporate, and action-oriented. Verbal techniques often rely on a single member speaking for the group; nonverbal strategies can be employed by each member of the choir. Most importantly, nonverbal teaching strategies place the learner in direct connection with the music under study rather than disrupting the music making to entertain a dialogue about the music.

In a hierarchical sense, nonverbal thinking is most characteristic of musical understanding. Informal, impressionistic, and supervisory knowledge is largely nonverbal, while formal knowledge is often verbal in nature and is a means of contextualizing the potent nonverbal understandings of the learner. As shown in Figure 1, a basic way to practice the shift from prescriptive rehearsals to action-oriented rehearsals is to brainstorm several different approaches that require musical judgment on behalf of the learner. In these examples, verbal strategies are used to clarify nonverbal action on behalf of the singers.

The Conductor/Teacher

The role of the conductor/teacher in the choral classroom is influenced by the historical view of conductor training and teacher training in the United States. In the university setting, for example, conducting majors are generally considered performance majors, whereas prospective teachers are education majors. This is a false distinction, however, because music educators must function both as conductors and teachers, regardless of their educational background. Indeed, one might argue that conducting gesture alone is a potent form of nonverbal teaching. Without words upon which to

Example 1

- Prescriptive:
  "Tenors, please sing an F-sharp in bar five."
- Action-oriented:

  Nonverbal strategy. (The teacher models the phrase by singing the faulty intonation.)

  Verbal strategy. "Tenors, how might we improve the leading tone in this phrase?"

  Nonverbal strategy. "Tenors, please raise your hand if we sing an incorrect interval."

  Verbal strategy. "Did any interval change? Can you now mark the appropriate accidental on the leading tone?"

Example 2

- Prescriptive:
  "On page two, we need much more sweep in the phrases. Please mark a piano in measure sixty with a long crescendo to the apex of the phrase in bar sixty-eight."
- Action-oriented:

  Nonverbal strategies.

  "Beginning in measure sixty, draw the phrase through the air, demonstrating your idea about phrase shape."

  "What is the most important word of text on page two? Sing the journey you must make for the listener to understand your idea."

  (Singers sit in a circle on the floor.) "Step page two and show me with your body where the most important musical idea resides."

Figure 1. Two examples of verbal strategies for clarifying nonverbal action

rely, students must respond to gestural cues from the conductor, whose task is to convey musical ideas through motion. These distinctions are drawn because the choral classroom may be the arena for important tacit philosophical assumptions relating to the role of the conductor. O'Toole (1994) distinguishes between expertise as described above and what she terms the "expert model" evident in some choral classrooms. In her analysis of choral pedagogy, O'Toole (1994) examines the assumptions made about the expert role granted the conductor. For example, the privileged position of the conductor before the rows of singers, the expectation that singers will monitor themselves by raising hands before speaking, and the understanding that singers will follow the spoken directions of the conductor all contribute to an implicit understanding that the conductor is granted power in the classroom.

It is likely that many teachers could characterize their own experiences in the choral ensemble from this paradigm. Lortie (1975) examined the myriad images that teachers may have encountered in their own experiences as students prior to the onset of their careers. He describes an "apprenticeship of observation" phenomenon wherein prospective teachers encounter thousands of hours of observation of teaching, likely shaping future teaching behavior (Lortie, 1975, pp. 61–65). Prospective novice conductor/teachers may have sung for conductors since junior high or even grade school. The expert model, if it is the dominant paradigm, is likely to be reenacted by the novice. In this paradigm, the ensemble members are expected to carry out the instructions of the conductor towards the refinement of the conductor's aural image. A danger of this approach, as outlined by Reimer's (1989) discussion of performance ensembles in the school setting, is that students often participate in ensemble experiences with a growing adeptness for following instructions, but little sense of their own musicianship, often evidenced by a lack of participation in musical activities beyond high school.

According to Brooks and Brooks (1999), "The American classroom is dominated by teacher talk." They point out that "student-initiated questions and student-to-student interactions are atypical" and suggest that "student thinking is devalued in most classrooms." (Brooks & Brooks, 1999, pp. 6–7). While models of teacher-directed learning might promote this devaluation, present-day understanding of learning would reject this approach in rehearsal settings if teacher/conductors are indeed promoting the development of musical independence. If students are to continue musical involvement as adults, they must learn to think for themselves, to solve problems, and to make musical decisions.

Consider the hypothetical case of a high school choral student taught by rote with no opportunity to grasp musical symbolism. After high school, the singer desires to continue singing and finds that the obligatory college choral audition results in placement in the "University Singers," a mixed group for inexperienced singers (i.e., "nonreaders"). The pace is laborious, the repertoire is easier and less appealing than what the singer experienced in high school, and the frustration level is higher. By the end of the fall semester, the singer decides not to return, stymied by the fact that what came so easily in high school is no longer accessible.

Who is to blame here? The student, the college director, or the high school teacher who made the singers dependent upon his or her teaching and discouraged, even prevented, the development of musical independence? Whose needs were truly met: the student's or the teacher's? With student learning at the core, schools can both acknowledge learners' present needs and learning preferences and help prepare them for the future. It is vital to recognize that "for students, schooling must be a time for curiosity, exploration, and inquiry, and memorizing information must be subordinated to learning how to solve real problems" (Brooks & Brooks, 1999, p. 9).

In the decade or more since the publication of *Dimensions of Musical Thinking* (Boardman, 1989), our world has been virtually transformed via technology and the Internet. We have ever more resources to develop higher-level thinking skills and less reason to resort to lower-level ones such as rote-learning. Admittedly, there will always be a place for rote-learning, as there are some facts we simply must "know," but to function in an increasingly complex world, we must rely on more sophisticated cognitive strategies. Teachers who model intellectual curiosity and risk-taking and who provide student-centered learning opportunities "honor students as emerging thinkers" (Brooks & Brooks, 1999, p. 10).

A current paradigm for teaching and learning, known as constructivism, holds promise for music education in the choral classroom. Traditionally, teacher-centered learning has focused on student recall and acquisition of a set body of knowledge, often as seen through adult eyes. Constructivist pedagogy, however, "helps learners to internalize and reshape, to transform, new information" (Moore & Moore, 1999, p. 15).

From new cognitive structures spring new understandings. Moore and Moore (1999) assert that constructivist teachers share twelve characteristics, among them the following four:

1. They "encourage and accept student autonomy and initiative." While some aspects of choral education must be collectively agreed upon (e.g., interpretive nuance for ensemble uniformity), these can sometimes be arrived at through a process of discovery and exploration set up by the teacher.

2. Constructivist teachers use cognitive terminology such as "classify," "analyze," "predict," and "create." These higher-level thinking skills require the students to invest themselves in the effort and to think independently.

3. Constructivist teachers encourage student inquiry by asking thoughtful, open-ended questions and encouraging students to ask questions of

each other. The art of good questioning is an essential skill for teachers. Simple yes-no and close-ended questions may appear efficient. There is a single right answer, and the student either gets it right or wrong, making the teacher's evaluation process very clear-cut. Such questions, however, do not nurture critical thinking.

4. Constructivist teachers seek elaboration of students' initial responses. How easy it is to accept the "right answer" when driven by deadlines. How often have we rejected one answer after another until some lucky student happens to read our minds? That kind of guessing game is discouraging to students who fear the risk of failure. Even a simple follow-up such as, "How did you figure that out?" or "Tell us more about that" will invite elaboration that provides the teacher and other students with a window into the learner's mind (Moore & Moore, 1999, pp. 103–18).

Developing expertise or choral artistry, then, built as it is on deep understanding, must necessarily focus on student learning. This does not imply that the choral educator is not ultimately responsible for instruction, nor does it preclude bringing a group of singers to an understanding of the teacher's conception about a musical work. It does suggest a reorientation during the rehearsal toward opportunities to engage the student in musical judgment and action. Further, it may inspire choral educators to include activities that have traditionally been relegated to the general music classroom, such as improvisation and composition.

Teacher Thinking

Research in the area of teacher thinking comprises important new understandings for educational practice. Two research strands relevant for conductor/teachers are the nature of teacher knowledge and the role of teacher image in teaching.

The Nature of Teacher Knowledge. Researchers in education are examining how teachers acquire content knowledge and how that knowledge changes over time. Teacher knowledge can be thought of as situated cognition that informs the teaching instance. Grossman (1990) identifies four areas constituting teacher knowledge: general pedagogical knowledge, subject matter knowledge, pedagogical content knowledge, and knowledge of context.

For choral educators, general pedagogical knowledge might be represented in foundations and methods classes that introduce broad-scale theories of how humans learn, behave, and function in the school setting. Subject matter knowledge relates to the specialized field of choral music and ranges from study of music theory and history, choral literature, and performance practice to personal study of a primary instrument or conducting. Pedagogical content knowledge is specific to a subject matter and includes the ability to develop instructional strategies, understand what makes the content accessible or challenging to learners, and how best to represent such knowledge to a classroom. As conductor/teachers, we may have the ability to conduct with great technical skill but lack the ability to develop teaching strategies to communicate these ideas. Likewise, we may understand how to teach a musical idea, but misrepresent the intent in our conducting gestures. A master teacher is able to bridge both verbal and nonverbal forms of teaching.

Knowledge of teaching context, according to Grossman (1990), relies on a teacher's ability to make sense of personal experiences. Such knowledge includes an understanding of the classroom, school culture, and larger community. As it relates to conducting/teaching, this knowledge is critical to the authentic perception of the learners' needs within a given classroom setting. Choosing repertoire, for example, should include contextual consideration and awareness of the local community and culture. Knowledge of context is important when working with the changing male and female voice, in order to meet the specific educational needs of a particular group of singers.

This growing body of research has important implications for the choral educator. In terms of teacher training, prospective teachers need opportunities to develop both global teaching strategies in relationship to broad theories of learning and behavior and specific content-bound teaching strategies that illuminate the musical idea at hand. This necessarily requires conductor/teachers to learn to evaluate and assess, in action, the musical product. One might plan to rehearse a series of steps in a given class but need to monitor and adjust the instructional plan as the rehearsal unfolds. Such action requires deep content knowledge by the conductor/teacher, both in terms of choral art and in the formulation of teaching strategies. Novice teachers may hear or diagnose a musical challenge, but be unable to identify how to solve a particular problem. Other teachers may ignore the musical challenge in favor of executing a teaching plan. Teacher training programs and ongoing professional development efforts might better address how prospective teachers could develop the varied forms of knowledge needed in the choral classroom.

The Role of Teacher Image. Another area of research interest is the effect of teachers' implicit beliefs on their teaching practices. Studies of teacher image are trying to answer questions such as the degree to which implicit belief affects teaching and whether tacit understandings can be made formal to interrupt the default application of past personal experience. Also of interest is the examination of personal practical knowledge, defined as learning gained through real-world practical experience (Clandinin & Connelley, 1986, 1988). Learning to teach, then, is dependent not only on the acquisition of skill but on everyday experience in the teaching act.

Areas affected by teacher image may include philosophy of classroom management, repertoire selection, curriculum weighting and design, and philosophy of select and nonselect choirs. In each instance, previous experience likely influences choral educators' choices. Regular opportunities for teachers to uncover their tacit beliefs might have a favorable impact on teaching practice.

The Choral Classroom

The choral classroom, as a primary performance vehicle, might best be characterized in terms of choral rehearsal. The structure of the rehearsal typically includes a warm-up; rehearsal of previously learned music, as well as introduction of new music; and a run-through of music nearing performance readiness. This section will examine ways of redefining the choral classroom to increase musical thinking and learning, including an expansion of the rehearsal model of choral instruction and the addition of special projects.

Expanding the "Rehearsal Model" of Choral Instruction. While the *National Standards for Arts Education* (MENC, 1994) are voluntary, they have had wide impact nationwide. The Standards often influence curricula through outright adoption or by being examined in the construction of local curricula. One readily noticeable feature of the Standards for performance ensembles is the inclusion of experiences in composition, improvisation, criticism and analysis, and varied multiethnic materials. It may well be time for the choral profession to reexamine the choral classroom and its function in the education of young musicians in the choral art. Choral educators will be held increasingly responsible for meeting these expanded tracks of learning in the choral setting. The old paradigm, rehearsing repertoire for performance, will likely need to change if these new demands are to be met.

A common complaint from teachers is the lack of time available to implement such instructional goals as composition and improvisation. Using a traditional rehearsal structure, however, it is possible to weave such activities into the everyday choral classroom. The time for warm-up, for example, is an excellent vehicle for inclusion of improvisatory or even compositional projects.

During this period, a conductor/teacher might regularly introduce improvisation. The teacher could, for instance, sing a bass line using the five pure Latin vowels. Once the pattern is established, the tenor, alto, and soprano sections might be responsible for improvising a harmony over the bass part. This could be done individually (assign sixty seconds to try out ideas and then present to section) or corporately (all sing and ultimately agree on a pattern). After several days with the established pattern, ensemble members might be responsible for notating their part on the board. The next day's challenge might be to vary the established pattern; the following day might shift the initial warm-up pattern to another section.

An out-of-class assignment might be the composition of a vocal warm-up for the choir by ensemble members. Teacher-directed parameters such as whether traditional or nontraditional notation is to be used, the number of vocal parts comprising the warm-up, or the starting key and tonality could help make the assignment accessible. Students can share these warm-ups over a period of time by singing them, presenting them visually, or playing them on a keyboard.

In many respects, the development of improvisational and compositional skill is related to an openness for new possibility as characterized by the expertlike mind set. Another effective means of encouraging students to think creatively is to encourage input by having them solve particular problems in the choral repertoire. In a middle school classroom, for example, choral educators routinely rewrite vocal lines to accommodate the special needs of the changing voices. With many teacher-provided models, students can be invited to help rewrite lines, a skill that develops over time.

Sectional rehearsals provide another opportunity for developing compositional skills. Technology will play an ever-increasing role in the school setting, and many schools already have established keyboard laboratories or multiple computer stations. While one section is rehearsing, another can spend time on individual or group choral composition projects. Important here is a careful progression of challenges provided by the choral educator. "Go compose a three-part madrigal" might be an initially overwhelming assignment. Providing an opening motive with specific instructions on length of phrase might be an initial step in what will be a closely guided project by the teacher. From this point, adding additional parts, discovering how to notate ideas, and analyzing creations in relationship to madrigals already encountered might represent the unfolding of the project over time.

The choral rehearsal also lends itself to increased participation by ensemble members. In addition to the involvement of students in the rehearsal process described earlier, additional assignments could be created from the repertoire under study that will enhance students' comprehension of musical context. Students might, for example, be required to write out the poetry of a given piece and be prepared to discuss their interpretations of the text. Another assignment could be for students to create a new verse, one that extends the original poetry in a personally meaningful way. New poetry provides an excellent means of assessing both text and the relationship of musical content as set by the composer. Students can debate what qualities make the new text appropriate or inappropriate and speculate as to how the original composer might have set the new verse.

Mini-research projects about the music under study can also be generated. One- or two-paragraph historical biographies are easily researched on the World Wide Web or in the school library. Structured assignments for score study are another vehicle that can increase student ownership over repertoire. Identifying phrase length and determining the key or mode, for example, are initial steps in score analysis.

Time, in a traditional school calendar, would likely be the primary deterrent to such a choral curriculum. Block scheduling offers an excellent vehicle for multiactivity teaching. In either case, it may be that choral educators will need to perform less music during a school year. If so, it becomes vitally important that the music chosen represents a variety of musical practices and styles, each of which is a compositional exemplar, to balance the offerings.

Special Projects. Alongside the reconception of the structure of the choral classroom might be the inclusion of special projects, particularly for those students needing additional challenges. A system of peer leadership greatly enhances a choral program and provides special opportunities for individual growth and progress. Examples include the use of student conductors, peer section leaders, or performance of a student composition. A select chamber choir might experiment with a "conductorless" performance.

Another area ripe for curricular change is the traditional musical, typically shared by music and drama teachers and in some settings the art and dance departments. Interdisciplinary learning is an important educational goal that musicians have been meeting for decades. An added dimension to this historical pattern of collaboration might be the generation of new work. Every fourth year, for example, the school might produce a new musical or opera. The forces required to mount such an effort can involve many areas of a school. Excellent models exist for those interested in such projects, including the *Education at the Met* original opera program by the Metropolitan Opera Guild for elementary and middle school classrooms (http://www.operaed.org/home.htm). Such a project could involve not only the choral area, but general music classes as well as other departments within the school.

Finally, an educational focus on performance opportunities can reorient the choral curriculum. Choosing one concert a year as an "informance" can involve students in the synthesis of learning for presentation to parents and community. An informance is geared to uncovering learning, whether providing historical information, demonstrating vocal challenges inherent in the music and revealing how the choir has solved these challenges, or exploring choral tone in relationship to a compositional style or text.

Implications

Musical thinking and learning in the choral context is maximized when the learner has multiple and sustained opportunities for musical judgment and decision making, when the materials presented represent the finest exemplars of choral music, and when the teacher functions as facilitator and coach.

Teacher and student knowledge are increased when the expertlike mind set is adopted. This process-based orientation reflects working at the upper edge of one's abilities, continually seeking new levels of understanding and challenge. Such knowledge is facilitated when the choral classroom functions as a reflective practicum. Reflecting on one's actions forms the metacognitive basis for thinking and learning. Reflection can be verbal, reflecting on one's actions, or nonverbal, as guided thinking during musical action such as singing.

A redefinition of choral curricula might include a richer palette of musical opportunity for the choral singer. In addition to singing, activities such as improvisation, composition, analysis, and self-reflection deepen knowledge. Assessment and evaluation should include traditional measures of formal knowledge, as well as performance measures of production such as singing skill. Such assessment might be woven into the daily rehearsal in addition to regular testing opportunities.

The choral classroom of the twenty-first century can be a site of deep learning, as well as a powerful vehicle for student expression. Understanding more about how humans think and learn will only enrich the choral educator's abilities to guide student learning and provide meaningful challenges that will shape young lives.

References

Apfelstadt, H. (1989). Musical thinking in the choral rehearsal. In E. Boardman, (Ed.), *Dimensions of musical thinking* (pp. 73–81). Reston, VA: MENC.

Bereiter, C., & Scardamalia, M. (1993). *Surpassing ourselves: An inquiry into the nature and implications of expertise.* Chicago: Open Court.

Boardman, E. (1989). *Dimensions of musical thinking.* Reston, VA: MENC.

Brooks, J. G., & Brooks, M. G. (1999). *In search of understanding: The case for constructivist classrooms.* (2nd ed.). Alexandria, VA: Association for Supervision and Curriculum Development.

Clandinin, D. J., & Connelly, F. M. (1986). The reflective practitioner and practitioners' narrative unities. *Canadian Journal of Education, 11* (2), 184–98.

Clandinin, D. J., & Connelly, F. M. (1988). *Teachers as curriculum planners: Narratives of experience.* New York: Teacher's College Press.

Elliott, D. (1992). Rethinking music teacher education. *Journal of Music Teacher Education, 2* (1), 6–11.

Elliott, D. (1995). *Music matters: A new philosophy of music education.* New York: Oxford.

Education at the MET (Metropolitan Opera Guild). <http://www.operaed.org/home.htm>

Grossman, P. L. (1990). *The making of a teacher: Teacher knowledge and teacher education.* New York: Teacher's College Press.

Jensen, E. (1998). *Teaching with the brain in mind.* Alexandria, VA: Association for Supervision and Curriculum Development.

Lortie, D. C. (1975). *Schoolteacher: A sociological study.* Chicago: University of Chicago Press.

MENC. (1994). *National Standards for Arts Education.* Reston, VA: MENC.

O'Toole, P. A. (1994). Redirecting the choral classroom: A feminist post-structural analysis of power relations within three choral settings. Doctoral dissertation, University of Wisconsin–Madison. *Dissertation Abstracts International,* 55, 07A, 1864.

Reimer, B. (1989). *A philosophy of music education.* (2nd ed.). Englewood Cliffs, NJ: Prentice–Hall.

Schön, D. (1983). *The reflective practitioner: How professionals think in action*. New York: Basic Books.

Schön, D. (1987). *Educating the reflective practitioner.* London: Jossey–Bass.

Sandra Snow is assistant professor of music in the department of music at the University of Michigan. Hilary Apfelstadt is professor of choral studies and coordinator of graduate studies at the Ohio State University.

13

TEACHING FOR UNDERSTANDING IN MUSIC TEACHER EDUCATION

JANET R. BARRETT

A familiar element of many general music methods classes is the exploration of various teaching approaches or methodologies such as Dalcroze, Generative, Kodály, Music Learning Theory, and Orff (additional options might include random hodgepodgism and principled eclecticism—currently known as "best practices"—as well). By way of introduction to this exploration, I frequently ask methods students these questions: "How would you know that a general music teacher was using a particular approach if you were to visit his or her classroom? What particular teaching practices would you see? What would the learners be doing that would be characteristic of the approach? If you interviewed the teacher, what key principles or beliefs would you expect the teacher to describe? What forms of music making would be emphasized? How would this approach fit the style of the teacher, needs of the learners, and context of the school community?" These questions frame the search for answers as we engage in discussion, study, and experiences that illustrate these prevalent approaches.

This chapter will address similar questions for exploring the teaching and learning found in music teacher education classrooms. Unlike the comparative approach described in the opening paragraph, however, this chapter will emphasize one framework, social constructivism, for educating music teachers. Five themes of social constructivism will be described as influences on the curriculum for undergraduate music education majors (or "preservice teachers") to emphasize their ongoing transformation of roles from student to teacher and the curriculum for practicing music educators engaged in graduate study or teacher-development activities.[1] Five examples drawn from classroom and rehearsal settings will show how preservice and practicing teachers develop ongoing models of musical development, lead students toward musical independence, develop insightful perception of student responses, model reflective thinking, and design educational experiences that stretch students' understanding. I have experimented with the application of these ideas in the context of undergraduate methods courses, field studies or practica, courses in the assessment of music learning, music for students with exceptionalities, foundations and principles of music education, and student teaching seminars. Courses for practicing music teachers have included the psychology of music teaching and learning, curriculum development, and graduate seminars on contemporary educational issues.

In the past decade, teacher education has been steadily moving away from an emphasis on training, or the transmission of technical knowledge as adequate preparation for the classroom, to a more constructivist approach. The environment of change in teacher education is ripe for this transition since teachers can hardly know what specific challenges may face them in future classroom settings. An education for principled action, which is based on constructivist ideas with epistemological roots in Piaget, Dewey, Bruner, and Vygotsky, holds special promise. Richardson (1997) reminds us, however, that the basic notion of constructivist teaching is not a "monolithic, agreed-upon concept" (p. 3). Some of the different constructivist approaches include Piagetian, situated-cognition, sociocultural, and emancipatory emphases. What is common among these approaches, asserts Richardson (1997), is a consensus that

> constructivism is a learning or meaning-making theory. It suggests that individuals create their own new understandings, based upon the interaction of what they already know and believe, and the phenomena or ideas with which they come into contact.

> Constructivism is a descriptive theory of learning (this is the way people learn or develop); it is not a prescriptive theory of learning (this is the way people should learn. (p. 3).

Music teacher educators constantly move back and forth to help teachers build descriptive theories in two complementary realms. The musical understanding of elementary and secondary students, a "first order" subject-matter focus, is examined through the processes of musical engagement including singing, playing, composing, improvising, describing, representing, evaluating, and responding to music. Through direct contact with students, teachers build a working model of students' musical knowledge and the ways that students make meaning of music. The pedagogical understanding that teachers use to enable students' musical growth is a "second order" focus in the teacher education classroom. Teachers draw upon their existing repertoire of practices and beliefs in social contexts that challenge them to describe, examine, confront, and revise their ideas about teaching. Shulman (1987) describes pedagogical content knowledge as the essence of domain-specific practice, which in the context of music education consists of the representative models, works, examples, and metaphors that help students learn music. Curriculum development, instructional techniques, and assessment strategies are the applications of this pedagogical knowledge.

To return to the opening paragraph of this chapter, we might ask, "What constitutes a social constructivist environment for music teacher education and how could we tell if we stumbled across one?" Five themes or crucial ideas are of particular importance for music teacher educators to consider in building such an environment: (a) the meaning of meaning; (b) an attention to context; (c) the nature of change; (d) the intersection of cognition and emotion; and (e) the interplay of intentions, actions, and reflections. After addressing each one of these themes, I will provide examples of applications for preservice and practicing teachers.

Themes of a Constructivist Classroom

The five themes of social constructivism (the meaning of meaning; attention to context; the nature of change; the intersection of cognition and emotion; and the interplay of intentions, actions, and reflections) are explored in the following discusssions.

The meaning of meaning. Meaning can be an especially slippery and ambiguous term. Often, constructivist notions of meaning are clarified through juxtaposition with "traditional" forms of learning. In this "old school" view, learning is portrayed as the acquisition of declarative knowledge in a collection of facts, disconnected impressions or information, or mere reiterations of ideas, often without a corresponding ability to clarify their significance. The teacher's transmission of knowledge and the learner's accurate acquisition of it are emphasized. Other means for helping teachers understand the different views involve dichotomous pairings—random versus ordered, separate versus integrated, or superficial versus deep systems of knowledge, for example.[2]

Although these comparisons are helpful, more distinction is needed. In teacher education, a search for meaning involves the formation of structures or schemes of knowledge about teaching, learners, subject matter, and schools, thereby emphasizing insightful relationships and substantive connections between what teachers already know and what they are learning in the present. Teacher education is also frequently seen as a context in which bridges are built between theory and practice; constructivism dovetails well with this metaphor in that the span is supported by both ends of the bridge, and travel flows in both directions across it. The relationship of parts to the whole is critical, as is the active process of assembling the parts and designing an educationally sound blueprint for thoughtful classrooms.

One of the challenges of this approach is that it may run counter to the expectations of teachers who have become accustomed to learning about bridges but who have seldom experienced bridge building firsthand. A constructivist classroom can be disorienting if your educational horizons have been narrowed to answering the questions at the end of the chapter and checking whether they match the answer key. Teacher educators often find themselves stumbling upon these robust expectations that hint at deeper epistemological conflicts. Many of us have overheard (or have had reported to us) the groaning of exasperated students who exclaim, "I wish my professor would stop making us think and just tell us what to do." It would be easier by far to download every iota of knowledge that one has about teaching to the cognitive "hard drives" of other teachers, but the file would probably be an unreadable jumble of characters and impressions.

Meaning is not only a matter of structure; it is a matter of utility as well. Teachers must be able to draw upon what they know to solve complex problems that are part of the fabric of classroom life. Action that arises from meaning demonstrates understanding. Gardner's definition of understanding draws on this notion: he states that "an individual understands a concept, skill, theory, or domain of knowledge to the extent that he or she can apply it appropriately in a new situation" (Gardner 1999, p. 119). This definition also saves us from the potentially tricky quagmire of relativism. It is not just any old meaning that teachers need to construct. Fundamental principles, concepts, ideas, and practices are the core of the musical and pedagogical content to be organized and applied. Gardner (1999) further relates understanding to the disciplinary expertise that teachers need to form the "construction of habits and concepts that reflect the best contemporary thinking and practices of the domain" (p. 123).

How does a music teacher educator assist teachers in the construction of meaning about music and pedagogy? Consider the following guidelines: design experiences that will acknowledge and rely upon prior understanding as a means to examine and evaluate new models for classroom practice; provide rich primary experiences that allow teachers to take new theories and models out for a spin, kicking the tires as they test and evaluate the strength and applicability of ideas; seek to inform the investigation of new models by observing best practices and relating them to pertinent readings in the field; focus on the sense that teachers make of the examples, often in terms of the principles that undergird specific instances; and test these principles by relating them to a variety of alternate instances as well.

An attention to context. Socially mediated inquiry is a central concept of social constructivism. Simply put, this means that our knowledge as teachers is formed through the questions we ask and the answers we form in interaction with the students we teach, our teaching peers, and mentors past and present. The music teacher education classroom fosters inquiry when beliefs about teaching and learning are brought into the ongoing discussion for examination. Teaching practices ("what works") are related to underlying principles whenever possible so that a particular strategy or technique can always be revised to fit the demands of a new context.

If participants in a college or university classroom can function as a community of learners, preservice and practicing teachers will experience firsthand the benefits of group inquiry. The more minds set to work on important teaching and learning problems, the greater the possibility for interesting insights. Through language, teachers give names to ideas and intuitions. Goals and accomplishments take on greater clarity as teachers describe them to others. The usual tools of a teacher education classroom—journals, guided discussions, group projects, case studies, and reflective critiques—make thinking public so that the group can develop, clarify, and refine ideas. Peer teaching, observation, and collegial critiques are also integral to this social milieu of the teacher education classroom.

As lively as the college and university classroom can be, it can never entirely simulate the complex and unpredictable worlds of the elementary, middle, or high school setting. Field experiences for preservice teachers or practicing teachers' own classrooms are the real laboratories of learning. School contexts are more than just the settings in which teaching and learning occur; the rituals, beliefs, and values of the surrounding community influence the learning that takes place. Music classrooms are especially rich social contexts since the goals of the group in making and creating music are often integral to the very nature of musical participation. Music classrooms also serve very important social roles within the school community since the music program is often a representation of the cultural identity and values of the school.

It is to the extent that the context of the university classroom can serve as a setting for thoughtful reflection on elementary and secondary school settings that the greatest possibility for transfer of insights can take place. The common assumption that understanding flows in one direction from the theoretical world of the university to the practical world of the elementary and secondary classroom is obviously too simplistic. Practice and theory reside in both contexts, and for teachers to grow, complementary relationships need to be identified and examined.

The nature of change. Growth in any domain is rarely orderly, continuous, and predictable. Learning to teach and developing one's teaching practices over a career span are especially evolutionary journeys. The challenge of music teacher education classrooms is to stimulate growth along a developmental continuum through meaningful experiences centered around music teaching and learning.[3]

Change in teaching practices or beliefs is not a matter of piling up an accumulation of techniques like layers of sedimentary rock. In fact, that analogy seems more fitting to describe the kind of acquisition and transmission of knowledge found in more traditional views of learning. The kind of change in teachers' thinking that will have long-lasting influence on classrooms is likely to be more transformative, like the shifting of tectonic plates that disturbs the smooth surface of habits and unquestioned routines.

"Shifting" is a useful term. A shift in understanding is a reorganization of what we know. This reorganization often comes as a result of wrestling with old and new ideas in juxtaposition. In the form of psychological constructivism represented by Piaget, the term "cognitive dissonance" is often used. This is the state in which a learner's prior framework of knowledge or scheme comes into conflict with some phenomenon that doesn't seem to fit the framework. Another constructivist view is represented by Gardner, who advocates an approach to understanding in which teachers orchestrate learning experiences that lead to the "direct confrontation of erroneous conceptions" (1999, p. 127). In his description of reflective teaching, Donald Schön refers to the importance of confusion in bringing about change in one's teaching practices. He asserts that "surprise and puzzlement are at the heart of reflective teaching" (Schön, 1988, p. 22).

One of the goals of the music teacher education program, therefore, is to promote the sort of metamorphosis that signals change in teachers' thinking about teaching. Prior understanding must certainly be acknowledged and drawn upon, but substantive growth will result as teachers confront longstanding misconceptions and gaps in knowledge to acquire new perspectives and roles. R. A. Hodgkin (1976) writes:

> We learn best as teachers; we teach best as learners. The effort to communicate strengthens knowledge and to be an authority is to know how to doubt. Many people have experienced this paradox, yet the deeper implications of the mutuality of teaching and learning are largely unexplored. ... Indeed the whole educational endeavor needs to be seen as more perilous and problematic than has been customary. "Problematic" here does not merely mean that education is puzzling, but that the essence of the process, from the first to last, has to do with the control of doubt, with problems seen in the shadows, with the models that we make and share when we think we have found a solution, and with the underlying faith that there are more problems round the corner (p. 3).

This sort of change can feel unsettling, especially to the beginning teacher, but it signals crucial shifts of understanding. Music teacher educators and other teachers in the classroom often act as midwives for this sort of transformation, offering reassurance or advising perseverance when it seems that problems are especially thorny. Odd as this may sound, this approach to change can be applied to instructional design. The careful orchestration of situations in which teachers must wrestle with old ways of thinking in hopes that they will create new shifts of understanding is an exciting prospect. Indeed, if we want to escape the cycle of always teaching in the way we were taught, this is not just an interesting intellectual exercise, but an imperative.

The intersection of cognition and emotion. Cognition and emotion, held at arm's length in intellectual traditions from Descartes onward, are beginning to merge as important elements in teaching and learning. In the current climate of standards-based instruction and accountability based on the scores of standardized tests, the acknowledgment of the affective side of teaching and learning in balance with the development of rational thought is a breath of fresh air indeed. Eisner (1991) reminds us that "what really counts in schools is teaching children that the exploration of ideas is sometimes difficult, often exciting, and occasionally fun" (p. 11).

Hargreaves (1998) asserts that the emotional dimensions of teaching are often ignored or neglected in teacher education or staff development programs, yet the emotional tenor of the classroom is of great significance to teachers. He writes: "Good teaching is charged with positive emotion. It is not just a matter of knowing one's subject, being efficient, having the correct competencies, or learning all the right techniques. Good teachers are not just well-oiled machines. They are emotional, passionate beings who connect with their students and fill their work and their classes with pleasure, creativity, challenge, and joy." (Hargreaves, 1998, p. 835).

Music teacher education is especially receptive to this mutuality, since thinking and feeling merge in the artistic processes of performance, creation, perception, analysis, and response as well as in teaching and learning music. Artistry in the classroom emerges in those teachers who are sensitive to the ways that meaning can be conveyed and expressed through sound, gesture, image, symbol, and word. Like other important but fairly intangible ideas, artistry can be modeled in the design of classroom experiences, even if it is difficult to teach directly. The emotional dimensions of the classroom influence what is remembered, what is acted upon, and what is incorporated into students' lives outside of the classroom.

The interplay of intentions, actions, and reflections. Studies of teacher thinking and teacher knowledge have focused on many dimensions of the mental lives of teachers. Some of these studies separate teachers' thinking into three functions: planning, teaching, and assessing. These are processes that teachers use before, during, and after direct interaction with students. It is helpful to think of these three aspects of teacher thinking as cyclical rather than linear, because teachers often change their plans "in flight" (Robbins, 1999, p. 26) or use what they learn in evaluating a class or rehearsal as the fodder for planning the next.

Much of what teachers know is revealed through action in this cycle. Teachers select materials and repertoire, design activities, create imaginative assignments, organize, and structure instructional time. In direct interaction with students, teachers remain on the lookout for evidence of learning, confusion, progress, and response. Music classrooms are especially dynamic and flowing, since musical understanding reveals itself in many ways and at many speeds. Students bring diverse skills, expressive capabilities, desires, intentions, and levels of understanding to bear while learning new works and concepts. The continual flux and movement that characterize a class or rehearsal can be unsettling for those who prefer a more stable environment. What is learned influences what is taught and vice versa. Smyth (1991) observes that, through this interaction between teacher and student, there is a "process of mutual modification underway" (p. xv).

Through reflection, teachers attend to their own ways of thinking and their interactions with students. Speculations about the processes of learning music are considered through reflection. The critical impulse of this reflective inquiry is often a need to explain or describe what is going on, and, surprisingly, differing perceptions and interpretations emerge disguised as descriptions. In order for change to take place, teachers must evaluate, sort, sift, borrow, adapt, and discard teaching practices on the basis of these reflections. The relationship of this reflective approach to constructivism is clear in that reflection helps teachers to uncover their underlying assumptions about teaching and learning; examine them in a supportive, collegial environment; seek alternative ways to think and act; and thereby move toward substantive changes of practice and belief.

Examples of Constructivist Contexts

Five examples of activities or assignments from music teacher education classrooms are provided to illustrate these themes of a constructivist approach. These activities are meant to illustrate some of the principles of constructivism, but no one activity incorporates all of them.

Secondary general music methods and the transport exercise. Three goals from a secondary general music methods class for preservice teachers form a context for an assignment called the transport exercise.[4] The goals are (a) to incorporate diverse musical experiences for students of diverse backgrounds into a secondary general music curriculum; (b) to articulate criteria for the selection of musical works in a secondary general music curriculum, incorporating principles of cultural authenticity for ethnomusical examples; and (c) to design valid interdisciplinary curricular experiences that relate music to culture, history, art, and literature.

Students are asked to choose a musical work from a culture relatively unfamiliar to them. The purpose of the exercise is to examine the process of familiarizing oneself with an unfamiliar work, which often leads to an examination of the cultural assumptions that we bring to the listening process. In class, we set up the assignment by listening to several examples of music from the former Yugoslavia as preparation. The examples include folk music in fairly traditional styles, as well as a particular form of singing known as *ganga,* which features vocal timbres and closely-packed harmonic relationships that usually challenge the class members. After the preservice teachers have chosen their own works, they are asked to listen to them repeatedly over the course of a week, keeping track of their progress from complete unfamiliarity to deeper understanding by writing about their "journey" and the strategies they use to inform their listening. Each student completes an extended journal entry to describe the stages experienced along the path. Several days are spent playing excerpts of the works in class, asking classmates to hypothesize origins on the basis of their musical characteristics, and then revealing the cultural contexts and meanings of the pieces.

The transport exercise is essentially metacognitive in character in that the subject of the exercise is both the musical work itself and the teacher's own thinking. Selecting a musical example from a relatively unfamiliar musical tradition often reveals prior knowledge as teachers bring robust, ingrained musical expectations to the exercise. As we discuss what we learned on our various paths, it becomes clear that the processes of getting to know a work are highly idiosyncratic, which is a good premise for thinking about the diversity of approaches to learning found in classroom settings. Working on our own knowledge is a prelude to the pedagogical step of constructing a classroom experience to introduce new musics to students. We work on the tacit understanding and beliefs that teachers bring with them to the study of a new work.

Teacher responses to this exercise are telling. One preservice teacher remarked that she had never kept track of her own thinking before and that it seemed as if this validated her intellectual contributions. Other teachers have remarked that although they often are exposed to new works as music education majors, they rarely take the time to delve into the ways that they hear the structure of the piece. It is relatively common for methods students to say that their formal training interferes in some way with the exercise, in that they have to deliberately shut down their analytical processes in order to consider other meanings and characteristics of the piece. Occasionally confusion breaks out, as teachers try to force what they hear into familiar musical structures; when this doesn't work, they have to realign their perceptions to hear shifting meters, timbres, or phrase structures. Throughout the process, participants function as hybrid teacher/learners, reflecting on their own discoveries while generating pedagogical possibilities.

Assessment class and the search for signs of musicality in the universe. A fundamental premise of an Assessment of Music Learning class for undergraduate and graduate students is that teachers need to articulate what musicality is before they can hope to assess students' musical growth. Perceptive and purposeful observation of students engaged in musical activities is one means for building a coherent description. Observation can allow teachers (a) to develop perceptual acuity; (b) to build a broader knowledge base for music teaching; (c) to help direct another teacher's growth; (d) to examine cases of practice in instructional settings; and (e) to develop professional judgment (Barrett, 2000). The very essence of observation rests on constructivist bedrock in that the meaning teachers bring to the exercise is infused with the prior knowledge, beliefs, values, and habits of the observer. Teachers use their abilities to represent what they see through descriptions that are also truly interpretive in nature. In the social context of the classroom, discussions centered around these descriptions bring out important patterns, relationships, and points of view about the nature of music learning and teaching.

Teachers in the class are given this assignment: "For the next week, observe those around you who are engaged in musical activity. What are the 'signs' that someone is musical? What is musical knowledge and understanding and how is it demonstrated? Are there different kinds of musical understanding? Describe them." Class members are encouraged to observe elementary, middle, high school, and/or college students and to bring several pages of field notes to class to use in building a model of musicianship. In order for the class to also have a common example to discuss in addition to their varied individual observations, I use a videotaped case of a high school concert band rehearsal in which the conductor solves problems of balance and stylistically appropriate rhythm in preparing *Orpheus in the Underworld* for performance (Olson, Barrett, Rasmussen, Barresi, & Jensen, 2000). The same questions are used to examine the musical understanding and knowledge of the band members, as well as the conductor, in the video case.

Armed with a wealth of observations and interpretations from the individual observations and the responses to the video case, the next challenge is to incorporate the ideas into some coherent overall model. A four-ring Venn Diagram based loosely on the Cognitive Skills Matrix of Davidson and Scripp (1992) allows teachers to organize their descriptions into a workable representation of musical engagement (see Figure 1). In small groups, class members hammer out a possible model before presenting it to the entire group for consideration.

In contrast to reading or memorizing someone else's definition of musicality, this exercise places teachers in the center of thinking about the diverse ways that students and teachers demonstrate their musical understanding. The observations and the video case allow us to derive important principles of musical engagement from watching students and teachers in action in relatively natural settings. The task of description challenges us to put our ideas in an articulate, clear form for others to consider. Throughout the discussion, teachers offer interpretations, rebuttals, clarifications, and examples to support their ideas.

An action research project for an elementary general music methods class. In an elementary general music methods class, preservice teachers need to correlate what they read about the generalized principles of children's musical development with the complex and multifaceted particularities of real children. An action research project integrates assignments and readings from the methods class with opportunities to plan instruction for children and to gather data on their responses to musical activities at the field-study site. Another goal of the project is to demonstrate how opportunities for composition and invented notation can grow from more traditional listening lessons.

In one project, preservice teachers made an inventory of the activities, musical works, and elements of music that were familiar to the fourth-grade students of the class chosen for the project at the elementary school. The teachers chose to use Grieg's "In the Hall of the Mountain King" as the centerpiece of a curriculum project that grew from the children's familiarity with the work in listening lessons. They designed a series of experiences that began with a movement exercise in which the children showed the melodic rhythm by tapping and stepping around the room to show long and short durations. Next, the children engaged in additional forms of description by answering questions about changes in tempo, texture, and dynamics. In a subsequent activity, students drew their own representations, or iconic maps, of the features of the work; the preservice teachers related these representations to class reading (such as Upitis, 1991). Finally, students took their maps and used them as the impetus for creating new works in small groups. Each group generated ideas, rehearsed their works, performed them for the class, and recorded them. The preservice teachers took turns leading the activities, while others made notes on the children's responses. Rubrics for evaluating movement and the iconic maps were developed. Finally, using guidelines for developing rubrics for evaluating creative products (Webster & Hickey, 1995), the preservice teachers assessed the small-group compositions.

Throughout the project, the preservice teachers moved from rather generalized views of children's musical capabilities to more specific and detailed examples drawn from their observations and evaluations. The tripartite nature of the design, which includes movement, visual representations, and compositions, allowed them to compare and contrast different ways that children demonstrate their musical understandings. As the group collaborated in planning, implementing, and evaluating the project, the teachers were intrigued by the children's perceptual abilities and originality. The cooperating teacher at the field study site enriched their understanding by helping them to connect the children's work on this project to previous activities that enabled sophisticated response. One of the most important outcomes was the cultivation of wonder at the children's wholehearted engagement in the activities, which was a vital affective dimension. Finally, preservice teachers learned how an ambitious project was transformed from paper to reality within the context of an elementary general music classroom.

A psychology of music learning and teaching class puts theory to the test. Practicing music educators bring a wealth of classroom examples and pertinent questions that arise from the puzzles of practice in graduate studies. In a summer class devoted to the examination of psychological principles of teaching and learning music, practicing teachers participated in an exercise that put theory to the test. A cognitive concept, principle, or model that is merely described may remain an inert abstraction if teachers do not have an opportunity to take the idea for a "test drive."

We decided to focus on an understudied but important context for music instruction (the applied lesson) as the vehicle for investigating Vygotsky's (1978) sociocultural theory of development.[5] We read about Vygostky's Zone of Proximal Development (ZPD) and scaffolding strategies used by teachers to enable students to solve more complex problems than they would be able to solve without assistance (Bordrova & Leong, 1996; Kozulin, 1990; Vygotsky, 1978). This basic idea was applied to a percussion lesson that the entire class observed, analyzed, and discussed through creating a working model of the applied lesson. We hypothesized that an applied lesson is like a work space or territory in which student and teacher make moves toward understanding. This work space is bounded by four sides, or factors, that influence the work that can be done. They include the following:

- the student's musical understanding
- the teacher's musical understanding
- contextual factors that enable or constrain learning
- features of the musical work itself, including formal, technical, and expressive qualities.

The percussion instructor at my university agreed to have ten of us sit in on a percussion lesson with a talented percussion student.[6] We all took notes on their interactions during the lesson, in particular keeping track of the moves that the instructor made and the moves the student made toward enhanced performance of a composition for marimba. We noted how the student monitored her own progress throughout the lesson, bringing up technical difficulties of sticking patterns and her sense of losing control in loud, forceful sections of the piece. The instructor used a variety of scaffolding strategies, including reducing the number of musical elements for the student to focus on and identifying smaller segments for concentrated work. He also modeled playing techniques, practicing strategies, and voicing options. As observers, we tried to note when strategies suggested by the instructor were incorporated into the student's playing for immediate results and also when efforts to communicate musical ideas seemed to be blocked in either direction. Of particular note was the instructor's admonition to perform the piece with the audience's perception in mind, trying to communicate musical ideas in a way that would make sense to the listeners. This had the effect of "turning up the heat" in the lesson as the student shifted her focus from successfully getting through the piece to communicating ideas to others through her performance. It was obvious to us that this move on the instructor's part was the beginning of a significant shift in the student's musical thinking and a sophisticated step toward change.

Contextual factors that influenced the lesson setting certainly included the presence of a roomful of observers, but also included the technical and expressive demands of the instrument itself in that the marimba, in the instructor's words, in an "instrument you don't get to touch to play." Control of the hand and mallets to produce a range of sounds is substantially different from playing techniques required for other instruments. In addition, the piece the student was performing was unusual in that it included improvisatory sections as well as thoroughly composed themes.

Using the Vygotskian-inspired notion of the "work space" proved to be beneficial in that it redirected the typical focus of teachers' observations on strategies, techniques, stylistic characteristics, and comparisons with their own practice to a more interactive middle ground. In this manner, their perceptions were focused on the intelligent moves of the student aimed at working through the problematic aspects of performance. In discussion, we were able to focus on this interplay between teacher and student and speculate how the notion of a work space would inform the interactions of teachers with students in small- or large-group settings as well as individual lessons. Although all of us had either taught or taken private lessons, the project offered an important window for us to observe the fluid interactions of teacher and learner in the applied studio from the sidelines.

The three-way conference after a student teaching observation. Student teachers in music face a multitude of challenges in learning to teach in the context of their cooperating teacher's classroom while demonstrating what they have learned during the course of their music teacher preparation to the supervisors who visit them periodically throughout their placement in schools. It is relatively easy to understand how a student teacher's focus could be drawn away from his or her primary center of attention—the musical development of the elementary, middle, or high school students in that classroom.

The most familiar context for integrating these various dimensions of student teaching is the supervisory conference that takes place after an observation. In the very best sense, this environment enables the student teacher, cooperating teacher, and university supervisor to work together to make sense of a particular lesson or rehearsal. Each brings a valuable point of view to the conversation, and the potential for articulating useful insights is high. These supervisory conferences, however, are infused with many emotional layers as the student teacher's thinking is on display, the cooperating teacher's program is open to examination, and the university supervisor's abilities to relate fundamental concepts are tested. Shared meanings are important for the three-way relationship to function well.

A constructivist approach to these conferences places the elementary, middle, or high school students' musical understanding as the centerpiece of the discussion. Often, initial questions relate to the student teacher's perceptions of students' work in the class or rehearsal ("What did you notice about the students' responses? In what ways did students demonstrate what they were learning?"). Questions that speak to the unexpected elements of a lesson often bring forth necessary differences between the student teacher's plan and what actually transpired ("Were there any surprises in the lesson? What happened that was unexpected?"). For responsive teaching to occur, a student teacher must be able to articulate how he or she makes changes in a plan to accommodate the students' discoveries, confusions, difficulties, or successes. Additional questions can focus on the evaluative aspects of the lesson ("What did the students learn, and how do you know that they learned?").

As all three participants in the discussion share answers to these questions, their relationship to the cycle of planning, teaching, and assessing becomes clear. In reflective practice, what is learned through collaborative examination of a lesson or rehearsal is folded into the next experience that a student teacher plans or implements. In addition, the mutual modification of the beliefs and practices of the cooperating teacher and university supervisor also occurs in this setting.

Summary

This chapter has illustrated ways that preservice and practicing teachers can apply contemporary principles of teaching and learning to create thoughtful classrooms centered on musical understanding. The design of a course for teachers is a test of professional judgment as goals are clarified, assignments are created, readings are selected, and the flow of the semester's work is mapped out. The implementation of a course is a test of critical and creative thinking, artistry and technique and involves a blend of idealism and realism as course corrections and adjustments are made throughout. Reflecting on the course at the end of the semester often causes us to examine what actually transpired and the way the events remained true to the spirit of initial intentions.

The ultimate goal, however, is to work toward music teacher education classrooms that are in direct contrast to static, stale, one-size-fits-all conduits for teacher training. The challenge is to design an environment that resembles the kinds of classrooms we hope to create. Music educators need to build an ongoing model of musical development; model musical thinking and reflective thought; design engaging, open-ended experiences; practice masterful perception; draw upon a repertoire of representations; collect evidence of students' thinking; and embed assessment in curriculum and instruction in order to create these mindful classrooms. Ultimately, the ways that teachers draw upon the insights and experiences in university classrooms will inform the way they design their own classrooms. The various meanings and models of teaching and learning music are put to use at the heart of understanding.

Footnotes

1. Throughout the chapter, I'll use "preservice teachers" when referring to undergraduate music education majors, "practicing teachers" for teachers already in the field who are participating in graduate music teacher education or professional development activities, and "students" to refer to primary and secondary school students.

2. See Webster (1998) for a concise overview of the shift from traditional to constructivist views of learning.

3. Richardson and Placier (2001) provide an especially thorough review of research on two views of teacher change from the perspective of the individual and from an organizational standpoint.

4. See Barrett, McCoy, & Veblen (1997) for a complete description of the transport exercise (in Chapter 4, "Getting to Know a Work of Art," and the cultural counterpoint described in Chapter 11, "Music and Culture").

5. See Kennell (1992) for more insights on examining the applied lesson setting.

6. My thanks to instructor Josh Ryan and student Holly Roth for agreeing to participate in this "experiment."

References

Barrett, J. R. (2000). Observing to learn: Connections to current practice. In G. B. Olson, J. R. Barrett, N. R. Rasmussen, A. Barresi, & J. Jensen, *Looking in on music teaching.* (pp. 52–68). New York: McGraw-Hill Primis.

Bodrova, E., & Leong, D. J. (1996). *Tools of the mind: The Vygotskian approach to early childhood education.* Englewood Cliffs, NJ: Prentice-Hall.

Davidson, K., & Scripp, L. (1992). Surveying the coordinates of cognitive skills in music. In R. Colwell, (Ed.), *Handbook of research on music teaching and learning* (pp. 392–413). New York: Schirmer Books.

Eisner, E. W. (1991). What really counts in schools. *Educational Leadership 48,* (5), 10–17.

Gardner, H. (1999). *The disciplined mind: What all students should understand.* New York: Simon & Schuster.

Hargreaves, A. (1998). The emotional practice of teaching. *Teaching and Teacher Education, 14* (8), 835–54.

Hodgkin, R. A. (1976). *Born curious: New perspectives in educational theory.* London: John Wiley & Sons.

Kennell, R. (1992). Toward a theory of applied music instruction. *The Quarterly Journal of Music Teaching and Learning, III,* (2), 5–16.

Kozulin, A. (1990). *Vygotsky's psychology: A biography of ideas.* Cambridge, MA: Harvard University Press.

Olson, G. B., Barrett, J. R., Rasmussen, N. R., Barresi, A., & Jensen, J. (2000). *Looking in on music teaching.* New York: McGraw Hill Primis.

Richardson, V. (Ed.). (1997). *Constructivist teacher education: Building a world of new understandings.* London: Falmer Press.

Richardson, V., & Placier, P. (2001). Teacher change. In E. Richardson, (Ed.), *Handbook of research on teaching,* (4th Ed.). Washington, DC: American Educational Research Association.

Robbins, J. (1999). Getting set and letting go: Practicum teachers' in-flight decision-making. *The Mountain Lake reader: Conversations on the study and practice of music teaching,* 26–32. Murfeesboro, TN: Middle Tennessee State University.

Schön, D. A. (1988). Coaching reflective teaching. In P. P. Grimmett & G. L. Erickson (Eds.), *Reflection in teacher education* (pp. 19–30). New York: Teachers College Press.

Schulman, L. S. (1987). Knowledge and teaching: Foundations of the new reform. *Harvard Educational Review, 57* (1), 1–22.

Smyth, J. (1991). *Teachers as collaborative learners: Challenging dominant forms of supervision.* Philadelphia: Open University Press.

Upitis, R. (1991). *Can I play you my song?: The compositions and invented notations of children.* Portsmouth, NH: Heinemann.

Vygotsky, L. S. (1978). *Mind in society: The development of higher psychological processes.* Cambridge, MA: Harvard University Press.

Webster, P., & Hickey, M. (1995). Rating scales and their use in assessing children's music compositions. *The Quarterly Journal of Music Teaching and Learning, VI* (4), 28–44.

Webster, P. R. (1998). The new music educator. *Arts Education Policy Review, 100* (2), 2–6.

Janet R. Barrett is professor of music education at the University of Wisconsin–Whitewater.